ADVANCE PRAISE FOR

Law, Media, and Culture

"At a time when hatred is on the national agenda, *Law, Media, and Culture: The Landscape of Hate* is a journey through a contemporary cultural exposé of hate. Judson and Bertazzoni examine their subject with clarity, sensitivity, and an eye to social justice."

Cynthia Burack, Associate Professor of Women's Studies,
Ohio State University, and Author of The Problem of the Passions:
Feminism, Psychoanalysis, and Social Theory

"In *Law, Media, and Culture: The Landscape of Hate*, Judson and Bertazzoni have written a highly accessible guide to the role of hatred in everyday American life. Rather than comfort the reader with the notion that hatred, somehow, is 'out there' on the margins, they show us that hatred infects virtually all avenues of public and private culture in contemporary society. This book particularly is a must-read for students of the media's impact on public opinion and social life."

Brian Steffen, Associate Professor and Chair of Communication Studies,
Simpson College, Indianola, Iowa

"This is an important and necessary book, one that captures the complexity, force, and yes, even the social value of the strongest—and most politically incorrect—of human emotions. Its discussion of digital hate speech moves well beyond the standard legal summary to raise sharp questions about the implications of hate sites on our national character and conceptions of community: have we truly become a culture in which hate is as much the basis of community as de Tocqueville's democracy ever was? It's a critical question—one that students across the disciplines should be urged to consider."

Dianne Lynch, Associate Professor in the Department of
Journalism and Mass Communications, St. Michael's College, Vermont,
and Editor of Stand! Virtual Ethics: Debating Media Values in a Digital Age

LAW, MEDIA, and CULTURE

Politics Media & Popular Culture

David A. Schultz, *General Editor*

Vol. 4

PETER LANG
New York • Washington, D.C./Baltimore • Bern
Frankfurt am Main • Berlin • Brussels • Vienna • Oxford

Janis L. Judson and Donna M. Bertazzoni

LAW, MEDIA, and CULTURE

The Landscape of Hate

PETER LANG
New York • Washington, D.C./Baltimore • Bern
Frankfurt am Main • Berlin • Brussels • Vienna • Oxford

LIBRARY OF CONGRESS CATALOGING-IN-PUBLICATION DATA

Judson, Janis L.
Law, media, and culture: the landscape of hate /
Janis L. Judson and Donna M. Bertazzoni.
p. cm. — (Politics, media, and popular culture; Vol. 4)
Includes bibliographical references and index.
1. Hate—Social aspects—United States. 2. United States—Race relations.
3. Hate speech—United States. 4. Hate crimes—United States.
I. Bertazzoni, Donna M. II. Title.
III. Politics, media & popular culture; vol. 4.
HN59.2 .J83   305.8'00973—dc21   00-062970
ISBN 0-8204-4981-4
ISSN 1094-6225

DIE DEUTSCHE BIBLIOTHEK-CIP-EINHEITSAUFNAHME

Judson, Janis L.:
Law, media, and culture: the landscape of hate /
Janis L. Judson and Donna M. Bertazzoni.
−New York; Washington, D.C./Baltimore; Bern;
Frankfurt am Main; Berlin; Brussels; Vienna; Oxford: Lang.
(Politics, media, and popular culture; Vol. 4)
ISBN 0-8204-4981-4

Cover design by Joni Holst

© 2002 Peter Lang Publishing, Inc., New York

All rights reserved.
Reprint or reproduction, even partially, in all forms such as microfilm,
xerography, microfiche, microcard, and offset strictly prohibited.

Dedicated to the men in our lives:

Jacob, and Michael and Wayne

Table of Contents

Introduction 1

CHAPTER 1
Hate and Society 7

CHAPTER 2
Hate and the Law 31

CHAPTER 3
Hate and the Internet 53

CHAPTER 4
Hate in the News 77

CHAPTER 5
Hate and Popular Music 99

CHAPTER 6
Hate and Television 117

CHAPTER 7
Hate and Film 135

CHAPTER 8
Hate and Gender 155

CHAPTER 9
The Future of Hate 171

EPILOGUE
Hate after September 11 193

References 201

Index 221

— Introduction —

> *Hate, like much of human feeling, is not rational, but it usually has its reasons. And it cannot be understood, let alone condemned without knowing them....There is hate that fears, and hate that merely feels contempt; there is hate that expresses power, and hate that comes from powerlessness; there is revenge, and there is hate that comes from envy...There is hate of the other, and hate that reminds us too much of ourselves. There is the oppressor's hate and the victim's hate. There is hate that burns slowly, and hate that fades. And there is hate that explodes, and hate that never catches fire.*
> (Sullivan 1999, 6)

As journalist Andrew Sullivan observes, hate is a commonly felt emotion. Present in our thoughts and sometimes even in our behavior, hate casts a wide net over the culture, the laws, and the politics of American life. Hate is manifested in words, symbols, and actions. It holds an unrelenting grip on our ideological landscape. How has such a horrific emotion become part of the national psyche? That is the theme we intend to address in this text.

Generally, when we think of people who hate, our minds turn to those at the extreme fringes of society—skinheads, white supremacists, and militiamen on the extreme right, and the Nation of Islam, the former Black Panthers, and the Weathermen on the extreme left. We point to the dragging death of James Byrd in Texas or the murder of gay college student Matthew Shepard, and we shake our heads and wonder how people can be so consumed with hatred that they commit such ugly crimes. We allow ourselves to feel superior because we would never permit our own minor resentments against affirmative action recipients or our own vague feelings of distrust of young black men to boil over into violence. We may not act on our feelings, but the sentiments are there. *Washington Post* journalist Donna Britt recites a similar mantra when she says, "You're civilized—so you dispense your enmity in doses so tiny and manageable, you'd hardly call it hatred at all. However, like the wind that finds a crack in a window, malevolence finds its way. Seeping through crevices in our good sense, exploiting the strains of everyday life, it chills our compassion" (Britt 1998).

A visit to the Museum of Tolerance in Los Angeles alerts us to just how omnipresent the feelings of hate really are. As you enter the museum, you walk through a long corridor of diverse portraits and enter a room with a man speaking to you from multiple screens. He appears to be articulating the need for tolerance, but his artificial and banal talk simply masks the prejudice and hate that reside in all of us. From that room, you are asked to choose one of two doors to enter—just like the television game show *Let's Make a Deal*. The green door reads "unprejudiced" and the red door holds the glaring sign "prejudiced." If you happen to try and open the green door, which many people do, you will discover the door is bolted and locked shut. No one, the message implies, is free of hatred. Even as you walk through the museum and participate in such interactive exhibits as "The Point of View Diner," there is always a voice overhead reminding the viewer that the potential for hatred and violence resides in us all. It is a moving experience that reinforces how normal hatred has become in each of our lives.

As we reflect on how hatred has become part of our national character, we must consider not only those on the fringe of society, but the rest of us who occupy that larger center of the political and social spectrum. We must examine our own intolerant attitudes toward immigrants, gays and lesbians, and other minorities. It is these attitudes toward the "other" that allow racial profiling and the use of deadly force, that lead to reverse discrimination lawsuits, and that block full civil rights for homosexuals and transgendered people.

We must also consider whether hatred may even be functional. Beverly Tatum argues in *Why Are All the Black Kids Sitting Together in the Cafeteria* that, like racism, hatred is a system of cultural messages (1997). These messages form an ideology or set of interconnected ideas that enables a ruling class to maintain its power. James Madison spoke magnificently to this idea in *Federalist No. 10* when he described how contentious factions, motivated by hate and distrust, have had a utilitarian purpose in securing dominant institutions. As a political theorist Madison understood just how hatred could be galvanized by the state for political purposes. Use the natural animosities that men have for one another, remove political power from the masses, and you have, as he wrote, "a well constructed Union" able to mediate the violence of factions. Madison cleverly understood that all citizens possess "a zeal for different opinions concerning religion, concerning government, and many other points," and that these inherent differences "inflamed them" with mutual animosity, hatreds, and "violent conflicts" (1787). For Madison hatred was the glue that kept society together—in an odd sort of way. What price, though, have we paid to utilize hate at the expense of generosity and tolerance?

Hatred is useful in other ways. It only takes a downturn in the economy or what is perceived as a decline in our moral constitution for those at the center to begin to play the blame game. Hatred is essential to blame and scapegoating. Aaron Beck points out in *Prisoners of Hate* that "during periods of social change and economic upheaval, people are more amenable to adopting a paranoid perspective, if that is communicated by an authority. This condemnation of groups of individuals as witches throughout history has provided the oppressed population with a convenient explanation for impoverishment, plagues, and famines" (1999, 150). For our moral guidance, we look to our national leaders. However, what we've gotten are presidents such as Ronald Reagan who branded poor black women as "welfare queens," candidates such as George Bush who allowed supporters to play the race card in the infamous "Willie Horton" campaign advertisement, and attorneys general such as John Ashcroft who have praised the leaders of the Confederacy. Their attitudes and beliefs have allowed the rest of us to feel comfortable accepting, rather than challenging, the stereotypes we are exposed to by our news media and popular culture. We can then use those stereotypes to justify our hatred of the "other."

The ability of the news media to reinforce preexisting hateful attitudes toward minorities is reminiscent of the tactics used by the Nazis to vilify Jews. Beck describes how the German propaganda machine was able to first draw upon long-held images of Jews as diabolical and vile so they could be blamed for the malaise that existed in the country after its defeat in World War I. "The diabolical image of the Jew as a central element in the German's information processing provided simple, acceptable explanations for adverse circumstances" (1998, 179). This negative image was then reinforced in schools, through courses in racial hygiene and biology, on posters that equated Jews with typhus, disease, and death, and in propaganda films such as *The Eternal Jew* (1940) that equated them with vermin. In contrast, the image of the Aryans, and especially that of Hitler, was shown as heroic and mythical. The classic propaganda film *Triumph of the Will* (1934) shows adoring crowds of young blond men and women, so illuminated they appear to be surrounded by halos, watching, waving, and saluting as Hitler is driven by. Beck argues that in such situations, people get caught in "groupthink" (1998, 155). The authorities are able to manipulate what he called the chosen in-group, in this case the Aryans, into believing that social and economic ills are the result of actions taken by the out-group, in this case the Jews. "Framing certain groups of people, placing them into a category, is an expression of the universal tendency to stereotype others" (Beck 1999, 150). It is not a surprise, then, that those in the in-group become willing to stigmatize, blame, and eventually attack those in the out-group. They subordinate and mesh their own personal interests to that of the group, thus energizing ethnic conflict, and acts of prejudice, persecution, and war (Beck 1998).

To further understand the role and significance of hatred in our culture, it is important to distinguish it from its frequent companion—rage. Salman Akhtar, M.D., observes that rage and hatred are different phenomena that can coexist within an individual (1995). Hate sticks to an individual in powerful and relentless ways. Rage is far less dangerous because it is often temporary or transitory. In comparing the two, Akhtar writes, "Rage is ontogenetically primitive; hate is a later development...rage is acute, hatred is chronic...rage has disruptive effects on intellect while hatred sharpens reasoning...rage results from the ego's conflict with an external object, hate from its conflict with an external and an internal object....Rage comes and goes with the inciting event. Hatred simmers" (1995, 89).

We would like to take this useful distinction between rage and hatred and apply it to the broader society. American life seems far less defined by rage or momentary aggressions than by a chronic commitment to festering hatreds. Like the individual, society uses hatred to link the past and future and to establish a sense of continuity and identity (Akhtar 1995). Overcoming hatred will take more than simply preaching to children how to mediate the differences that arise from highlighting multiculturalism in school.

It will require a deeper attitudinal change, which may be difficult to achieve. Often we are prejudiced against different races or ethnic groups without even realizing it. American life is defined and identified by its ideology of hatred. This fact, however, would be vehemently denied by the majority in the center whose unacknowledged attitudes toward the "other" may never lead to violence, but whose rhetoric nevertheless infuses our national conversation with a subtext of hatred.

Self-hatred is another form of hatred important to our study, and we will explore some of its consequences. Why, for example, do so many young boys adopt the philosophy of white supremacist hatred? Are they so unsure of their own self-worth, so consumed with self-disdain, and so desperate to exert their superiority that they must resort to violent action against the "other"? Conversely, is their self-hatred internalized, resulting in self-mutilation and suicide? What role does self-hatred play in the lives of young girls who are now showing more willingness to participate in thoughts and deeds of hate? What about societal self-hatred?

The topic of hate breeds many profound disagreements in American society about the need to enhance punishments of "hate crimes," to take steps toward treating "hate speech" differently from other forms of protected speech, and to accentuate the experiences of victims of hate crimes. Conservatives argue that all crimes include an element of hate, so crimes directed against particular minorities should not be singled out for enhanced status. Free speech advocates argue that the First Amendment was adopted to protect the expression of ideas that the majority does not agree with, even if they are hurtful. And some black scholars argue that the concept of "victimology" actually hampers the progress of African Americans. John H. McWhorter, in his book *Losing the Race*, writes, "Victimology is today nothing less than a keystone of cultural blackness....Victimology today pulses through the very bloodstream of African-American identity" (Asim 2000, C3). He believes that the accent on victims must stop. We also intend to confront these controversial arguments in this book.

We intend to explore our national attachment to hate in the following chapters. Chapter 1 introduces the argument that hate is not just peripheral to fringe segments of our society, but rather finds itself at home at the very center of our culture and politics.

The rhetoric of hatred is often present in mainstream dialogue and in the discourse of our political parties. Chapter 2 looks at hate crimes, and shows how the law is being used to control chronic and even growing hatreds. Chapter 3 examines hate speech through the lens of the Internet, a new terrain of hatred that permits this chronic condition to spread. In chapter 4, we will examine how the news media have covered hate crimes and whether that coverage can actually reinforce hatred. In chapter 5, we switch our attention to popular culture and examine how the subtext of hatred is translated to our youth through music. In chapter 6, we examine how television, as both a news medium and an entertainment medium, reinforces hatred by stereotyping the "other," primarily the African-American "other." We use chapter 7 to look more closely at the effects of hatred on the victim through their portrayal in popular films such as *Rosewood, American History X*, and *Boys Don't Cry*. Chapter 8 documents the growing number of women who are now joining the ranks of men in proselytizing and championing the cause of hatred and dissension. Finally, in chapter 9, we discuss whether it is possible to define and to redirect the national conversation of hatred.

We are about to begin our discussion of hate as a central feature of our national ideology by defining hate and by examining how it has moved into the mainstream of our society. First, though, we must thank our colleagues, especially Dr. Hoda Zaki, for their comments, series editor David Schultz for his insightful critique and support, Hood College and The Hodson Foundation for financially supporting our sabbaticals so we could develop this manuscript, and The Teagle Foundation for supporting our initial research into hate speech on the Internet. We would also like to thank the Berry family of Charles Town, West Virginia, without whose cooperation much of chapter nine of our book would not be possible, George Rutherford, president of the Jefferson County, West Virginia, chapter of the NAACP, Bob Winget, president of FAIR, Dr. Molly Strauss, David Judson, Nan Doss, our students, and especially our families for their support, encouragement, and understanding.

— Chapter 1 —
Hate and Society

A black man is dragged to his death in Texas. A gay student is beaten and left hanging on a fence to die in Wyoming. An abortion doctor is fatally shot in his home in New York. An immigrant is beaten to death at a bus stop in Washington state. Athletes are targeted in a high school shooting rampage in Colorado. Young children at a Jewish community center in California are shot by a white supremacist. Houses under construction in a suburb on Long Island are destroyed by fire. Laboratories that house research animals are destroyed. Why did these incidents occur? What do they have in common? Hate. For one reason or another, the victims in these incidents were despised by their attackers. They were hated because of their race, their ethnicity, their sexuality, their profession, their talent, their religion, or their treatment of animals or the environment.

In the United States today, crimes spawned by hate grab headlines, shocking the nation with their viciousness and increasing regularity. We are living in an era in which hatred has become a part of our national ideology, a subtext of our national conversation. Hatred against the "other" is an endemic and unforgiving aspect of our popular culture. It can be found in contemporary cinema, in television news and entertainment programs that reinforce racial and ethnic stereotypes, on talk shows that rail against affirmative action, in schools that are reluctant to allow children to read books about alternative lifestyles, and on web sites that assert that "God hates fags." Why this reemergence of violent hatred in our society today—decades after the struggle for civil rights should have placed us beyond the scope of that virulent emotion? It seems that the more we tout the virtues and values of a multicultural society, the more we see a growing intolerance, not just from fringe extremists but also from an expanding center of the population. This expanding center of intolerance is influenced by rhetoric from politicians, pundits, and religious leaders on both the right and the left wings of the political spectrum.

It is relatively easy to pinpoint how conservative rhetoric promulgated by right-wing politicians has influenced some of society's hateful attitudes. In *Roads to Dominion: Right Wing Movements and Political Power in the United States*, Sara Diamond traced the rise of the Right and its successful forty-year campaign to insert its message of "capitalism, militarism, and moral traditionalism" permanently into the national conversation (1995, 9). Their rhetoric of moral traditionalism and traditional family values—antigay, anti-Hollywood, antiabortion, pro-Christian, pro-white patriarchy—has become part of the national debate over cultural values, especially during political campaigns. The Right has made "liberal" a dirty word, using language designed to encourage hatred by calling women who have had abortions "baby killers," women who fight for equal rights "feminazis," and people who favor environmental protections "tree huggers." In addition, their view of capitalism has had a hateful effect on less privileged members of society. Right-wing groups have consistently challenged the government's attempts to raise the standard of living for all Americans by opposing affirmative action programs on the grounds that they discriminate against whites (overall the most privileged group in the country). They have attempted to keep the "other" marginalized by fighting government programs that award college scholarships and set aside a certain percentage of contracts to minorities and women, and that attempt to ensure a more racially and ethnically balanced workforce. The message their arguments send is that the vast majority of racial or ethnic minorities who are accepted to college, hired for a job, or promoted to a new position instead of a white person are "less qualified." Over time, that message has become part of our national subtext of hatred. After all, it is much easier to blame the "other" for your inability to get into your number one college choice than to blame your grades.

It is less easy to see how members of the "liberal" left can be viewed as purveyors of hate. After all, they're the ones who, for the most part, advocate equality, support a woman's right to choose, and oppose attempts to reintroduce prayer in public schools. Even so, the anti-Semitic attitudes held by some members of such organizations as the Nation of Islam rival the beliefs of some neo-Nazi groups. In addition, the violence carried out by protestors at World Trade Organization meetings, members of radical environmental groups, and radical animal rights activists promotes hatred of entities as varied as multinational corporations, builders of suburban housing developments, and cancer researchers.

As we will see shortly in our discussion of Levin and Paulsen's typology of hate (1999), it is not necessary to be an active, violent member of a radical racist neo-Nazi group to be a hater. Our societal acquiescence of hatred allows us to sympathize with the ideas, the concepts, and the rhetoric of hate without resorting to action. Ironically, our reluctance to tackle these issues head-on has allowed hatred to flourish and to remain a subtext of our conversation. This message of hate has become so mainstream that elements of it are espoused by members of President George W. Bush's Cabinet.

Before we discuss how hatred has become part of our ideology, it is important to understand what we mean by hate. There is no one clear definition of hate, so in some ways, it is hard to pin down. Instead, we will be offering a variety of definitions, each of which will illustrate a different aspect of hate. In the book *Love, Hate, Fear, Anger and the Other Lively Emotions*, June Callwood asserts that hatred is necessary. She titles one chapter, "Everyone hates, including mothers, lovers, and patriots."

> [H]ate gets the personality moving. Without hate, humans would languish all their lives in a warm stupor of passive contentment; without hate they would need no companion but mother, since mother would be perfect....Few adults hate openly, many believe they don't hate at all. What mankind hates most of all is hatred (1965, 21).

Children are not born hating. They must learn to hate from parents, peers, and other authority figures. As Callwood notes, we live in a contradictory world. Society appears to need and crave hate. We require an "other" to scapegoat, to target, to revile, to blame. At the same time, however, we condemn the outward manifestations of hate. We rail against First Amendment protections for hate speech because of its negative influence on children and its effect on victims and the civic good. We legislate against crimes driven by hate, enhancing penalties for those who commit crimes of bias. We appoint special commissions and support organizations that study, track, and pontificate about hate. We host seminars and conferences to examine the various manifestations of hate. Nevertheless, despite our hatred of hate, society has been unable to eradicate its hold on us. It is part of the American psyche.

Hatred finds its way into American society through words, actions, and symbols. When young children in school taunt one another with such epithets as "gay" and "faggot," they are learning early the language of hate speech. Students, especially those in middle school, often use such words to insult anyone who is different. One middle-school student told *The Washington Post*, "If you're too short, too tall, too fat, too skinny, you get targeted in middle school. Kids sign their yearbooks, 'See you next year, fag'" (Stepp 2001, A7). However, those students who truly are gay are hurt and angered by the casual use of the epithets. Justin Deal, a gay high school student from West Virginia, waged a one-person campaign to stop the harassment of gay students. He drafted a harassment policy for his high school that included sexual harassment, lobbied the governor for a task force to investigate harassment of students, and testified before the legislature, which was considering adding sexual harassment to its hate crimes law. Unsuccessful on all fronts, he finally decided to transfer to another high school with a sizable population of openly gay students. "My friends don't understand that every time I hear the word 'fag' it really hurts," he said. "It reminds me that I'm so far away from what kids see as normal" (Stepp 2001, A7).

A hate action occurs when a person is physically assaulted because of his or her skin color or ethnicity. In April 2000, for example, a suburban Pittsburgh man opposed to immigration went on a rampage, killing an Indian man at a grocery, two Asian men in a Chinese restaurant, a Jewish woman who lived next door to him, and a black man at a karate school. Earlier, the man, Richard Baumhammers, had put up a Web site in which he had advocated less foreign aid, an end to Third World immigration, and making English the nation's official language (Associated Press 2000c). Baumhammers was later convicted of first-degree murder in the hate crimes.

Finally, symbolic expressions of hate occur when nooses, burning crosses, or Nazi regalia are used to intimidate. On the Quantico Marine Base in Virginia, "a headless black mannequin with an iron collar where its neck would have been was tied to a steel rod at the wastewater treatment plant" (Glod 2001). This symbolic display of hatred prompted the NAACP to ask the Marines to investigate. One black employee who worked nights on the base was fearful because, as she said, "not long ago, James Byrd was dragged behind a car in Texas until he was decapitated" (Glod 2001).

What is it about hate that makes it such an enduring emotion? Why is it so central to our culture? Writer Franz Fanon, in his book *Black Skin, White Masks*, argues that "Hate is not inborn; it has to be constantly cultivated, to be brought into being....Hate demands existence, and he who hates has to show his hate in appropriate actions and behavior; in a sense, he has to become hate" (1967, 53). Hate is constantly cultivated in our society through both political rhetoric and cultural offerings such as film and music. The story of Benjamin Smith, to be presented later in this chapter, will illustrate how an individual can become, as Fanon writes, hate incarnate.

Fanon, a black psychiatrist born in Martinique and educated in France, and African-American author Toni Morrison help us to understand why hate has found such an unrelenting foothold in our cultural thinking and worldview. Madison and Callwood have indicated that hate serves a purpose. For Fanon and Morrison, hate actually shapes the lives of all people. Without an "other" our sense of self would have limited meaning. Remember Callwood's contention that without hate we'd spend our lives in a "warm stupor of passive contentment" (1965, 21).

During Algeria's struggle for independence in 1954, Fanon treated both dark-skinned Algerians and white Frenchmen for mental illnesses caused by the war. He vividly described how whites defined themselves in terms of their connection to blacks. For Fanon, the relationship was one of hate and desire—"the act of racism becomes the denial of desire." He examined the relationship of the colonizer and colonized as one in which the slave and the master were interdependent. The slave struggled to win recognition from the master, yet the master was dependent on the recognition of the slave for his validation.

Morrison argues that the white American identity is constructed through its relationship with and representation of an African other (1992). This powerful argument helps to explain why the emotion of hate drives so many people. In *playing in the dark: whiteness in the literary imagination* [*sic*], she contends that white characters in contemporary fiction find their place in the world by measuring themselves against their poorer, darker, powerless counterparts. Morrison writes, "[B]lack slavery enriched the country's creative possibilities. For in that construction of blackness and enslavement could be found not only the not-free, but also, with a dramatic polarity created by skin color, the projection of not-me" (1992, 38).

Fanon and Morrison both believe that the definition of a person's worth and value is dependent on a comparison with a valueless "other." In Morrison's case, this "other" is defined by black/white relations. However, Fanon expands the definition of the "other" to include anyone to whom a person could feel superior, including members of his or her own race or other ethnic minorities. For example, Fanon discusses how natives of Martinique who had visited France felt and acted superior to those who had never left the island. A contemporary example can be found in Spike Lee's 1989 movie *Do the Right Thing*, in which Asians insult Jews, Blacks insult Hispanics, and Hispanics insult Asians. Callwood, too, focuses on hatred of the "other." In her essay she points out, "In the southern United States, poor whites are weirdly comforted by hating Negroes, just as the Germans beaten in World War I were able to regain their battered pride by refining anti-Semitism" (1964, 22).

Elisabeth Young-Bruehl offers us another explanation for the omnipresence of hate in society in *The Anatomy of Prejudices*. She defines three distinct types of hates: obsessive, hysterical, and narcissistic. Obsessive hate is so powerful it may involve a "visceral recoil from the objects of detestation" (Sullivan 1999, 6). Obsessive haters see the "other" as sick and diseased and in need of cleansing from society altogether. Hitler and the Nazis are examples of obsessive haters. They were obsessed by a fantasized threat from a minority that they determined had to be eliminated. In their treatment of Jews, homosexuals, and Gypsies, the Nazis demonstrated what can happen as a result of obsessive hate. It can lead first to laws that segregate those who are hated by making them wear special markings, then to portrayals that demonize them, such as in the film *The Eternal Jew* (1940), and consequently to the "final solution," the Holocaust. Once you have made the "other" less than human, comparing them with rats and vermin, it becomes easy to eradicate them.

The second type of hate Young-Bruehl identifies, hysterical hate, is more complex with respect to the relationship between hater and hated. Hysterical hate involves appointing "a group to act out in the world forbidden sexual and sexually aggressive desires that a person has repressed" (1996, 34). As Andrew Sullivan points out, some racists seem to fit the pattern of hysterical hatred. For some whites, their hatred of blacks results from "sexual and physical envy....A certain kind of white racist sees in black America all those impulses he wishes most to express himself but cannot" (1999, 7). Hysterical hatred can be found on white supremacist Web sites that condemn miscegenation (marriage between whites and people of other races), and in such books as *The Turner Diaries*, which includes a description of "The Day of the Rope," which is the first day of a fictional white rebellion. In the passage, the narrator describes thousands of hanging female corpses with placards around their necks that say, "I DEFILED MY RACE....They are the white women who were married or living with Blacks, with Jews, or with other nonWhite males" (Blythe 2000, n.p.).

Hysterical haters fear that nonwhite men hold a special fascination for white women and, in turn, that men of color cannot resist white women. Trumped-up charges of rape and advances toward white women were used as excuses for repeated lynchings of black men and boys in the South throughout American history. The racially mixed marriage of a white colleague at the University of Colorado at Boulder served as an early impetus along the path of white supremacy for William Pierce, author of *The Turner Diaries*. "I couldn't understand why a white guy would pick a nonwhite woman, because to me they weren't attractive. Still, my idea at the time was that marriage was a strictly private matter" (Blythe 2000).

The third type of hate Young-Bruehl identifies is narcissistic hate, or sexism. "Women are not so much hated by most men as simply ignored in nonsexual contexts, or never conceived of as true equals. The implicit condescension is mixed, in many cases, with repressed and sublimated erotic desire. So the awareness of women is commingled with a deep longing or contempt for them" (Sullivan 1999, 7). The "wilding" incident in New York's Central Park during the Puerto Rican Day festival in which young men harassed and terrorized women speaks volumes about Young-Bruehl's theory that men simultaneously desire and yet harbor great hatred toward women.

Even though Young-Bruehl's categories of hate involve racism, prejudice, and sexism, hatred involves much more than just those elements. Hate is defined in the dictionary as "intense hostility and aversion usually deriving from fear, anger, or sense of injury; an habitual emotional attitude of distaste coupled with sustained ill will; a very strong dislike or antipathy." The verb "hate" means "to feel extreme enmity toward; to have a strong aversion to: detest; to express or feel extreme enmity or active hostility." Synonyms for hate include detest, abhor, abominate, and loathe. Notice what words are not in the definition of hate—prejudice, bias, racism, gay-bashing, anti-Semitism. These are society's manifestations of hate, deriving from such emotions and actions as intolerance, abhorrence, disgust, and moral condemnation. They are part of the cultural messages that are sent through political rhetoric, movies, music, and media. Notice, too, from where these emotions tend to come: fear, anger, or a sense of injury.

In the *Encyclopedia of Human Emotions*, Levin and Paulsen offer a typology of hate, identifying four distinct types of haters (1999). In the hierarchy of hatred, the first type they identify is a hatemonger. These people believe "that the very presence of certain groups of people in *their* town, *their* state, *their* country represents an intolerable threat to their personal well-being and to the survival of their group's way of life" (1999, 327). Hatemongers, who are also known as mission haters, are on the fringe of society. As members of such organized hate groups as the White Aryan Resistance or the World Church of the Creator, they proselytize hate by passing out leaflets, recruiting on college campuses, and producing programs to air on cable access television stations.

A dabbler is the second type of hater. Levin and Paulsen describe dabblers as young people, usually teenage boys, who have trouble getting along "at home, in school, or on the job." As a result, they say, these young men "may hate themselves as much as they hate their victims." These haters are also known as "thrill seekers." They commit most of the hate crimes against blacks, gays, Latinos, Asians, and Jews, and by doing so, they gain "bragging rights" (Levin and Paulsen 1999, 328). Dabblers and hatemongers are at the extreme edges of the hate movement; many of them identify themselves as members of organized hate groups. They commit most of the violent acts against the "other," and their messages of hate and intolerance make their way into the mainstream through media coverage of their actions. Their philosophies can also be found on innumerable Web sites, and the harm caused by their hate speech will be examined more fully in a later chapter.

To better understand the hatemongers and dabblers, it would be useful to discuss some of the major hate groups operating in the United States today and what they believe. According to the Southern Poverty Law Center (SPLC), which tracks hate movements in the United States, the number of Americans who belong to organized hate groups ranges from about 20,000 to 50,000. In 2000, 602 identified hate groups were operating; that represented a 10 percent increase in the number of groups from 1999. The center attributed the increase to "white power rock, racist neo-Paganism, and the ethnic nationalism that is growing in places from the deep South to the nation's inner cities" (SPLC 2001). The center also noted that "multiculturalism and globalism" are among the issues driving the increase in membership in hate groups. As Beck noted in *Prisoners of Hate*, economic woes can also focus hatred against the "other." Joe Roy, director of the Intelligence Project, agreed: "If the economy goes sour, we can expect more scapegoating violence especially against immigrants. Hard times have a way of making things worse" (SPLC 2001).

International conflicts involving the United States are another catalyst for hatred against ethnic minorities. In 2001, for instance, Chinese Americans were targeted after an American surveillance plane was forced to land in China after a collision with a Chinese pilot. In Springfield, Illinois, a disc jockey for a local radio station suggested that Chinese Americans be placed in internment camps similar to the ones set up by the U.S. government during World War II to hold Japanese Americans—a horrific example of institutional hatred—and that all Chinese be sent home to "their country" (Golden 2001). The attack against Chinese Americans mirrored similar attacks against Arab Americans during the Persian Gulf conflict, and the U.S. government's knee-jerk reaction after the bombing of the Murrah Federal Building in Oklahoma City. In that instance, it was immediately assumed that the building had been destroyed by Arab terrorists, and an Arab-American man was held at an airport in London on suspicion of planting the bomb. These incidents emphasize that hatred of ethnic minorities and immigrants is so close to the surface that it takes little to bring it to the forefront.

The increase in hate groups in 2000 represented a reversal from 1999, when the number of organized groups declined. In its 2000 Intelligence Report, though, the SPLC pointed to three reasons that the decline in hate groups could be deceiving—the Internet, consolidation of smaller groups into larger groups, and, most importantly for our viewpoint, the mainstreaming of radical right issues. The center reported that "many of the key issues of the radical right—especially those related to race—have been siphoned off by more 'respectable' groups. Immigration, affirmative action, race-based IQ theories, black crime, and similar matters are key issues for groups like the racist Council of Conservative Citizens, an outfit that includes many southern lawmakers" (SPLC 2000b, 6). Among mainstream politicians who have had contact with the Council of Conservative Citizens are Sen. Trent Lott, R-Miss., Attorney General John Ashcroft, and Rep. Bob Barr, R-Ga., one of the House impeachment managers (Conason 2001).

Hate groups are clustered under several umbrella categories. The oldest and perhaps best-known group is the Ku Klux Klan, which has operated since after the Civil War, and currently has more than 130 chapters, mostly in the South. The SPLC breaks the hate groups into five additional categories: neo-Nazi, racist skinhead, Identity churches, black separatist, and others, which include such groups as the National Association for the Advancement of White People, the Council of Conservative Citizens, and some publishing and record companies (SPLC 2000b). Except for the black separatist movement, which focuses on antiwhite propaganda, most of the remaining hate groups share common beliefs. They include the natural rights of whites in a "Christian" nation; the dangers of Jewish dominance in government, finance, and the entertainment industry; the breakdown of the family that would result if "special rights" were given to gays and lesbians; the unfairness of affirmative action programs that allow "unqualified" minorities to take jobs away from deserving white males; and the fear of race-mixing that would result if more white women married men of color.

Affirmative action and protection for gays and lesbians are among the issues that divide middle America today. These are right-wing issues that have found a voice at the center of mainstream discourse. Loretta Ross argues that white supremacist ideologies have become part of the "social fabric of our politics, our institutions, and our laws:"

> With time and repetition, white supremacists have fused many fringe far right beliefs together into acceptable mainstream values. While hate groups have previously relied on violence, their new manipulation of ultra-conservative rhetoric has combined with this to provide a deadly acceptance of intolerance in this country (1995, n.p.).

We are concerned about this mainstream acceptance of once-radical white supremacist ideology. This acceptance of intolerance is at the heart of the chronic nature of hate in our society. The rhetoric described by Diamond has long been embraced by the right wing of the Republican Party, which over the past several decades has been willing to use race, homophobia, and opposition to affirmative action to appeal to white conservatives during presidential elections. The party has come to be dominated by conservative Southern white men, and the voices of moderates in the party have increasingly been drowned out. Sen. Jesse Helms, the "unabashed white racist politician" (Broder 2001, A21), has dominated North Carolina politics for more than thirty years. Helms decided in 2001 not to seek reelection, but will the hatred that he has nourished in his own state and elsewhere dissipate? Even the departure from the party of Sen. James Jeffords of Vermont, which led to it losing control of the Senate in May 2001, may not be enough to temper the entrenched hatred of Southern voices.

This intolerance is found among the final two categories of haters in Levin and Paulsen's typology, the sympathizers and the spectators. These people represent the hidden majority of haters, those who secretly harbor fear, anger, and resentment against the "other." Sympathizers do not act on their hate, but they agree with those who discriminate or commit violent acts. Even more importantly, they do not make any move to stop hatred. "Because of their refusal to cooperate with those who seek to bring bigots to justice, sympathizers also share responsibility for the acts that their sympathetic stance makes possible" (Levin and Paulsen 1999, 328).

Spectators may passively support equal rights and equal treatment for ethnic minorities and people of color. Nevertheless, they rarely put themselves out to support equality in fact. They are "indifferent or apathetic rather than hateful.... In the context of everyday decision making, they stand idly by, hoping not to get personally involved" (1999, 329). They do little to stop the rhetoric against "welfare queens," gays seeking "special" rights, and "unqualified" students helped by affirmative action.

Sympathizers and spectators rarely commit violent acts. However, their support of the rhetoric of hatred and their failure to counter that rhetoric have allowed negative attitudes about the "other" to become part of mainstream discourse. The political success of the Christian Right indicates that many sympathizers and spectators vote based on these attitudes. As Levin and Paulsen point out, "when a particular hatred becomes part of the culture—the way of life—of a group of people, sympathy for that hatred may become a widely shared and enduring element in the normal state of affairs for that society. As such, sympathizers (through reinforcing contact with parents, friends, teachers, and the mass media) develop their hate from an early age" (1999, 329). This normalization of hatred reminds us of Hannah Arendt's classic study *Eichmann in Jerusalem: A Report on the Banality of Evil*, in which she describes how evil can become all too commonplace in any society (1994).

This normalization of hatred is influenced by the moral leadership, rhetoric, and attitudes of the politicians and political parties who influence mainstream discourse. While their message of hatred pervades the national conversation, it is rarely overtly racist, sexist, or anti-Semitic. (The exception seems to be in campaigns against gay rights, which are often openly homophobic.) Instead, symbols and code words are used to denigrate the "other" and to evoke long-ingrained stereotypes and fears. The codes have become a regular part of our political campaigns. Diamond, for example, cites the infamous Willie Horton advertisement used against Democratic presidential nominee Michael Dukakis in 1988. "The Willie Horton spots made no claims about genetic racial differences, as the organized neo-Nazi movement would have done" (1995, 270). Instead, the ad, with its revolving prison door, was aimed at hysterical haters, and not-so-subtly played on white fears of the sexual prowess of black men. Similarly, Craig Horowitz noted Vice President Dan Quayle's attack on "the cultural elite" of

Hollywood during the 1992 presidential campaign. "Many people simply saw *cultural elite* as a euphemism for *Jewish elite*. Addressing a Clinton fund-raising dinner, in fact, director Mike Nichols opened by saying, 'We can drop the Republican code for 'cultural elite.' Good evening, fellow Jews'" (1996, 23). Before the 2000 presidential election, advertisements were run on television stations and in newspapers in the Washington, D.C., area linking immigration policies to commuter traffic problems and runaway development (Laris 2000). Without strong counterarguments from sympathizers and spectators, these advertisements against the "other" rile up voters who are frustrated by problems that seem unsolvable. It is much easier to blame the immigrants (most of whom cannot afford new houses in northern Virginia anyway) than the real culprits—the politicians who will not say no to the developers and the commuters who will not say yes to car pools.

This message of hatred and intolerance is an underlying theme of our national political discourse. Diamond points out that the Christian Right and the New Right, which tend to use these code words, enjoy more political influence than the extremists on the racist Right. David Duke is one of the few representatives of the racist Right who was elected to public office (1995). However, politicians less radical than Duke have helped spread the message of the racist Right, so spectators and sympathizers can hear it and discuss it. Pat Buchanan, the Reform Party's candidate for president in 2000, is a good example of a right-wing politician whose intolerant beliefs have found their way into mainstream discourse. After Buchanan's book *A Republic, Not an Empire* was published, Rabbi Marvin Hier, dean and founder of the Simon Wiesenthal Center (SWC), called Buchanan "the preeminent guru of America's haters." Referring to Buchanan's anti-Semitic attitudes, he said, "Buchanan speaks in a code that his constituents understand very well. When describing who he alleges forced America into World War II, he says it was the fault of 'Wall Street bankers, plutocratic newspapers, magazine writers, the intelligentsia, communists, Hollywood...'—all code words for Jews" (SWC 1999). It is ironic that the infamous "butterfly ballot" in Palm Beach County, Florida, was blamed for the number of elderly Jewish voters selecting Buchanan as their choice for president in the 2000 election.

As the Reform Party candidate for president, Buchanan failed to attain even the 5 percent of the national vote his party would need to receive public funding in the 2004 presidential election. Perhaps that is because the issues he champions—limiting immigration and bilingual education, curtailing gay rights, and ending affirmative action—have been adopted by mainstream candidates. For example, he called immigration "America's most pressing foreign policy crisis." His argument has been mirrored in mainstream attacks on bilingual education and proposals across the country to initiate "English only" programs. In a referendum, for example, California voters limited bilingual education. In addition, President Bush's initial nominee for Labor Secretary, Linda Chavez, criticized bilingual education in her first book.

Buchanan makes no secret of his abhorrence of the "gay rights agenda." In an interview with National Public Radio's "Talk of the Nation" program in May 2000, he said,

> On your point about all Americans are equal, there's no doubt all of us have the same constitutional rights. I agree. However, I think a real problem America has is we've taken this idea of equality and extended it so beyond where it belongs. All lifestyles are not equal. All ideas are not equal. Some are wrong; some are right (Issues 2000, n.p.).

One need look no further than Attorney General John Ashcroft's views on homosexuality to find a more mainstream version of Buchanan's beliefs.

Buchanan also opposed what he calls "government-sponsored prejudice." "A true respect for civil rights requires that we put an end to all racial, ethnic, and gender entitlements. No quotas, no set-asides, no forced busing, no mandatory hiring, no affirmative action. As President, I will eliminate all forms of discrimination in federal agencies, including reverse discrimination" (Buchanan 2000). Again, President Bush's Cabinet nominees Linda Chavez and John Ashcroft espoused similar beliefs. As attorney general and governor of Missouri, for example, Ashcroft fought court-ordered desegregation of St. Louis schools.

Pat Buchanan may represent a far right-wing view of what America ought to resemble, but as we have seen, he is far from alone in questioning the worth of such programs as affirmative action, minority set-asides, gay rights, and bilingual education. Of the contentious issues that are part of mainstream discourse, affirmative action seems to resonate loudest. Many middle-class Americans believe this government policy undermines rather than promotes equality because it offers what some consider preferential treatment for particular people. However, the vocal opponents of affirmative action—those who sympathize most strongly with these views—choose to ignore the advantages that white people enjoy in this society. In *White Man Falling: Race, Gender, and White Supremacy*, Abby Ferber argues that some segments of society believe that white masculinity is in crisis and is in need of reaffirmation (1999). (This belief plays into both the criticism of affirmative action and the traditional white patriarchy supported by the Christian Right.) Once private reflections criticizing affirmative action are now common to public discourse. People are no longer afraid to articulate their bias against what they believe is coerced multiculturalism, and their opinions have influenced federal, state, and local policies. These attitudes have led to backlashes against affirmative action in such states as California and Texas. Both states have limited affirmative action programs in education, leading to demonstrable reductions in black admissions to colleges, universities, and graduate schools. During a presidential debate with Al Gore, Republican nominee George W. Bush, then the governor of Texas, refused to acknowledge that he even understood what affirmative action was all about. Instead, he insisted that he supported "affirmative access."

The argument over affirmative action serves as a good example of how the attitudes of the extreme right wing have become part of mainstream discourse. "Americans don't merely talk about affirmative action, they shout about it," according to an article in *The Washington Post*. "Blacks walk around with a chip on their shoulder like we owe them something, I don't feel that we do," a Texas housewife told reporters. "They talk about a glass ceiling for women and minorities, but there's a glass ceiling for middle-age white male managers too," said a middle-aged technical specialist for the EPA in Georgia. "Affirmative action to me was supposed to be used to equal things out. Now it's used as an excuse," said an Army specialist in California (Morin and Warden 1995, A1).

A national survey conducted in 2001 by *The Washington Post*, the Henry J. Kaiser Family Foundation, and Harvard University found that 40 to 60 percent of whites believe that blacks are as well off, or even better off, than they are in terms of their jobs, incomes, schooling, and health care. However, statistics indicate that the gap between whites and blacks in terms of their positions in the workplace, their earnings, and the amount of schooling they receive continues to be wide. The median household income for whites in 1999 was $44,366, while it was $27,910 for blacks. Only about 17 percent of blacks have completed college, compared with 28 percent of whites. About one-third of whites hold managerial positions, compared with one-fifth of blacks (Morin 2001, A1). The survey suggests that "among whites, the pervasiveness of incorrect views seems to explain, at least in part, white resistance to even the least intrusive types of affirmative action" (Morin 2001, A1). A consultant on the survey project, political scientist Keith Reeves of Swarthmore College, said the results suggest that most whites do not believe that in 2001 problems could still exist. The attitude among whites is, "we could not possibly be saddled with segregation and discrimination, and therefore things can't possibly be as bad as black Americans say they are" (Morin 2001, A1).

These whites fit squarely into the spectator category. They do not believe the type of discrimination that was prevalent years ago still exists, so they see no need for any type of programs that would give minorities additional opportunities. Many of them oppose even the mildest of affirmative action programs, such as preference or outreach programs that recruit minority job candidates. A thirty-year-old firefighter from Rockford, Illinois, reflected that view for the survey. He opposes such programs if the result is that blacks receive more consideration than whites. "That boils down to reverse discrimination," he said. "I think education and jobs should be open to everybody. If they want to recruit minorities, fine, as long as an equally qualified white isn't replaced. If that's a problem, make the school bigger" (Morin 2001, A1).

The problem with this attitude is that neither employers nor schools can just make themselves bigger. An employer can easily find a reason to hire the "equally qualified" white person instead of the black person or another ethnic minority. This attitude contributes to the difficulties that blacks and other minorities are having in achieving economic and social parity. This difficulty is exacerbated by the fact that many white people who compete one-on-one with minorities for jobs and for college scholarships are working-class whites. As Beck points out in *Prisoners of Hate* (1999), economic woes can lead to scapegoating and hatred. When it is more difficult to find jobs, it becomes easier to hate those people who are perceived as receiving special treatment and special opportunities. White "spectators" can move easily into the sympathizer or the dabbler category when they believe they have been victims of reverse discrimination. They then become more susceptible to the rhetoric of white supremacist organizations.

The rhetoric condemning affirmative action from such white supremacists as David Duke, William Pierce, and Matt Hale is not that far removed from the comments made by the everyday Americans in *The Washington Post*. A former member of the Ku Klux Klan, Duke founded the National Association for the Advancement of White People, served in Louisiana's state legislature, and ran for governor of that state. He says, "[D]iscrimination against White people must be ended. We must end set-asides in contracting, and stop the massive racial discrimination against Whites in jobs, promotions, college entrances, or scholarships. Whether it is called quotas or "goals," racial preference must be ended: PERIOD! The only preference must be for the best qualified" (2000). This statement reinforces the hateful notion, held by many sympathizers and spectators, that racial and ethnic minorities are hired or accepted to college because of special programs, not because they are qualified.

Pierce, of the National Alliance, writes, "Whites—even Whites who never think about crime statistics—resent programs which give Blacks an advantage over them. They resent having academic standards lowered and work performance standards lowered just to make it easier for Blacks" (1997a). One of the most radical white supremacists is Matt Hale of the World Church of the Creator. He calls equality "a mythology embraced either by the inferior as a way of achieving social gain, or as an opportunistic method by which politicians pander to the masses in an effort to obtain their votes." Equality is at the heart of the democratic ethos that guides our nation. However, Hale calls it a "dangerous" mythology because, for example, it affords equal weight to the votes of whites and blacks. He says, "That the future of our people may be decided by such a scenario clearly reveals the poisonous nature of the equality mythology" (2000a).

In reading these quotes, you can see how close the rhetoric advanced by many mainstream politicians is to the messages advanced by Pierce, Duke, and Buchanan. Only Hale seems truly radical, as he boasts openly of the need to hate:

> We Creators recognize that in order to create, one must first often destroy what stands in the way in the process, and necessarily, in order to destroy, the emotion of hatred must be involved. To think otherwise is folly. To think and express the idea that we don't hate the Jews and mud races but only love our own is a flight from reality—one which many in the White racial struggle all too often choose to indulge in (2000b).

Few Americans, of any racial or ethnic group, are ready or willing to accept Hale's extremist views. They are not "hatemongers." However, as sympathizers and spectators, many are willing to listen, discuss, debate, and accept these same ideas when presented in a more reasonable fashion, such as in speeches by legitimate right-wing politicians. Does that make most Americans haters? Certainly not in a fashion that is going to prompt them to commit violent acts against people who are unlike themselves. Even so, many Americans who consider themselves mainstream hold views that contain elements of hate. How much of the rhetoric against affirmative action, immigration, and gay rights is prompted by fear, anger, or a sense of injury? Ross writes:

> White fears of change or difference are exploited by hate groups. At the same time, they are expanding their targets of hate. They have adopted not only homophobia as a prominent part of their new agenda, but are forcefully anti-abortion, pro-family values, and pro-American, in addition to their traditional racist and anti-Semitic beliefs (1995).

In essence, she says these groups are using "conservative buzzwords" to recruit white sympathizers and spectators.

This rhetoric constitutes a harmful manifestation of the culture of hate, moving it from the radical fringe into the mainstream of society. The city of Charlottesville, Virginia, has grappled with whether it should invite this rhetoric of hate into the community by allowing the Thomas Jefferson Center for the Protection of Free Expression to erect a "Community Chalkboard." There would be no restrictions on what people could write on the board, and many residents fear that it would become a magnet for hatred and intolerance. Local resident Barbara Merriwether, a retired educator who grew up in Mississippi, opposed the chalkboard at a public hearing. "There will be hate messages, messages of intolerance. My white friends think it's going to happen, too. It's in our society already. What's the purpose of inviting it?" (Morello 2001). In defending the board, J. Joshua Wheeler, associate director of the Jefferson Center, said, "We know there's going to be some offensive writing on the wall. The question is, do we just tolerate free expression or welcome it?" (Morello 2001). Here, residents of Charlottesville are confronted with the difficult conundrum of how to allow free speech without appearing to condone the inevitable hate speech that flourishes because of the First Amendment.

These messages of intolerance have even found their way into the police force of a major metropolitan city whose residents are majority African American. In March 2001, it was revealed that in internal e-mails, police officers in Washington, D.C., regularly used racial epithets to describe suspects and committed acts that could result in charges of racial profiling. Police Chief Charles Ramsey immediately reprimanded members of the force for their actions, and asked for a Department of Justice investigation (Santana and Lengel 2001a, 2001b). This intolerance is also found in one of the bedrock institutions of this country—the military. Numerous incidents have been reported through the years of military personnel engaging in hatred.

Intolerance and hate come in many guises. While George W. Bush was declared the ultimate winner of the 2000 presidential election, he received only 8 percent of African-American votes nationwide. Despite his pledge to be a "uniter, not a divider," he nominated for his Cabinet three people who drew fire for expressing intolerant attitudes and beliefs. None of them uttered the word "hate." None of them could be considered a "hatemonger." Even so, they all had expressed views that reinforce our concern about hatred as a subtext of our national ideology. The first was Chavez, who eventually was forced to withdraw as Labor Secretary nominee because she did not reveal to Bush transition officials that she had housed an illegal alien in her home. Labor and civil rights groups opposed her nomination because of her well-known antipathy toward government programs that benefit minorities and immigrants, and her opposition to bilingual education. The second nominee who drew fire was Interior Secretary Gale Norton, not only for her environmental views, but also for her support of the Confederacy. After visiting a Confederate cemetery in Virginia, she defended the concept of states' rights, and said that the country "lost too much" when the South lost the Civil War. She did not condone slavery, but instead referred to it as "bad facts in that case where we were defending state sovereignty" (Blight 2001). Norton's reference to slavery as a "bad fact" raises questions about her ability to understand the harm caused by the subjugation and dehumanizing treatment afforded African-Americans under slavery and the Jim Crow laws that eventually followed emancipation. In addition, her defense of the Confederacy, even in the guise of supporting states' rights, mirrors the attitude of many Americans who choose not to acknowledge that maintaining official symbols of the Confederacy serves as a message of hate toward African-Americans.

The nominee who generated the most controversy was former Missouri Senator John Ashcroft, selected to be attorney general. Ashcroft, described in *The Washington Post* as a "longtime hero to the Christian right," was faulted, among other reasons, for his strong opposition to abortion, his opposition to school desegregation in St. Louis while he was attorney general and governor of Missouri, his meeting with the head of the racist Council of Conservative Citizens, his defense of leaders of the Confederate States of America, his acceptance of an honorary degree from Bob Jones University, and his successful campaign to block the elevation of an African-American judge to the federal bench. In his confirmation hearings, Ashcroft pledged to uphold the law despite his personal views (Eggen and Vise 2001). However, his views may exacerbate problems with hate in our society. As attorney general, he sets the tone for the justice system in the country. He has leeway on how many resources to devote to enforcing laws that protect the civil rights of all Americans, including homosexuals and women seeking abortions. He will be asked for legal opinions, and can intervene in federal court cases. He also may have some influence over the selection of nominees for federal judicial appointments, and abortion rights groups fear he will use abortion as a litmus test in the judicial selection process.

Even outside the United States questions have been raised about his appointment. In a commentary, Martin Kettle of *The Guardian* criticized Ashcroft's remarks to *Southern Partisan* magazine, in which he defended "Southern patriots" like Jefferson Davis and Robert E. Lee. Ashcroft told the magazine, "We've all got to speak up in this respect, or else we'll be taught that these people were giving their lives, subscribing their sacred fortunes and their honor to some perverted agenda." As Kettle pointed out, "[T]o many people, the meaning of such words is difficult to misunderstand. Preserving slavery, Ashcroft is implying, is not a perverted agenda" (2001). At the beginning of the twenty-first century, do we want our president to be advised by a man who holds such hateful beliefs, even if he has pledged to "uphold the law"? A good bit of the United States Senate did not. Ashcroft won confirmation, although 42 Democratic senators voted against him. Shortly after his confirmation, Ashcroft met with members of the most prominent gay Republican organization, the Log Cabin Republicans, and he appointed a commission to study racial profiling. Perhaps the fears that his personal views will affect his public actions will prove to be unfounded. As of this writing, it is too soon to tell.

For the most part, the effect of the mainstream rhetoric of hate is subtle, yet insidious. It keeps African Americans, other ethnic minorities, gays, lesbians, and immigrants marginalized. They are unable to access the full range of civil rights that should be available to members of a free society. They are discriminated against in a variety of small and subtle ways that support a system of institutional intolerance and hatred. However, when they seek programs that would level the playing field, they are accused of demanding "special" rights. The vast majority of white Americans do not resort to violence to maintain their position in society. They don't need to. The way society is structured, whites enjoy natural advantages. However, for a few people, alienated young men especially, the message of those who preach fear, anger, hatred, and intolerance against the "other" resonates and leads to the commission of hate crimes.

For several years, the Federal Bureau of Investigation has been maintaining statistics on hate crimes. A hate crime is defined as a traditional offense that is motivated by the offender's bias. Statistics are currently kept on crimes committed because of a person's race, religion, sexual orientation, ethnicity/national origin, or disability.

In 1999, nearly 7,900 hate crimes (including 9,301 separate hate incidents involving 9,802 victims) were reported to the FBI. Of those, 4,295 were racially motivated, 1,411 were religiously motivated, 1,317 were based on the victim's sexual identity, 829 on the ethnicity or national origin of the victim, and the remaining 24 incidents on the basis of disability or for multiple reasons (FBI 2001). The largest number of incidents based on race were antiblack, 2,958, compared with 781 antiwhite, 298 anti-Asian/Pacific Islander, 47 anti-American Indian/Alaskan native, and 211 anti-multiracial group. The largest number of religious hate crimes were targeted against Jews, 1,109. Other categories, such as anti-Catholic, anti-Protestant, and anti-Islamic, reported fewer than 50 crimes each. Finally, male homosexuals were the targets of the greatest number of incidents based on sexual orientation, 915 of the 1,317 crimes reported.

The following story illustrates how hatred against the "other" can consume a person and lead to pain, suffering, and even death. Benjamin Smith, a follower of Matt Hale's World Church of the Creator, allowed his hatred to boil over, destroying the peace and security of his victims, and ultimately leading to his own death. Smith's story is frightening to parents, educators, and social observers because of the ease by which the seduction and allure of hatred manifests itself in modern life and culture. Smith burst into the national consciousness on Independence Day in 1999. Generally, Independence Day is a time to reflect on the positive aspects of the United States—the notions of freedom, justice, and equality for all. However, that year it was a time of terror for religious, racial, and ethnic minorities in the Midwest when Smith went on a shooting rampage that killed two people and injured nine others. The terror finally ended when he killed himself.

Smith's background does not fit the stereotype of someone who ends up a racist murderer. News stories written at the time of the incident indicate that Smith did not grow up in poverty, and he did not openly denigrate minorities through high school. In contrast, he roomed with an African-American student in college, had Jewish friends, and dated an Asian-American woman. After the incident, his parents issued statements disavowing their son's racist beliefs. What caused Smith to snap? At the time of the shooting spree, interviews with Smith that had been videotaped before he died were broadcast on national television. One of the tapes, made by Beverly Peterson, was entitled "Invisible Revolution." On the tape, Smith cited the Internet as a potent source for information. "It's a slow, gradual process to become racially conscious. ...I thought about these issues before, but it wasn't really until I got on the Internet, read some literature of these groups that it really—it really all came together" (*Dateline NBC* 2000).

Smith's attitudes about Jews, African Americans, and other people of color came to reflect those of WCOTC leader Matt Hale. In April 1999, Smith was arrested on a nuisance charge after trying to distribute hate literature in his hometown of Wilmette, Illinois. In the video, Smith said, "If they violate our constitutional rights and say we can't put out our literature, we have no choice but to resort to acts of violence and really to plunge this country into a terrorist war they've never seen before" (Sawyer, McFadden, and Donaldson 1999).

Soon after, Hale was denied a license to practice law by the state of Illinois because of his racist views. (In June 2000, that decision was upheld by the U.S. Supreme Court.) After the shooting spree, Hale was quick to take advantage of Smith's actions, answering questions from print and broadcast reporters. He told reporters that Illinois's decision to deny him a law license "likely triggered" Smith's actions (Elliott 1999). He also described Smith as a "martyr for free speech" and told Reuters news service that Smith turned violent because he felt "oppressed" by those who sought to protest his hate speech.

No one will really ever know what was the compelling moment or the exact set of circumstances that coalesced to push Smith in the direction of violent action. We do not know why he was not able to undo the damage done by the cultural messages of hate. We can ask, though, what it is about young white males that makes them targets for hate recruiters and pushes them from spectators and sympathizers into the hatemonger category? What factors influence young people's views of society, their socialization into its culture, and their ensuing civic responsibilities? As Young-Bruehl points out, "[T]he case literature available for studying the origins and developments of the various prejudice types suggests that adolescence is the key period for the conversion of incipient prejudices into fully articulated prejudices and acts of discrimination or violence" (1996, 299). Are young women as vulnerable to that seduction? Gender assumptions about hate and socialization will be addressed at a later juncture.

Benjamin Smith, Matt Hale, and William Pierce represent the hatemongers among us, yet they do not fit the common stereotype of a hater. Smith grew up in a wealthy suburb of Chicago. Hale graduated from law school, and Pierce holds a Ph.D. in physics. No one common circumstance turned them from hate sympathizers or spectators into hatemongers. However, our political discourse, laws, media, and popular culture—our cultural messages of hate—all contribute to an atmosphere in American society that makes it easy to hate. They make it easy for any one of us to become a Smith and to allow our hate to explode.

Hate is an integral part of American society. We would prefer that this hate be the type that, as Sullivan writes, either "soon fades" or, better yet, the type that "never catches fire" (1999, 5). Only then can we begin to chart a different course toward creating a more tolerant, civil, and caring community. Until that happens, though, our society must find other ways to express its disapproval of hate. One of the ways we have done that is through passage of a series of laws that enhance the punishment of those who commit hate crimes. In the next chapter we will examine the rationale behind those laws, and why they are controversial.

— Chapter 2 —
Hate and the Law

His smiling face looks out at you from the newspaper. You cringe at the description of him being stabbed to death in broad daylight in front of his playmates and siblings. Eight-year-old Kevin Shifflett was brutally attacked in April 2000 on an Alexandria, Virginia, street. His death aroused a sense of profound grief, not only among those who knew and loved him, but in the broader community as well. Federal authorities, who later arrested Gregory D. Murphy on an unrelated drug charge, believe Murphy is the man who murdered Kevin Shifflett. They asked a federal grand jury to investigate possible civil rights violations in connection with Kevin's death because Murphy is black and Kevin was white. The grand jury was asked "to determine whether Kevin's slaying violated federal statutes that make it a civil rights crime"—a hate crime—"to interfere for racial reasons with someone's right to live in their home or use the public street" (Masters and Davis 2000, B9).

Why might Kevin's slaying be a hate crime? When officials first arrested Murphy, they discovered a handwritten note in his motel room advocating the killing of "racist white kids." What difference would it make if Kevin's death is found to be a hate crime? If Murphy is convicted of a crime that is motivated by "racial animus," he will receive a harsher penalty than someone who commits a parallel crime, a crime that lacks "bias motivation." For example, if John S., a white man, walks up to James G., a black man, and stabs him to death simply to rob him of his briefcase and wallet, John S. would be guilty of committing a parallel crime—a crime without racial motivation. John S. did not select his victim because of his race, whereas it appears Murphy did choose Kevin because of his race. Does Gregory Murphy deserve a harsher penalty than John S.? Should the law treat crimes of hate differently from so-called parallel crimes? Is Kevin Shifflett more of a victim than our fictional James G.?

This conundrum of hate and the law is one of the several issues to be examined in this chapter.

How has the law actually dealt with individual and societal manifestations of hate? Lawrence Friedman identifies several functions of law—among them social change, social control, and social maintenance (1984). While society and culture have forced us into a grim awareness of the presence of hatred and the need to control such behavior, the law simultaneously permits that hatred to flourish under the rubric of constitutionalism. Before we consider how society has allowed such a paradox, we need to identify the structures of law that have been pressed into service to react to hate. The Congress, the Supreme Court, and the various state legislatures have all been faced with the task of hate control. These institutions have defined the parameters of hate, either through statutory legislation or through judicial interpretation.

In analyzing how institutions have broached the problem of hate, we must distinguish between hate language and hate action. Hate speech has the unequivocal protection of the First Amendment, a fact that has polarized scholars and antagonized the national community. This chapter will explore how our formal law controls, changes, and yet maintains hate; how the critical institutions approach these tasks; and how the problem of hate has now coalesced into a battle over the limits of speech and conduct. The following questions will be useful in helping us to analyze this issue: When did hate crime legislation first emerge? What types of statutes have been put in place to combat hate? What kinds of conduct are covered by the various statutes? What future policy issues will be raised by new hate crime legislation?

In looking at the history of how American law has addressed the problem of hate, we can easily argue that our formal institutions at one time clearly fostered hate—an integral component of racism. The crimes of slavery, the Black Codes, and decisions of the Court such as *Dred Scott v. Sanford* (1857) were all structural embodiments and reinforcements of hate. When the Supreme Court failed to identify Scott's right of citizenship, it was ultimately codifying an emotion of hatred against people of color. Despite the passage of the Fourteenth Amendment, which held the promise of due process and equal protection for all, the reality of hate prevailed as whites continued to believe that blacks were not fully human. Even a constitutional amendment could not ensure racial tolerance, as the *Civil Rights Cases* (1883) and the *Plessy v. Ferguson* (1896) decisions would illustrate. As Nathan Rutstein writes, "[T]he pattern of racial thinking had been set." Today, Toni Morrison describes this same phenomenon as the "race talk" of whites who use a distorted lens to examine human equality (1992).

While we recognize the importance of the legacy of slavery, our analysis does not begin from that chronological point, nor from other moments in history when American institutions codified and legitimized hate. Rather, this study addresses the contemporary question of hate and begins at the point where state legislatures first began to incorporate a reference to hate in their statutes regulating speech and action. The Supreme Court began its assault on hate when it advanced its "fighting words" doctrine in the 1942 case of *Chaplinsky v. New Hampshire*. Chaplinsky was convicted of a breach of public order for calling a local politician a "god-damned racketeer" and a "fascist" in front of an already unruly crowd. On appeal, the Supreme Court ruled that the First Amendment did not guarantee protection for speakers espousing certain categories of words, such as fighting words or hateful speech. Writing for the Court majority, Justice Murphy ruled that fighting words "by their very utterance inflict injury or tend to incite an immediate breach of the peace." Murphy further argued that speech that plays no part in "any exposition of ideas" cannot expect constitutional protection (1942).

In successive fighting words cases, however, the Court began to retreat from the *Chaplinsky* ruling. In *Terminiello v. Chicago* (1949), the Court invalidated the conviction of a Catholic priest who had verbally denigrated African Americans and Jews at a veterans rally. The Court ruled that while speech which provoked a breach of communal interest could still face restriction, the "injurious" element of the *Chaplinsky* doctrine could not be defended here. The *Terminiello* decision asserted the view that free speech, even a speech as incendiary as that of the Rev. Terminiello, was a vital ingredient to the ideal of democracy.

Another important case that tested the limits of hate was the case of *Brandenburg v. Ohio* (1969) in which the Supreme Court vacated the conviction of a KKK leader for advocating violence. Building on its precedents in *Yates v. US* (1957) and *Noto v. US*

(1961), the Court declared that "the mere abstract teaching...of the moral propriety or even moral necessity for a resort to force and violence is not the same as preparing a group for violent action and steeling it to such action" (1969). Thus the Court had now concluded that advocacy of an abstract idea (no matter how hateful) is not necessarily tied to advocacy of imminent lawless action. This attempt by the Court to secure a distinction between speech and action reveals itself again in later hate crimes cases such as *RAV v. St. Paul* (1992) and *Wisconsin v. Mitchell* (1993).

The decades between *Terminiello* and *Brandenburg* were, of course, still rife with the civil rights struggles that stemmed from the passions of hatred. However, society would make progress in the 1960s on the issue of mandating and protecting rights. As Congress passed such momentous legislation as the *Civil Rights Act of 1964* and the *Voting Rights Act of 1965*, the nation appeared to be on a trajectory toward greater equality and tolerance. By the 1980s, however, a different story began to emerge. As Michael Omi and Howard Winant write in their seminal work *Racial Formation in the United States*, "no sooner did egalitarian and anti-discrimination policies emerge from the political tempests of the 1960s than they began to decay" (1986, 71). Omi and Winant, for example, use the following incident as an example of how Ronald Reagan's leadership in the 1980s would begin to "marginalize and transform the reforms won in the earlier decade":

> In 1983 after extensive maneuvers, the Reagan administration completed reorganization of the U.S. Commission on Civil Rights, a state watchdog organization which had been established to monitor the progress and problems in the achievement of racial equality. Under its new leadership the Commission defined reverse discrimination (i.e., discrimination against whites resulting from affirmative action) as its first priority (1986, 71).

Racial sensibilities were heightened, as many in mainstream America (spectators and sympathizers) took their cues from the Reagan presidency and again began to embrace the cycle of hatred and intolerance that defined the decades before the Civil Rights movement. As suggested in chapter one, the George W. Bush presidency may very well offer a similar leadership, unconsciously or not, supporting the politics of this terrible hatred.

In the 1980s, as hateful ideas spawned an increase in hateful and often violent acts, both the federal and state governments were forced to address this growing concern. FBI statistics corroborate this rise in reported hate crimes in the 1980s. In 1981, the Anti-Defamation League was the first to draft model legislation to counter hate-motivated crimes. The text of the ADL legislation addressed institutional vandalism, intimidation, and civil action for institutional vandalism and intimidation. It also included a section on bias crime reporting and training. Central to the ADL model's legal approach to hate crimes was the idea of penalty enhancement, which provided harsher sentences when bigotry prompted an individual to engage in criminal activity (Hate Crimes Laws 1994). Soon several states would use the model ADL legislation as a "prototype" for their own hate crimes ordinances (Jacobs and Potter 1998).

By the early 1980s, five states had actually passed hate crime legislation. New Jersey was one of the first. The initial New Jersey statute was a limited effort to outlaw the burning of crosses and the placing of swastikas on public or private property with the purpose of terrorizing others. As society began to witness an increase in the nature of hate activity, New Jersey expanded its hate crime legislation by enacting the Ethnic Intimidation Act of 1990. Under this broadened hate legislation, two defendants were charged after they spray-painted a Nazi symbol and words that seemed to spell "Hitler rules" on a synagogue in Rumson, New Jersey (Morgenstern 2000). In another case, two juveniles were charged with spray-painting hate-filled words on the garage door of a Pakistani's home in East Brunswick, New Jersey (Hate Crimes Laws 1994, 17). Hate, it seemed, was on the rise as everywhere one looked there were stories of intolerance, violence, and fear. As hate moved its way back into mainstream thought and culture, more states began to understand the urgency for anti-hate ordinances.

Forty-three states and the District of Columbia now have anti-hate legislation loosely based on the ADL model, and "almost every state has some form of legislation which can be invoked to redress bias-motivated crimes" (Hate Crimes Laws 1999). State statutes are classified according to the specific language they employ to prohibit certain behaviors. In general, states have enacted two types of statutes. The first prohibits intimidation or interference with civil rights, and the second creates separate bias-motivation crimes.

This second category is further broken down to include

a) statutes creating a separate crime where a defendant commits an enumerated crime "by reason of" the victim's characteristic
b) statutes creating a separate crime where the defendant commits an enumerated crime "because of" the victim's characteristic
c) statutes creating the crime of ethnic intimidation or malicious harassment (Hate Crimes Laws 1999)

States also differ as to the kind of prohibited prejudices that are included—race, color, religion, national origin, ancestry, physical disability, gender, sexual orientation, blindness, mental disability, age, and marital status are just some of them. The distinctions among these types of laws are complex and difficult to understand. Another aspect of state laws—the penalty enhancement for bias-motivated crimes (remember the Kevin Shifflett case)—is particularly complicated and rife with controversy, as we will see later in the chapter.

The U.S. Supreme Court had its first chance to interpret the constitutionality of these state statutes with its plenary review of *RAV v. St. Paul* in 1992. In *RAV*, the Court addressed the meaning and intentions of antibias-motivated legislation. It was in the context of the old "fighting words" doctrine that the Court made its pronouncement. The defendant in the case, Robert Viktora, a minor at the time of his arrest, burned a cross inside the yard of a residence owned by the Jones family, who are African American. Viktora was charged with violating St. Paul's ordinance that made it a crime for a person to place

> on public or private property a symbol, object, appellation, characterization or graffiti, including, but not limited to a burning cross or Nazi swastika, which one knows or has reasonable grounds to know arouses anger, alarm or resentment on the basis of race, color, creed, religion or gender (*RAV v. St. Paul* 1992).

In a decision that shocked many observers, the Court invalidated Viktora's conviction on the grounds that the ordinance was "under-inclusive," meaning it did not take into account all the possible classifications of people who could be offended by hate actions. The ordinance, for example, did not include prohibitions against speech that might arouse someone to anger based on other characteristics, such as homosexuality, political affiliation, or marital status. In the majority decision, Justice Antonin Scalia wrote, "[T]he First Amendment does not permit St. Paul to impose special prohibitions on those speakers who express views on disfavored subjects" (1992). Because the statute could not curtail all types of hateful language, no discriminatory speech could be censored. The *RAV* ruling implied that the fighting words test, which once had been used to moderate the impact of hate speech, was now a "dead" legal doctrine. For Russ and Laura Jones, whose home was targeted by Viktora, the ruling was devastating. After the decision, Laura Jones said, "The skinheads wouldn't let us alone. Now we started to see them gathering right across the street from our house. They did it blatantly, even tauntingly, flaunting it in our faces—as if to say, 'We won. We can do whatever we want to.' They were letting us know that even the Supreme Court was going to protect them...before the decision the skinheads were anonymous...but afterward, they were in our faces. And you could see the hate in their eyes" (Lederer and Delgado 1995, 31).

In 1993 in *Wisconsin v. Mitchell*, the Supreme Court took another hate case. This time it squarely addressed the controversial issue of state penalty enhancement provisions for hate crimes. The *Mitchell* case was unusual in that it involved an incident of black on white hate. After viewing the powerful film *Mississippi Burning*, which some agree is a diatribe of white-on-black hate, a group of black youths, urged on by the defendant Mitchell, decided to "fuck somebody up." When a boy approached the group, Mitchell called out, "there goes a white boy; go get him" (1993). Several of them chased and beat the white youth so severely he remained in a coma for days. Mitchell was found guilty of aggravated battery and the trial court enhanced his punishment when it concluded his crime was bias motivated. Mitchell challenged the penalty enhancement portion of his sentence on the grounds that it violated his First Amendment right to freely express racist thoughts. Mitchell's reasoning twists free speech into its worst manifestation—using protected thoughts to justify illegal action. The Supreme Court did, in fact, reject Mitchell's claim by again differentiating protected speech from unprotected conduct. The Court determined that Mitchell was punished by the state's prohibition against racist action, not racist thought.

Although penalty enhancement was squarely addressed in *Mitchell*, two earlier cases—*Barclay v. Florida* (1983) and *Dawson v. Delaware* (1992)—actually broached the topic of enhancement in light of First Amendment concerns about free speech. Barclay addressed the use of aggravating circumstances in death penalty sentencing for a hate crime. Barclay and four other men were part of a group called the Black Liberation Army whose sole purpose was to indiscriminately murder white people and to initiate a virulent racial war. After killing a white hitchhiker, eighteen-year-old Stephen Orlando, the men left the following note attached to his body: "Warning to the oppressive state. No longer will your atrocities and brutalizing of black people be unpunished. The black man is no longer asleep" (1983).

Barclay was convicted of first-degree murder in Orlando's death. At the sentencing phase of the trial, the two aggravating circumstances of bias motivation and posing a threat of race war were used to condemn him to death. Barclay then challenged his sentence on the grounds that bias motivation was not one of Florida's statutory aggravating circumstances. His argument was that "Florida law does not permit non-statutory aggravating circumstances to enter into the weighing process" (1983). The Supreme Court, however, disagreed with Barclay and upheld his death sentence, saying that bias motivation was a legitimate aggravating circumstance that could result in the imposition of the death penalty (1983). Barclay's sentence was not based on a set of philosophical beliefs, but rather on concrete action. By looking at the Dawson case next, you will be able to understand the difference.

Dawson v. Delaware (1992) forced the Court to entertain the possibility that the First Amendment guarantee of free speech can conflict with penalty enhancement considerations. Dawson had escaped from prison and had murdered Madeline Kisner while hiding in her home. Dawson was convicted of first-degree murder. At the sentencing phase of the trial, state prosecutors introduced evidence that Dawson was a member of the Aryan Brotherhood— a white racist prison gang. Dawson argued that this evidentiary information was inflammatory and irrelevant and that its admission would violate his First and Fourteenth Amendment rights.

Interestingly enough, Dawson's victim, Mrs. Kisner, was white like Dawson. In fact, his membership in the gang was not introduced to show that his crime was bias motivated, but rather to aid in the determination of generally aggravating circumstances for a death penalty conviction. However, the Court ruled that the admission into evidence of Dawson's membership in the Aryan Brotherhood was irrelevant to the sentencing procedures in this case. The Dawson decision reminds us that it is still constitutional to belong to a hate group or association, as long as that membership is unencumbered by criminal activity. That was the fundamental difference between the Barclay case and the Dawson decision. "Unlike Dawson's membership in the Aryan Brotherhood, Barclay's membership in the Black Liberation Army was directly related to his crime: the murder of a white hitchhiker. Barclay's sentence was not based on 'his abstract beliefs,' whereas Dawson's was" (Jacobs and Potter 1998, 127).

The *Barclay* and *Dawson* cases explore the inherent tensions between thought and deed—a critical issue raised in both *RAV* and *Mitchell*. Recently, prominent journalist William Raspberry has written that hate crimes legislation and penalty enhancement, specifically, are "just an attempt at thought control. It says we'll punish you for what you did, yes, but also for what you are thinking when you did it. It [legislation] says we'll punish you not merely for your racist or anti-gay behavior, but also for your bigoted beliefs" (Raspberry 2000, A23). What do you think of Raspberry's analysis? Is thought as well as deed being punished with penalty enhancement provisions? Does penalty enhancement really raise First Amendment questions, or does the effect on the victim justify the harsher penalty?

Even with the *Barclay*, *Dawson*, and *Mitchell* decisions in place, penalty enhancement debates continue to dominate the legal landscape. New York offers one example of the contentiousness of the debate on penalty enhancement. It is interesting to note that New York, a state which has witnessed so many high-profile hate crimes—Yusef Hawkins in Bensonhurst; the killing of Guinean immigrant Amadou Diallo by police, which some view as a hate crime; and the assault on women in Central Park—joined the penalty enhancement bandwagon very late. New York Gov. George Pataki signed New York's hate crime law in 2000. State Senate

Republicans had blocked the bill, arguing that "singling out some crimes was unfair to the victims of non-bias crimes" (Fitzgerald 2000). This view on penalty enhancement clearly ignores the uniqueness of hate and its virulent impact on victims.

It was no surprise, then, that the Supreme Court would hear still another challenge to penalty enhancement—this time in the case of *Apprendi v. New Jersey* (2000).

Apprendi v. New Jersey involved that state legislature's attempt to apply the enhancement penalty approach to hate crimes. The *Apprendi* case differed from *Wisconsin v. Mitchell*, in that this appeal addressed two statutory questions—first, whether a judge or a jury should determine whether a crime was bias motivated, and second, whether that determination could be made by a preponderance of the evidence or by the higher reasonable doubt standard. Only in New Jersey and North Carolina was a single judge allowed to apply the lower evidentiary standard of preponderance of the evidence and to decide whether to enhance hate crime penalties.

In the *Apprendi* case, the petitioner, a white male, was arrested for shooting at the home of a black family. When arrested, Apprendi told police that he was giving the family a message that because they were black, they were not welcome in the community. Apprendi pleaded guilty to unlawful possession of a firearm and faced a five- to ten-year sentence. However, the judge concluded by a preponderance of the evidence that Apprendi's act was racially motivated, and he sentenced him to an enhanced penalty of twelve years in prison. Apprendi's attorneys argued that the defendant suffered from psychological difficulties that impaired his judgment and impulse control, thereby diminishing his capacity to fully understand his violent actions. The trial and appeals court judges rejected this defense and decided that Apprendi's actions were solely the product of racial bias (*Apprendi v. New Jersey* 2000). In accepting Apprendi's appeal, the Supreme Court again faced the constitutional conundrum of bias-motivated legislation and the enhancement of penalties for hate crimes.

In *Apprendi*, the Supreme Court did not abandon the idea of penalty enhancement. Instead, it ruled by a 5 to 4 vote only on the narrow procedural question of who should determine the sentence—a single judge or a jury. The Court ruled that juries, not judges, must decide whether someone charged with a hate crime was motivated by bias and therefore could be given an enhanced penalty for that crime. Justice John Paul Stevens, writing for the Court majority, found that the case was one of procedure—that any factor, except for a prior conviction, that "increases the maximum penalty for a crime must be submitted to a jury and proven beyond a reasonable doubt" (2000). Justice O'Connor, writing for the dissenters, argued, "[O]ur court has long recognized that not every fact that bears on a defendant's punishment need be charged in an indictment and submitted to a jury....Legislatures can define the elements of an offense" (2000).

Did the ruling in *Apprendi* mean that the Court tacitly approved of enhanced penalties, in general, as long as they were imposed by juries? It certainly seems so, although some observers suggest that the Court really ducked the central, substantive issue of whether penalty enhancements are actually constitutional. What do you think of the Court's ruling in *Apprendi*? What are the consequences of having jury members decide penalty enhancement rules? If, as we have been arguing, the rhetoric of the conservative right prevails, many juries may not support penalty enhancement for bias-motivated crimes, particularly when the offender is white and the victim is black or Hispanic. Jury composition may also have an effect on decisions of whether or not to enhance penalties.

The argument against penalty enhancement laws makes several points—that statutes perpetuate the victimization of already stigmatized minorities, and that they create a favored status of victims. Consistent with this view is the idea that penalty enhancement laws violate the Equal Protection Clause of the Fourteenth Amendment. It is suggested that these statutes unconstitutionally benefit minorities, who are more likely to be the victims of hate crimes, and burden majority members, who are more likely to be the perpetrators of such crimes. This reasoning seems ridiculous. State courts have already rejected this contention, insisting on the neutrality of their hate crime legislation. The opposition to penalty enhancement laws by so many may be a reflection of mainstream discourse that subconsciously reflects the politics of hatred. Why else is there so much vehemence against broadening the penalties for individuals who commit horrific hate crimes?

Frederick Lawrence makes a compelling argument for penalty enhancement laws in his book *Punishing Hate*, when he writes, "If bias crimes are not punished more harshly than parallel crimes, the implicit message expressed by the criminal justice system is that racial harmony and equality are not among the highest values in our society" (1999, 8). Penalty enhancement laws also allow us to provide a voice to the victim, not only to give credence to the victim's pain and anguish, but to politicize their status as injured parties. In effect, they deserve that attention as the unfortunate participants in this new archival history on hate. This concept of victimology has come under attack by John McWhorter in his book *Losing the Race: Self-Sabotage in Black America*. McWhorter argues that "there is lying at the heart of black American thought a transformation of victimhood from a problem to be solved into an identity in itself" (2000). Contrary to McWhorter, giving credence to the victim is necessary if we are to come to terms with the consequences of the politics of hatred.

The previous discussion has addressed how the states have attempted to deal with the matter of hate crimes and punishment. What role has the federal government played in addressing the meteoric rise of hate since the 1980s? Have federal initiatives against hate provided any leadership in the quest to control prejudice and violence? Some commentators argue that the already existing federal criminal civil rights statutes, such as *18 United States Code Section 241* and *18 USC Section 242*, could be utilized as hate crime laws. These statutes were two post–Civil War initiatives designed to "authorize federal prosecution of the KKK and others, including law enforcement and government officials, who denied the newly freed slaves their civil rights" (Jacobs and Potter 1998, 36–37). *18 USC 241* reads,

> [I]f two or more persons conspire to injure, oppress, threaten, or intimidate any person...in the free exercise or enjoyment of any right or privilege secured to him by the Constitution or laws of the United States....[T]hey shall be fined not more than $10,000, or imprisoned not more than 10 years or both.

18 USC 242 reads,

> Whoever, under color of any law...willfully subjects any person...to the deprivation of any rights, privileges, or immunities secured or protected by the Constitution or laws of the United States, or to different

punishments, pains, or penalties, on account of such person being an alien, or by reason of his color, or race...shall be fined...or imprisoned.

Where 241 prohibits private action of discrimination, 242 prohibits official or institutional deprivation of civil rights. Los Angeles police officers Stacey C. Koon and Laurence M. Powell, for example, were convicted under *18 USC 242* for the brutal beating of Rodney King in 1992. However, the two guilty officers were sentenced to only thirty months in prison and two years of supervised release for this institutional hate crime seen by millions on national television.

Two other federal laws used to combat and prosecute discrimination are *The Church Arsons Prevention Act, 18 USC 247*, and *The Fair Housing Act, 42 USC 3617*. *The Church Arsons Prevention Act* protects religious property and the free exercise of religious beliefs. According to Justice Department officials, the incidents of arson at places of religious worship increased dramatically between 1995 and 1998, "especially in the context of places of religious worship that serve predominately African-American congregants" (Hate 1999). Douglas Lee Barlow and Patricia Baron were prosecuted under this federal law for shooting four members of a congregation in front of their church. *The Fair Housing Act* allows for the punishment of anyone who interferes with a person's right to convey or hold property. In one case, a defendant was convicted under a provision of the Act for burning a cross on the lawn of a white family, who were entertaining black friends for a Labor Day weekend.

With these federal laws in place, it would seem that we have ample structural remediation to combat hate crimes, yet the problem of hate continues. As Jacobs and Potter suggest in their book, these federal laws, particularly *18 USC 241* and *242*, were never intended to be used as broad-based hate statutes, and did not include an authority to enhance penalties. Consequently, as the terrain of hate began to widen in the 1980s and 1990s, Congress passed three additional federal initiatives to address the problem.

The *Hate Crimes Statistics Act, 28 USC 534*, was enacted in 1990, and it authorized the Justice Department to acquire data on crimes "which manifest prejudice based on race, religion, sexual orientation, or ethnicity" from law enforcement agencies across the country. Data collection and reporting guidelines for hate crimes became the province of the FBI and its Uniform Crime Reports section. While the *HCSA* has had some difficulties with incomplete reporting, many believe it is a crucial piece of legislation. As the ADL reports, "[S]tudies have demonstrated that victims are more likely to report a hate crime, if they know a special reporting system is in place" (Hate 1999). However, women's groups were outraged when the *HSCA* passed because "gender" was not included in the language of the statute. In response to the criticism, the government noted that statistics on rape and domestic violence were already being collected. The debate about gender prejudice did not dissipate, though, and was partly addressed four years later in the *Violence Against Women Act*.

The second federal law was the *Hate Crimes Sentencing Enhancement Act of 1994*, which was the federal counterpart to state penalty enhancement statutes. The Act authorized the U.S. Sentencing Commission to provide a sentencing enhancement "of not less than 3 offense levels for offenses that are...hate crimes" (Hate 1999). Additionally, the *HCSEA*, this time, included gender and disability offenses on its list of protected crimes. The *HCSEA* was widely supported, for, as Robert K. Lifton commented, "the criminal law is an expression of the nation's basic moral standards" (Jacobs and Potter 1998, 76).

Congress finally passed the *Violence Against Women Act of 1994* as its third effort at anti-hate legislation. The passage of *VAWA*, clearly a political response to the failure to include gender bias in the *HCSA*, was a comprehensive attempt to address the increasing problem of violent crime against women. The law mandated that "all persons within the United States shall have the right to be free from crimes of violence motivated by gender" (Hate 1999). The *VAWA* also included a federal civil remedy for victims of gender-based violent crimes, which provided them with a right to sue for compensatory and punitive damage awards. However, this provision came under scrutiny in the 1999 case of *US v. Morrison*.

The *Morrison* case directly challenged the private right of action for victims of gender-motivated violence. The plaintiff in *Morrison* was Christy Brzonkala, a student at Virginia Polytechnic Institute, who filed a civil suit against two varsity football players whom she accused of raping her in her dormitory room after the start of her freshman year at the college. When Brzonkala learned that the college would not be disciplining the two alleged attackers, she filed the suit under the newly passed federal law. On appeal, though, the Supreme Court invalidated this civil remedy as an inappropriate use of Congressional authority under the Commerce Clause. Congress had frequently employed the Commerce Clause, along with the Fourteenth Amendment, to enforce legislation designed to prevent discrimination. However, Chief Justice William Rehnquist wrote that the *Violence Against Women Act*, which passed in 1994 to protect women's civil rights, could not be a regulation of interstate commerce because violence against women was not economic— "even if the violence had real and palpable economic consequences" (*United States v. Morrison* 2000). Simply put, the Court had decided that victims of rape did not have a federal civil remedy for damages done to them. The defeat in *United States v. Morrison* was considered a major setback for protecting women against violence.

The Supreme Court's unfortunate decision in *Morrison* was announced the very week that a horrific gender-bias incident occurred in New York City. The outrageous events in New York make the failure of the Court's jurisprudence on gender-bias hate crimes that much more apparent. The incident in New York's Central Park began at a Puerto Rican Day Parade. What began as harmless water balloon antics soon escalated into a scene where young men were caught on camera chasing, sexually assaulting, and generally terrorizing up to fifty women, in broad daylight, with New York City police standing less than twenty feet away! Women were videotaped screaming and cowering in abject fear. "'Get them!' the men shouted as they chased their victims down the park pathways and surrounded them with a ring of inexorable hands. 'Get the bitches!'" (Quindlen 2000). Several witnesses told *The New York Times*, "[W]ait a minute, this is not acceptable behavior, this is criminal behavior. Why aren't we calling it what it is? It's a crime. A hate crime" (Purnick 2000, B1). Journalist Joyce Purnick also wrote, "[W]omen were the victims not only of violent thugs but also of some police officers who, people have charged, ignored reports of the park's rampage and of threatening behavior before and during the parade" (Purnick 2000, B1). Remember Elisabeth Young-Bruehl's theory of narcissistic hate—one could certainly see that type of hate manifested by the young men involved in this terrible event. Additionally, the reticence of law enforcement officials to get involved in this incident was another example of mainstream acceptance of intolerance and hate.

Gender-bias hatred's worst manifestation occurred in the case of Marc Lepine, a Canadian man who killed fourteen women with a hunting rifle in December 1989. Lepine separated the women from the men whom he was holding hostage at the University of Montreal. Before shooting the women, he called them, "a bunch of feminists" (Lawrence 1999, 15). Lepine's crime makes it all the more imperative to recognize that crimes of violence motivated by gender are, in fact, hate crimes. Despite the argument that women are already protected under existing criminal laws such as rape statutes, several scholars argue that not including women under bias protection laws "implies that women are not as deserving of protection as racial, religious, or ethnic minorities" (Lawrence 1999, 17). By invalidating the civil remedy provision of the *Violence Against Women Act*, the Court once again failed to address what Lawrence and others feared most—that offenses against women would not be elevated to the status of hate crimes.

Even in the presence of the remaining federal laws and state ordinances, the landscape of hate continued to grow and include more and more tragic victims. As a result, the 106th Congress introduced still another bill—*The Hate Crimes Prevention Act of 1998* (*HCPA*). This bill stated among its findings that (1) "the incidence of violence motivated by the actual or perceived race, color, national origin, religion, sexual orientation, gender or disability of the victim poses a serious national problem," (2) that "such violence disrupts the tranquility and safety of communities and is deeply divisive," (3) that "existing federal law is inadequate to address this problem," ...(8) that "violence motivated by bias that is a relic of slavery can constitute badges and incidences of slavery," and (10) that "many states have no laws addressing violence based on the actual or perceived race, color, national origin, religion, sexual orientation, gender, or disability of the victim, while other States have laws that provide only limited protection" (1998). The *HCPA* made recommendations regarding the sentencing of defendants accused and convicted of hate crimes, and addressed the issue of studying adult recruitment of juveniles for hate crimes. It also would have authorized the Justice Department to assist in local prosecutions by investigating and prosecuting cases of bias violence because of the victim's sexual orientation, gender, or disability. This provision was critical because previously, federal law did not provide authority for involvement in these types of cases at all.

The *Hate Crimes Prevention Act of 1998* did not pass, as partisan politics and debate over the preferred status of victims signaled the death knell for the proposal. However, congressional supporters of the bill introduced a virtually identical federal hate crimes bill at the start of the 107th Congress. This bill, interestingly enough, employs the language of the "culture of hate" as a part of its philosophical justification.

What does the battle over the passage of the 1998 federal hate crimes act reveal about the intolerance of our modern spirit? Does the defeat of the 1998 federal law show how ingrained and accepting we are of societal hatred? Have we learned anything from these statutory attempts at social control? If a new federal law is passed, will it really deter behavior in any way? Actually, the discussion about the alleged favored status for minority victims seems inadvertently to be fueling more anger and subsequent hatred among hate sympathizers and spectators. It is equally doubtful that a federal hate crimes law will receive support from President Bush, given his refusal to sign a hate crimes law in Texas after James Byrd's murder.

The passage of a national law against hate crimes is not imminent, but other options are available to modulate the effects of hatred. One method allows victims to sue their hate tormentors. We have seen how one federal civil remedy was limited in the *US v. Morrison* case. However, many believe that victims should be encouraged to seek compensatory and punitive damages in civil court. The ADL model hate crime statute included a provision for civil suits that could be used for a private right of action, and some civil suits have been litigated successfully. The *Del Dotto v. Olsen* case is one example of a civil suit brought with the aid of the ADL. Mrs. Del Dotto, a Jewish woman living on the north side of Chicago, was the target of white supremacist neighbors who harassed and terrorized her and her family. Although members of the Olsen family faced minor criminal charges, the hate activity continued. Finally, Mrs. Del Dotto contacted the local ADL and eventually filed a civil suit seeking injunctive relief and damages. After a jury trial, Mrs. Del Dotto and her family were awarded $1.8 million in damages against the Olsens (Hate 1994, 22–23). In another case, three neo-Nazi skinheads repeatedly threatened and sprayed a Mace-type substance in the eyes of Mary Lampkin, an African-American bus driver. In addition to facing criminal charges, the skinheads were hit with a civil suit, and Lampkin was awarded $1.75 million in compensatory and punitive damages (Hate 1994, 23). While the plaintiffs in both these cases succeeded in convincing a jury of the rightness of their suit, it is unclear whether they actually collected their monetary judgments. Will these additional civil penalties work as deterrents to hate crimes? Are these just Pyrrhic victories? The data are not yet in.

More recently, the Southern Poverty Law Center helped win a major victory against the Aryan Nations in Idaho. The suit began when security guards at the Nations' compound shot and attacked Victoria Keenan and her son Jason, who are Native Americans, as Keenan drove by the white supremacist organization's headquarters on 1 July 1998. Morris Dees, founder of the Southern Poverty Law Center, initiated a lawsuit on their behalf. The Keenans won their suit and Richard Butler, guru of the Nations, and other Aryan Nations members were fined $6.3 million by the local courts. Butler was forced to sell the 20-acre Aryan compound to satisfy the debt, and the Keenans actually purchased the property at a bankruptcy auction. As Jason Keenan said, "[W]e hope to get the evilness out of there" (Neiwert 2001). The Keenans sold the property for $250,000 to Greg Carr, a former chairman of Prodigy. Carr, the head of the Carr Foundation, a human-rights group in Cambridge, Massachusetts, planned to turn the compound into a human-rights center (Associated Press 2001). The loss of the compound did not mean the end for Butler, though. He intended to plan another "Aryan Congress" for the summer of 2001.

Dees and the center will continue to follow their strategy of depriving hate groups of the assets necessary to advocate the cause of white supremacy. "In recent years civil suits have been filed by Dees that have financially crippled a half dozen or more white supremacy groups. They include a $15 million judgment against Horace King and a $12.5 million award in 1990 to the family of an Ethiopian student killed in Portland, Oregon, by a skinhead gang organized by the White Aryan Resistance (WAR) led by Tom and John Metzger. In 1994, the U.S. Supreme Court refused to review

Metzger's appeal of the award, and WAR's assets were seized and distributed primarily to the victim's son" (SPLC 2000b). Although civil suits against hatred seem appealing, some believe that tort law is a "two-edged sword that can be arrayed against the good guys as well as the bad guys" (*Washington Post* 2001). Some cite the compensatory damage suit brought against the NAACP's boycott of businesses in Mississippi. However, that judgment was reversed by the U.S. Supreme Court.

A final plan to address hate involves revisiting old criminal cases that were clearly hate-motivated. Several jurisdictions have investigated the possibility of resurrecting or reinvestigating violent acts perpetrated on racial and ethnic minorities long before the language of "hate crimes" entered our legal landscape. An example of such an investigation is the 1994 retrial of Byron De La Beckwith, the man long known to have murdered Medgar Evers, the Mississippi NAACP field secretary in 1963. In two previous trials, Beckwith, a well-known white supremacist, was freed when both juries were unable to reach a verdict. Because of the tireless work of Mississippi prosecutor Bobby Delaughter, Beckwith was finally convicted in 1994, thirty-one long years after Evers was brutally assassinated in front of his wife and children in the family driveway. As the film *Ghosts of Mississippi* poignantly revealed, Myrlie Evers was overcome with relief and a sense of justice at Beckwith's conviction for the vicious act of hate that took her husband's life. Beckwith died in prison in 2001.

Today, more and more prosecutors are opening Pandora's box by seeking new criminal penalties against those who may have escaped accountability in the past. Some other recently opened hate crimes cases include the deaths of Harry and Harriette Moore. Moore, an NAACP official, and his wife were killed in 1951 after a bomb exploded in their home. No one was ever charged in that crime. William Edwards Jr. was murdered by four Klansmen who threw him into the Alabama River. The case was considered an accidental drowning until investigators reinvestigated the incident. Another case involves Henry Dee and Charles Moore, two young civil rights workers whose decomposed bodies were discovered in the Mississippi River in 1963. The FBI has now reopened the case. O'Neal Moore and Creed Rogers were the first black sheriff's deputies in Washington Parish, Louisiana, when they were shot in an ambush in 1965. Local prosecutors are also reexamining that incident as a hate crime. Ben Chester White was a plantation caretaker shot to death in Mississippi in 1966. Only now have authorities filed charges against former Klansman Ernest Avants for that crime. Wharlest Jackson, NAACP treasurer in Natchez, Mississippi, was murdered by a car bomb in 1967, after he had been promoted at a local tire plant to a position that had previously been reserved for whites only. Now some thirty years later, police are reinvestigating the death as a hate-motivated crime (Fletcher 2000, A1).

One of the most celebrated crimes to be reopened is the 1964 slayings of civil rights workers James Chaney, Michael Schwerner, and Andrew Goodman near Philadelphia, Mississippi. The story of their murder was the subject of the film *Mississippi Burning*, which was the catalyst for the actions in the *Wisconsin v. Mitchell* case. Investigation into the killings resulted in the conviction of seven Klan members on conspiracy charges. None, however, were convicted of murder. New evidence has now emerged that may help Mississippi prosecutors bring the hate perpetrators to justice (Borger 1999).

Still another infamous case was the bombing of the 16th Street Baptist Church in Birmingham, Alabama, thirty-eight years ago. That bombing, which was considered "one of the most dastardly acts of the civil rights era," resulted in the deaths of four young black girls—Denise McNair, Carole Robertson, Addie Mae Collins, and Cynthia Wesley—who were in the church preparing for a Sunday morning service. One Klansman, Robert Chambliss, was convicted in 1977 and died in prison eight years later. A second suspect died in 1994 without ever being charged. Finally, in 2001, the remaining defendants, Bobby Frank Cherry and Thomas E. Blanton Jr., were indicted for their role in the bombing. However, only one of the two men actually faced justice. A state court judge ruled that Cherry, now 71, is mentally incompetent to stand trial. His trial, which some promised would provide a "civic catharsis" for the Birmingham community, was indefinitely postponed. That decision led one angry member of the church, associate pastor Joseph E. Decauter, to comment "[T]he government could have prosecuted them before, but they let them get old...they allowed them to lead full lives" (Sack 2001). However, in early 2002, Cherry was ruled competent to stand trial. The trial against Blanton proceeded as expected, and on 1 May 2001, he was found guilty of the quadruple murder and sentenced to life in prison. His attorney, however, argued that Blanton did not receive a fair trial and he plans to appeal.

These are just a handful of cases that are presenting state and local officials with a renewed opportunity to resolve hate crimes of the past. An article in the 26 September 2000 *Washington Post* reported that "these investigations were possible because of the profound changes that have transformed racial sensibilities in the South and have allowed African Americans to build significant political power" (Fletcher 2000, A3). Yes, the power base has changed. However, a society that permits so much racial and ethnic hatred to prevail certainly challenges the notion that the South has really been transformed. How successful will these reinvestigations prove to be? Some observers argue that these new probes of past civil rights slayings will finally provide closure to the "region's tortured history." Others, though, counter that reopening old wounds under the rubric of hate remediation is just a way to promote more anger and hatred.

While most of this chapter has addressed the brief history of legal remedies to combat hate, it should be noted there is a school of thought completely opposed to the use of such hate laws. Historian Arthur Schlesinger outlined this philosophy in his book *The Disuniting of America*. His position, widely supported by conservative politicians, argues that hate crime laws overemphasize the differences among people rather than the commonalities of citizens. Schlesinger believes that such separatism "encouraged by law...nourishes prejudices, magnifies difference and stirs antagonisms" (1991, 58). This criticism is known as the "balkanizing effect of hate crimes." Schlesinger went even further by arguing that the commitment to recognize ethnicity and its consequences has sidetracked America in its quest for the common good. He argues that we now have a legacy of minorities only concerned with their own "culture of victimization" (1991, 64). Now, James Jacobs and Kimberly Potter have advocated the Schlesinger position in their 1998 book *Hate Crimes: Criminal Law and Identity Politics*. Jacobs and Potter insist that the effort to pass increased hate legislation is a result of what they consider to be the problem of "identity politics." They argue that identity politics encourages people to relate to one another through their membership in competing groups classified by race, gender, religion, or sexual orientation, thereby encouraging a hierarchy of victimization. So the "greater a group's victimization, the stronger the moral claim on the larger society." Jacobs and Potter see this as problematic—identity politics causes the "splintering of society" (1998). It also permits government to select which prejudices become hate crimes and which do not. This argument echoes the majority opinion in *RAV v. St. Paul*. The authors support their arguments by denying the existence of a hate crimes epidemic. Citing a failure of the government to implement a reliable hate crimes accounting system, Jacobs and Potter try to minimize the reality of hate. It would be interesting to discover what the families of victims targeted by hate and violence would have to say about Jacobs and Potter's thesis. How would the grieving mothers and fathers of the four girls killed in the Birmingham bombing feel about this? How would Kevin Shifflett's parents feel?

Some final questions for reflection. Can our existing laws do the job? Are they sufficient to stem the tide of harm toward targeted populations? Can we even agree on which targeted groups need the protection of hate laws? The debate about gender and sexual orientation still clouds the picture. Will the constitutional protections of free speech, due process, and equal protection continue to be offered up as a smokescreen to weaken already existing legislation against hate crimes? Are Schlesinger and Jacobs and Potter right when they insist that such legislation perpetuates the racial, ethnic, and gender divide? Or is Frederick Lawrence (1999) correct when he insists that we have a moral obligation to the tenets of equality and democracy to raise the bar and insist on a higher ethical ground of expected behavior? Can laws alone govern and/or change people's behavior? Without the benefit of hate crimes legislation, are we doomed to return to Hobbes's state of nature, where not only a few commit heinous crimes, but where all have the potential to do so, and will!

Our next chapter explores the transition of moving hateful action from the streets, where it often occurs, to the privacy of the home through Internet use. Just how pervasive is hate on the Internet, and can anything be done to curtail incendiary hate speech?

— Chapter 3 —
Hate and the Internet

In 1997, several University of California at Irvine students opened their e-mail to find this message:

> From: Mother Fucker (Hates Asians) <mfucker@uci.edu>
> Subject: FUck You Asian Shit
> Hey Stupid fucker
> As you can see in the name, I hate Asians including you. If it weren't for asias at UCI, it would be a much more popular campus. You are responsible for ALL the crimes that occur on campus. YOU are responsible for the campus being all dirty. YOU ARE RESPONSIBLE. That's why I want you and your stupidass comrades to get the fuck out of UCI. IF you don't I will hunt all of you down and Kill your stupid asses. Do you hear me? I personally will make it my life career to find and kill everyone of you personally. OK?????? That's how determined I am.
> Get the fuck out,
> MOther FUcker (Asian hater) (Ingall 1998, 136).

This message, typos included, was sent by Richard Machado, one of the few people ever convicted of perpetrating hate on the Internet. But Machado was not convicted because of the ideas that he expressed, or because he hates Asians. Rather, he was convicted because his e-mail contained threats of violence against the Asian students.

Machado's e-mail is just one of the ways that hate is manifested in this country. Today, the Internet has become the vehicle of choice for hatemongers to spread their message and to recruit new converts. The Anti-Defamation League, the Simon Wiesenthal Center, and the Southern Poverty Law Center, all of which monitor incidences of hate on the Internet, report that the number of hate Web sites has grown exponentially since former Ku Klux Klan organizer Don Black began his Stormfront site in 1995. Today, such organizations as the National Alliance, the World Church of the Creator, the Ku Klux Klan, and the Nation of Islam maintain Web sites that offer varying degrees of racist, anti-Semitic, anti-abortion, and white supremacist material. Anyone with access to the Internet can find these sites easily. While the messages found on the sites are repugnant to many Americans, they serve as a rallying cry for hatemongers. Hate sympathizers are especially susceptible to being recruited by the propaganda on these sites because they are already predisposed to the messages. However, little can be done to shut down these sites because they, like other forms of hate speech, are protected by the First Amendment.

Hate speech denigrates a person because of an immutable characteristic of that person. It is important to distinguish hate speech from hate crimes. Speech, thoughts, and ideas are protected by the First Amendment; criminal behavior is not. Only a hate crime can be punished, although law enforcement agencies also keep track of hate "incidents" that include hate speech. As a result of the First Amendment protection for free speech, it is unlikely that a statute that severely restricts the dissemination of hateful information on the Internet, or elsewhere, would pass constitutional muster. In fact, in the 1997 case *Reno v ACLU*, Justice John Paul Stevens recognized that the Internet deserved full First Amendment protection:

> This dynamic multifaceted category of communication includes not only traditional print and news services, but also audio, video, and still images, as well as interactive, real time dialogue. Through the use of chat rooms, any person with a phone line can become a town crier with a voice that resonates farther than it could from any soapbox. Through the use of Web pages, mail exploders, and newsgroups, the same individual can become a pamphleteer (1997).

The *Reno* case arose after Congress passed the *Communications Decency Act (CDA)* as a part of the *Telecommunications Act of 1996*. The *CDA* was designed to limit access to "indecent" material by minors, but it was challenged because it also had the potential effect of limiting adult access to protected speech. In the decision, the Court struck down the *CDA*, saying it "threatens to torch a large segment of the Internet community" (1997).

Stevens's opinion spoke to the concept of the marketplace of ideas, first advanced by Justice Oliver Holmes in his 1919 dissenting opinion in *Abrams v. United States*. That concept is now a richly prevailing viewpoint among First Amendment scholars. In *Abrams*, Holmes argued that "the ultimate good desired is better reached by free trade in ideas—that the best test of truth is the power of the thought to get itself accepted in the competition of the market" (1919). The marketplace leaves it up to individuals to decide for themselves what to consider worthwhile, what to buy, and ultimately, what to believe.

This marketplace of ideas concept has bolstered First Amendment protection for the dissemination of hateful ideas. Non-controversial speech does not need to be protected. Neither the government nor the courts can censor your thoughts or your words. Only when those words cross the line into action can legal authorities step in and stop you. However, the Court's laissez-faire attitude toward hate speech has recently come under fire from a school of thought known as critical legal studies (CLS). Scholars who subscribe to this philosophy question the applicability of the marketplace metaphor for legal analysis. They believe that the First Amendment should not bar the government and the courts from limiting hate speech. Instead, CLS scholars argue that hate speech is not truly "speech" because it is not designed to examine ideas or to advance a common good. Instead, for them, hate speech is more like action. By hurling an invective against a member of a targeted minority, the speaker wants to stop speech. The goal is to deliver a rhetorical sucker punch that leaves the victim so devastated that he or she is unable to respond. For example, some of the students who testified at Machado's trial said they felt threatened and afraid, and refused to go out alone at night. Sabina Lin, one of the recipients, said "getting the message shattered her sense of safety." "I started carrying Mace. I had two friends walk me to class and pick me up after class" (Ingall 1998, 147).

The victim's inability to respond points up the flaw in relying on the marketplace metaphor to counter hate speech. Without the victim's response, the marketplace cannot function properly. Those of us who are not affected directly by the hate speech find it difficult to decide which speech is "true" because we do not have access to all the wares in the marketplace. We hear and, in the case of the Internet, we see primarily one side—that of the haters.

CLS writer Mari Matsuda writes, "[H]uman experience teaches us that certain ideas are wrong. Presumably we would all agree that slavery, the Holocaust, and apartheid are evil. On issues such as these...opposing viewpoints do not need a hearing in the marketplace of ideas" (Fraleigh and Tuman 1997, 187). A comparison can be made between what is legal and what is right. For groups that consider hate a valuable product, the Internet has given them a new, legal outlet to propagate their message that slavery, the Holocaust, and apartheid were not evils at all. However, is it right that the other side, that of the victims, is drowned out by the plethora of ways the Internet can be used to spread hate?

Today we have become accustomed to using e-mail, usegroups, the World Wide Web, and other Internet features to communicate with friends, relatives, and colleagues. While many of us have concerns about privacy, most of us take for granted our freedom to write and read what we want. That freedom has been bolstered by court decisions that have upheld the rights of individuals to spread hateful messages on the Internet. In 1995, for example, a University of Michigan student, Jake Baker, was charged with transmitting a threat to kidnap or injure a person after posting a fantasy about raping and killing a named female student to an Internet usegroup. However, Baker's case was dismissed by U.S. District Judge Avern Cohn, who ruled that the story was protected by the First Amendment. In his ruling, Cohn called the posting "only a rather savage and tasteless piece of fiction," and wrote, "musings, considerations of what it would be like to kidnap or injure someone, or desires to kidnap or injure someone" do not violate the Constitution unless some intent to commit the acts is expressed" (Yuhn 1995). A federal appeals court later upheld the dismissal of the charges. Despite the psychic harm to the woman involved, no actual, physical violence was involved. The court again drew the line between speech and conduct, and upheld the right of the speaker.

It has only been in cases where actual threats of committing violence have accompanied the ideas in the e-mails, as in the Machado case, that convictions have been sustained. Richard Machado was the first person convicted of a hate crime on the Internet (Hernandez 1998). The law he was charged under did not specifically address the Internet. Instead, he was charged under a 1960s civil rights statute that was aimed at segregationists who tried to prevent African-American students from attending public schools in the South. The law criminalized the behavior of those who "by force or threat of force attempt to injure, intimidate or interfere with...any person because of his race, color or national origin and because he is or has been enrolling in or attending any public school or public college" (Ingall 1998, 138). Machado was not charged because of his hateful ideas, but because he had included a threat of violence in his e-mail. After a first jury was unable to reach a verdict in the case, Machado was tried again and found guilty. Because he had already spent more time in jail than the recommended sentence for the crime, he was released. Instead, the judge sentenced him to supervised probation and tolerance training.

Soon after Machado's conviction, the federal government prosecuted an Asian-American student for sending anti-Hispanic e-mail death threats to sixty-seven students and employees of the California State University in Los Angeles, the Massachusetts Institute of Technology, and other institutions. The e-mail said in part, "I hate your race. I want you all to die...I'm going to come down and kill your wetback, affirmative action ass." The sender was sentenced to two years in federal prison (Potok 2000, 48).

E-mails and usegroup postings may have led to a few prosecutions and convictions, but the great majority of hate messages on the Internet have gone unpunished. The World Wide Web has become an especially fertile area for hate groups to spread their messages. The ADL noted a substantial increase in on-line discussions and postings on racist Web sites as a result of the racial protests in Cincinnati that followed the killing of a black man by a white police officer (U.S. Newswire 2001).

Hate Web sites are different from other forms of hate speech in one important way—in most instances, recipients of the messages need to access them deliberately. If a person wants to find out about a white supremacist group, he or she must deliberately search for it. E-mail is more frightening because it is unsolicited and it can be anonymous. The ADL's publication *High Tech Hate: Extremist Use of the Internet* cited a number of examples in which targeted individuals received hateful messages, but the perpetrators were never found or prosecuted (ADL 1998b).

Using the Internet to spread hate is not a new phenomenon. The ADL issued its first warning about Internet hate in a January 1985 report, "Computerized Networks of Hate," which examined a computerized bulletin board for white supremacists. In the report, the ADL explained five ways that the white supremacist movement was served by the bulletin board. In its publication "Poisoning the Web: Hatred Online," the ADL argued that those elements are still important today:

> First, the bulletin board was designed to draw young people to the hate movement with appealing propaganda. Second, the network helped to stir up hatred against the "enemies" of white supremacy. Third, the bulletin board was a means to make money. Fourth, the system offered the potential for circulating secret, coded messages among extremists, and finally, it bypassed embargoes that nations outside of the United States placed on hate literature (ADL 2000b).

We can demonstrate in a variety of ways that these five elements are important ways that hatemongers and the radical right use the Internet to insert their messages into our national conversation. As we saw in chapter one, the propaganda Benjamin Smith found on the World Church of the Creator Web site helped crystallize his white supremacist leanings and turned him into a hatemonger and killer. Publicity about the church then led other people to investigate its teachings, and since Smith's shooting spree, the WCOTC has become the fastest-growing white supremacist organization in the country. Hale has used the World Wide Web as a way to spread his message of hate to a much larger audience than he could reach by leaving leaflets in driveways and in college campus common areas. In interviews he finds ways to plug his Web site, attracting the curious and the disaffected. Devin Burghart of the watchdog group Center for New Community called Hale "very media savvy." "He knows controversy sells and he looks for it at every opportunity. When he finds it, he jumps into the fray with great gusto" (Elliott 1999).

Militia groups active on the Internet posted a "Call to Vigilance" during the 2000 presidential vote recount in Florida. Using inflammatory language, the posting urged militia members to "be prepared to rally at a moment's notice," and to "begin using encryption to thwart the ongoing efforts of the 'legal authorities' to monitor such preparations and to infiltrate and prepare action plans against free American Militias" (2000). As the ADL pointed out, postings such as these are also designed to stir up hatred against "enemies." In this case, the enemy was Vice President Gore, who was referred to as "Stalinist Gore," whose "long standing ties to the communists and communist sympathizers is well established" (2000).

Fund-raising is another important function of hate Web sites. Don Black, who was one of the first white supremacists to recognize the power and scope of the Internet, started a Stormfront Legal Defense Fund "to pay legal expenses for selected First Amendment-related cases," and he uses the site to solicit contributions to the fund (Don Black 2000). During the civil trial against Aryan Nations head Richard Butler, his site solicited financial support to pay his legal bills. In an interesting twist that recalls the Rev. Jim Bakker, former KKK grand wizard David Duke has been investigated for misuse of contributions to his white supremacist causes. FBI agents, postal inspectors, and the Internal Revenue Service raided Duke's house while he was abroad, seeking proof that he gambled away hundreds of thousands of dollars of contributions, and used other funds to pay off credit cards and to play the stock market (Martel 2000).

One of the longest surviving hate webmasters is Don Black. He started the Stormfront bulletin board in 1990 with three subscribers and opened it to the public in 1994. He started the Stormfront Web site in 1995 (Don Black 2000). The site opens with a Celtic Cross surrounded by the words "White Pride World Wide." Stormfront compiles sites that advocate white supremacy. Black writes that when he first started Stormfront, he could find only three sites worth linking to. Now, his Web site offers several pages of links to such categories as White Rights and Racially Conscious Conservatism, Eugenics, Revisionism, the Ku Klux Klan, Skinheads, and White Power Music. Black does make some concession to the "marketplace of ideas" by including links to what he considers "The Other Side," although he warns his readers that these sites are not complimentary to white supremacy. He writes, "These are sites opposing our use of the 'Net to promote our point of view. Some openly support censorship (though they don't call it that) while others claim that they only want to 'expose' us for 'what we really are'" (Don Black 2000). In that section, he links to such organizations as Nizkor, the Simon Wiesenthal Center, The Anti-Defamation League, and the Jewish Defense Organization.

Two groups that offer particularly unsavory messages on their Web sites are the National Alliance, headed by Dr. William Pierce, and The World Church of the Creator, whose pontifex maximus is Matt Hale. Both organizations walk a fine line between protected speech and advocacy of violent action. The ADL recently called the National Alliance "the single most dangerous organized hate group in the United States today" (ADL 2000a). The National Alliance is headquartered in West Virginia, but owing to the World Wide Web, its reach is international. Pierce uses the Web site to promote his group's other media operations, which all proselytize hate. They include his weekly radio commentary and an archive of recent broadcasts, available in both audio and text versions; a white supremacist book publishing firm, National Vanguard Books; the monthly newsletter *Free Speech*; the monthly *National Vanguard Magazine*; and Pierce's latest acquisition, Resistance Records, "the pro-white alternative" (National Alliance 2000a). The Web site's home page also offers a foreign language section, including Pierce's novel *The Turner Diaries* in French and German, and articles in Swedish, Dutch, German, and Portuguese (National Alliance 2000a). France, Germany, and Austria all have laws limiting access to racist material and Nazi propaganda. However, as the ADL pointed out, hate literature is available on the Web, and it allows white supremacists and neo-Nazi sympathizers in those countries easy access to material that they cannot get at home.

The National Alliance's site offers a glimpse into the mind-set of many of the white supremacists who spread hateful messages on the Internet. Its goals, as outlined on their Web site, include a white living space, an Aryan society, a responsible government, a new educational system, and an economic policy based on racial principles. Implicit in its goals is a threat of violence against non-whites. Legally, the Web site does not cross the line from protected speech into unprotected threats of action, because the threats are not specifically directed to any one person or group of people. However, CLS adherents would disagree that the messages contained on the site are not a threat. For example, the section on white living space includes the following statement:

> We will do whatever is necessary to achieve this White living space and to keep it White. We will not be deterred by the difficulty or temporary unpleasantness involved because we realize that it is absolutely necessary for our racial survival. The long-term demographic trend toward a darker world...must not only be halted; it must be reversed (National Alliance 2000b).

The National Alliance also promotes hatred of all aspects of society that do not subscribe to its white supremacist philosophy. Pierce maintains, for example, that the United States government will be "responsible" only if it is "wholly committed to the service of our race and subject to no non-Aryan influence." He argues in his on-line publication *Free Speech* that the "controlled media" spreads myths about his organization. He claims that his organization does not comprise haters. Instead, the real haters are the "propagandists who write news stories about so-called 'hate groups' in an attempt to make ordinary people hate me....Over the years they have done enormous damage to our people with their poisonous propaganda, and they aspire to do even more. One way or another we must stop them and make sure they can never harm our people again" (Pierce 1997b).

Pierce denigrates "Blacks, mestizos, and Asians who have made so much of our country an enemy-occupied wasteland" (Pierce 2000). However, his worst venom is directed against Jews and what he considers to be Jewish-influenced stereotypes of white supremacists:

> The Jews have used their control of the media to create certain images in the public minds, and one of their most effective creation is the image of the White racist. He is portrayed as a Neanderthal whose knuckles drag on the ground, a violent and hateful person who lives in a trailer with a yard full of derelict cars, has no education, does only manual labor, and hates Blacks because that makes him feel better about himself (Pierce 2000).

Pierce does not hesitate to stereotype non-Aryans, but he resents the stereotype of white racists—the "chicken-pluckers" as he calls them. Pierce's goal is to recruit a higher class of whites to his organization. He wants to recruit the people who sympathize with his cause but are now unwilling to be directly associated with it because of the stereotype of white racists. He says, "We try much harder to recruit teachers and engineers and successful businessmen, because they have the skills and the character traits we need to do our work successfully. Furthermore, they already wield much more influence than the average chicken-plucker, and we need all the influence we can get" (Pierce 2000). Remember Levin and Paulsen's typology of hatred (1999). Pierce's propaganda is aimed squarely at the sympathizers.

The National Alliance Web site tries to counter the chicken-plucker stereotype by featuring brief profiles of members in a section entitled "*Who* Is the National Alliance." It tries to recruit sympathizers by voicing concerns that many people share about education for young people and Hollywood's influence on our culture. The section reads as if it were written by a direct mail marketing professional, even ending with an exhortation to act right away. "Be a winner. Work with the winners in the National Alliance. Don't Wait" (National Alliance 2000c). Interested individuals can then download a membership application form.

White supremacist Matt Hale, of the World Church of the Creator, also spreads his message of a racial holy war—RAHOWA—via the Internet. The World Church of the Creator is different from other religious organizations. It has no churches or worship services. Instead, it is headquartered in the spare bedroom of Hale's father's house, and it exists primarily on the World Wide Web (Stephenson 2000). Its religion is the propagation and the advancement of the white race to the exclusion of all others. Everyone else is considered an enemy, a member of a "mud race" who should eventually be driven out of the United States in the upcoming racial holy war.

On the Web site, Hale propagates a message of violence and hatred, although he denies on the Creator home page that the church advocates violent action. He stays on the side of the law by not specifically threatening anyone, but CLS adherents would argue that his viewpoint is still a threat. Unlike Pierce, who tries to argue that the real haters are those who oppose the National Alliance, Hale tackles head-on what he calls "The Value of Hatred." "One of the many particulars that distinguish our World Church of the Creator from the other White racial organizations is the fact that we Creators refuse to shun what has been called a negative emotion: hatred" (Hale 2000b). As we saw in chapter one, WCOTC disciple

Benjamin Smith took that message of hate literally, killing two people and wounding several others. In that case, Hale has not been criminally charged with advocating violence, but he does face civil lawsuits from the families of Smith's victims (Associated Press 2000a).

Smith is not the only adherent of the WCOTC who has been involved in violent activities. In 1997, a group of skinheads distributing WCOTC flyers at a rock concert in Florida attacked a father and a son, beating and kicking the men in the back, chest, and face, and smashing beer bottles over their head. Also in 1997, WCOTC members disrupted a gun-rights rally at California's state capitol building by running through the crowd, distributing WCOTC flyers, and yelling "freedom of speech" (ADL 2000c). Hale, himself, was arrested several times because of his extremist activities, although he served no jail time (ADL 2000c). The Illinois State Bar Association pointed to those activities when it denied Hale a law license, even though he had graduated from Southern Illinois University's law school and passed the state bar exam.

This dispute once again illustrates the conflict between protected speech and unprotected action. In his appeal to the U.S. Supreme Court, Hale argued that it was his First Amendment protected beliefs that were under attack, and that the Illinois bar had established "orthodox religious and political beliefs to which (an aspiring lawyer) must subscribe as a condition of admission" (Carelli 2000). However, bar officials countered that because of his past conduct, Hale had "failed to provide he has 'good moral character.'" "As opposed to being excluded from Illinois' bar on the basis of beliefs or speech, Hale's past conduct, lack of credibility and inability to meet his burden of (good character) proof doomed his bar application" (Carelli 2000). After the U.S. Supreme Court rejected Hale's appeal, he sought admission to the bar in Montana (Hale 2000c). However, early in 2001, a committee of the Montana State Bar Association denied his request to take the exam. Bar Admissions Administrator Jay Weber wrote to Hale, "the committee does not feel that your file and application establish by clear and convincing evidence that you possess the requisite character and fitness to practice law in Montana" ("Montana Blocks" 2001). Hale planned an appeal of Montana's decision, but it had not been resolved as of the publication of this book.

The conflict between protected speech and unprotected action arises again when examining some of the antiabortion sites on the World Wide Web. In 1999, a federal district court in Oregon levied a $107.9 million fine against a group of antiabortion activists. Called to testify during the trial was Neal Horsley, the developer of The Nuremberg Files, a Web site devoted to collecting and maintaining dossiers on physicians who perform abortions. The line between speech and advocacy of violent action is muddier on this Web site than on some of the sites devoted to white supremacy. This site solicited and recorded physicians' addresses, pictures, license plate numbers, and other related information for visitor dissemination. Abortion providers who were murdered were listed on the site with a line through their name (Horsley 2000). During the trial, doctors testified that they lived in fear: They disguised themselves when they went out; they drove different routes to work; and they instructed their children to hide in the bathtub if they heard gunshots.

After the decision was reached, attorneys for the physicians said in interviews on national television that they planned to seek an injunction to shut down the site. However, before they were able to request the injunction, the Internet service provider that hosted The Nuremberg Files pulled it off the World Wide Web. That did not stop Horsley. In June 1999, he sued the ISP that had taken down the site for breach of contract. The Nuremberg Files site is now back on the Web, hosted by the ISP netfreedom.net, which is located in London. (A mirror site has been set up in Amsterdam.) The Web site contains the same graphic pictures, the same pleas for information, and the same pleas for contributions that it did before the 1999 trial (Horsley 2000). Chris Ellison of Internet Freedom, the organization that runs the netfreedom server, argues in an on-line article that the site must be defended. "The belief that restricting what people express will somehow restrict what people do (and thus will stop attacks on doctors) is sadly mistaken. Thus it is that those who value free speech must defend this repugnant site. There is nothing to be gained by giving up one freedom in the vain hope that it will secure another" (Ellison 2000). That defense, however, begs the question of which freedom is more valuable—speech or the right to life.

Early in 2001, the 9th U.S. Circuit Court of Appeals in San Francisco ruled that the contents of the Web site were protected free speech, and threw out the $107 million verdict against the defendants. Writing for the court, Circuit Judge Alex Kozinski said that the defendants could "only be held liable if they authorized, ratified, or directly threatened violence." In a 1960s case, the U.S. Supreme Court had ruled that speakers could be held liable only if their threats were explicit and were likely to cause "imminent lawless action" (*Brandenburg v. Ohio* 1969). Kozinski wrote that the defendants came "closest to suggesting violence on the Web page, where the names of murdered doctors are stricken and the wounded ones are grayed." However, whereas the markings "may connote approval" for past violence, they "cannot fairly be read as calling for future violence...otherwise any statement approving past violence could automatically be construed as calling for future violence" (American Health Line 2001). Once again, this decision points to the difficulty of regulating speech either on the Internet or in everyday conversation. The courts have given wide latitude to hateful words, as long as they do not result in immediate violent action. The difficulty comes when trying to link violence against a particular doctor to the Web site. It apparently does not count that the site makes it easier for antiabortion activists to find their targets.

This explosion of hate speech on the Internet leaves some hoping there is a counterargument to unfettered free speech. For many, the arguments advanced by critical legal studies scholars resonate. As we have pointed out, CLS scholars argue that hate speech deserves little, if any, constitutional protection. Assaultive speech usually targets outsiders—the traditionally disenfranchised such as women and people of color. In their 1993 book *Words That Wound* [sic], Professors Mari Matsuda and Charles Lawrence write about the ways in which such speech causes severe and irreparable harm. Hate speech based on a person's immutable characteristics, things they cannot change, causes self-hatred and diminished self-esteem for the victim. "Victims of vicious hate propaganda experience physiological symptoms and emotional distress ranging from fear in the gut to rapid pulse rate and difficulty in breathing, nightmares, post-traumatic stress disorder, hypertension, psychosis, and suicide. Patricia Williams has called the blow of racist messages 'spirit murder' in recognition of the psychic destruction victims experience" (Matsuda et al. 1993, 24). CLS scholars argue that this is an extraordinary price to pay for society's tolerance of virulent speech. Hate speech should not be evaluated according to sterile legal formalism or constitutional doctrine; rather it must be examined in the context of human experience and emotion. We examine how victims experience hate in our chapters about music and film.

Language causes harm in ways that many legal analysts could not have predicted. CLS scholars contend that it is easy to lurk behind such constitutional defenses of free speech as the marketplace model and wholly forget the impact that language has on self and identity. Although the injury to the recipient may be silent and invisible, it is no less abhorrent. Even with the possibility of recovering damages in a civil action for severe emotional distress, the impact of injury from hate speech can be profound and noncompensable. In addition, CLS writers are concerned with "the paradoxical pitting of the First Amendment against other forms of injury" and how this analysis results in the "specter of legal censorship blocking further discussion of moral censure" (Fraleigh and Tuman 1997). Critical legal analysts such as Matsuda and Lawrence et al. want desperately to add a moral texture to the complex discussion of hate speech.

How are we, as a society, to reconcile the competing demands for the individual freedom to construct heinous Web sites with the opposing need of the community to protect itself and reside in harmony? Can The Nuremberg Files, for example, a testimony to the very limits of free speech, coexist with the simultaneous reality of young children hiding in terror for fear of being gunned down along with their parents? Pierce, Hale, Horsley, and Black all rely heavily on the now unregulated Internet to spread their messages of hate, and they do it in the name of free speech. Pierce's Web site, for example, features the blue ribbon of the Free Speech Online Blue Ribbon campaign. Black makes himself available to media scrutiny. Besides his Web site, he has been willing to be interviewed by ABC's Ted Koppel in an appearance on *Nightline*; he has been quoted on ABC News, CBS News, in the *Birmingham News*, and newspapers in Florida, where he resides. Articles about Black began appearing as early as 1995, when the Fort Lauderdale *Sun-Sentinel* and the Miami *Herald* both published articles about his on-line activities. The *Sun-Sentinel* headlined its article, "Former KKK leader transmits his hate through cyberspace," while the *Herald's* headline proclaimed, "High-tech hate: Ex KKK member goes on line" (Black "Homepage" 2000).

Black recognizes that many people are unhappy about the information that he gathers, but he argues that he has a First Amendment right to disseminate his point of view. He compares the United States with its "strong First Amendment tradition guaranteeing freedom of speech" with countries such as Germany where, he says, "a Web site operator was arrested for merely including a link to Stormfront on his page" (Black "Stormfront" 2000). While we may abhor the material Black disseminates, the marketplace of ideas philosophy that we subscribe to allows unpopular ideas to be heard. We rely on the marketplace to counter his message, and such organizations as the Simon Wiesenthal Center, the Anti-Defamation League, and the Southern Poverty Law Center work diligently to counter the message these hate groups spread.

Conversely, countries without a First Amendment guarantee of free speech have taken more drastic measures to stop the dissemination of objectionable material. They have limited what information their citizens can read and write on the Internet. Human Rights Watch's World Report 2000 on Freedom of Expression on the Internet is replete with examples of countries requiring filters, ratings, and blocking systems that limit access to the Internet in a variety of ways:

- Australia approved a Broadcasting Services Amendment that would force Australian Internet service providers to "remove objectionable material from Australian sites and to block access to similar sites overseas." The blocks are to be based on current film and video classification standards, and HRW argues that the law will keep adults from accessing material considered unsuitable for minors.
- In Tunisia, Iran, and Bahrain, state-controlled or state-influenced ISPs blocked access to sites that contained political or human rights criticisms of their government.
- In India in June 1999, during the height of the Kashmir crisis, residents were blocked from accessing the on-line news site of the Pakistani daily *Dawn*, which offered independent coverage of the crisis.

- Other nations that blocked access to Web sites based on content included Saudi Arabia, the United Arab Emirates, and Yemen. In Saudi Arabia, for example, users who requested blocked sites received a message on their screens that all access attempts were logged.
- Even the United States is not immune from attempts to block access to sites that might be considered harmful to minors. Congress passed the *Child Online Protection Act* (also known as "Son of CDA") in 1998. A federal appeals court ruled the law was unconstitutional (Human Rights Watch 2000).

The issue of hate speech was not mentioned in the Human Rights Watch report. However, an article in the *Cyberlaw Journal* in CyberTimes, *The New York Times* on the Web, pointed out that "countries with more democratic traditions, such as the United States and members of the European Union, are considering policies that, in an effort to control problems like racism and pornography, could end up restricting legitimate speech on the global network" (Mendels 1998). The article pointed out that the European Union "is examining proposals that would require Internet service providers to block 'harmful speech' like sites promoting racism, or hold them accountable by law when they make such information available" (1998). At a conference in Berlin about hate speech on the Internet, co-organized by the Simon Wiesenthal Center, German President Johannes Rau called for rules to combat the rise of Web sites promoting racism and xenophobia. "We need a framework that sets boundaries for the use of modern information technology....We cannot just stand by and watch while opponents of human rights and those contemptuous of democracy exploit these new technological possibilities" (Thomasson 2000).

The conference discussed the need for international cooperation to combat hate on the Web. Ulrich Sieber, a professor of information law at Munich University, pointed out that the First Amendment to the U.S. Constitution makes it difficult to devise a global approach to combating hate speech. "The Internet is a global medium so we need global strategies....Most of the countries in Europe have gone further than the United States. I respect the U.S. Constitution, but you would think they could do more to try and find common minimum standards" (Thomasson 2000). At the conference, it was pointed out that in Germany, the number of far right-wing home-pages had increased to 330, about ten times more than four years ago, and that many neo-Nazi groups had moved their home-pages to servers outside of the continent to sell books and insignia and to promote their theories. Germany's Justice Minister Herta Daubler-Gmelin argued that while European initiatives had to be established, there was a need for action beyond Europe. She sought global rules against hate speech on the Internet. "What is forbidden off-line must be forbidden online....Our goal must be to achieve a global value consensus and to agree to an international minimum level of regulation" (Reuters 2000).

Two international cyberspace controversies that deal with hate have arisen recently, both as a result of the U.S. First Amendment's protection for objectionable speech. They involved attempts by European countries to prohibit companies and Internet servers in the United States from marketing products and making available Web sites that would otherwise be illegal in those countries. These controversies reveal a clash of values between the United States and European countries about the limits of free speech, and raise questions about whether international law will allow countries to apply their own laws to Internet servers outside their borders.

The first controversy involves the on-line auctioning of Nazi paraphernalia. France, Germany, and Austria have laws that prohibit its citizens from buying or selling racist and Nazi material. A French court ordered Yahoo! to block French citizens from accessing that portion of its auction site where Nazi items are sold. Lawyers for Yahoo! argued in court in France that it would be technically impossible to block the site from French citizens. However, Internet experts testified that new filtering software could make it possible to identify and bar up to 90 percent of French users. Yahoo! was then ordered to pay fines of up to $13,000 a day if it did not comply with the French court's ruling within three months. After the ruling, an attorney for Yahoo! argued that France has no jurisdiction over the company. He said that Yahoo! would ignore the decision unless it was enforced by a U.S. court and would refuse to pay the fines (Souchard 2000b). Yahoo! later filed suit in the United States to block the order, saying that France did not have jurisdiction (Jesdanun 2001).

Early in 2001, though, Yahoo! decided to stop carrying all on-line auctions of Nazi artifacts and other hate-related material. The senior auction producer for the company said that outside of raising awareness within the company and speeding up the decision, the French court's order played no role in the new policy. Brian Fitzgerald told The Associated Press, "[W]e decided we don't necessarily want to profit from items that promote hatred or glorify hatred and violence" (Jesdanun 2001). However, others questioned the timing of the decision. "In a way it's a preemptive strike in making sure this (the French ruling) doesn't become a serious issue. International law has a unique was of evolving," a consultant at Gomez, Inc. told The Associated Press (Jesdanun 2001).

The controversy over the sale of Nazi memorabilia raises new questions about restricting speech on the Internet. Given the international reach of the Internet, can one country use its laws to regulate Web sites based in other countries? At the time that the *Communications Decency Act* decision was handed down, the Supreme Court acknowledged that the technology did not yet exist to block pornographers overseas from making their wares available to citizens of the United States. However, several years have passed since that decision, and filtering technology has improved. A *Washington Post* column pointed out that the tactics of those who favor regulating the Internet have also changed. In the column, Sebastian Mallaby writes, "The old idea that you could never enforce rules against millions of far-flung webmasters is giving way to the realization that you don't need to. It is enough to pressure the Internet's big players and get at the small ones through them" (2000).

Another large on-line auction service, eBay, also revised its policy on items that "promote or glorify hatred, violence, or racial intolerance, or items that promote organizations with such views." It listed several items that would "generally be removed" from sale, including "[i]tems that bear symbols of the Nazis, the SS, or the KKK, including authentic German WWII memorabilia that bears [*sic*] such marks." However, it will still allow the sale of "German coins and stamps from the WWII era, regardless of markings; WWII memorabilia that does [*sic*] not bear the Nazi or SS markings; and books and movies about WWII or Nazi Germany, even if the Nazi symbol appears on the item" (eBay 2000).

Previously, eBay allowed the sale of Nazi memorabilia that were at least fifty years old. eBay added the age restriction after it was accused of marketing hate by Kweisi Mfume, president of the NAACP, because of an auction for a racist Web domain name. In December 1999, a seller who used the name "animius" tried to sell the domain name "niggers.org." Bidding began at $500,000, and twelve bids had been received before eBay pulled the auction after being alerted to it by *The Washington Post* (Dennehy 1999). A number of civil rights groups, including the NAACP and the Anti-Defamation League, then registered several domain names that are variations of other racial epithets to prevent hate groups from registering and using them (Associated Press 1999).

The decision by the French court to hold Yahoo! responsible for prohibiting the sale of racist material there met with stiff criticism from Internet free speech advocates. After the decision, The Associated Press quoted an attorney with the Center for Democracy and Technology in Washington, D.C.: "The French approach would lead to a lowest common denominator world where the most restrictive rules of any country would govern all speech on the Internet. What happens when the government of China decides to prosecute a human rights group in the U.S. for publishing dissident materials that are legal here but illegal there?" (Souchard 2000a)

One element that has been missing in the argument over whether on-line auction companies should allow sales of Nazi and neo-Nazi memorabilia is the effect such sales have on still-surviving victims of the Holocaust and their relatives. We live in a free market system where presumably everything is for sale to the highest bidder. It is also true that in order to bid on such items, a person must deliberately access the section of the on-line auction where they are being sold. However, just knowing that these items are available must produce painful reminders of imprisonment, degradation, and forced labor for the victims. It cheapens the memory of the experience of the survivors, and it lessens the memory of the ones who died by making symbols of this mass hatred available to the highest bidder.

These symbols and the memories they evoke are at the heart of a second new international cyberspace controversy over hate. This one involves the rise of far-right groups in Germany. To circumvent German laws that make it a crime to deny the Holocaust or to disseminate Nazi propaganda, these groups are now posting their Web sites on servers in the United States, where they are protected by the First Amendment. According to an Interior Ministry survey, the number of neo-Nazi sites based outside Germany, but aimed at Germans, has increased to nearly 800, a significant increase over the previous year when there were 330 (Finn 2000). The German Supreme Court has ruled that German laws about Nazi materials can be applied to people outside the country if the Web sites are accessible to Internet users inside Germany. It would be difficult to try to extradite U.S. citizens who host such sites to Germany for prosecution because, as a spokesman for the U.S. Justice Department said, to have extradition, "you have to have dual criminality in both countries, and this doesn't meet that standard" in the United States (Finn 2000). However, German Interior Minister Otto Schily said other possible actions to stop the dissemination of the material in Germany include filing civil suits in U.S. courts against people who target neo-Nazi sites at Germany, and trying to shut down such sites by overwhelming them with traffic (Finn 2000).

The controversy over cyberspace regulation tends to be posed in either/or terms. Either the United States will be grouped with countries that block access to information on the World Wide Web or it will allow any material short of obscenity to be available. It is difficult to reach consensus on the best approach to take. Our current laws allow adults to make up their own minds about whether they want to access hateful material on the Internet. However, an added concern about hate speech on the Internet is the effect it might have on children.

The number of families buying computers and accessing the Internet increases each year. Over the years, politicians, child advocates, and social scientists have pointed to everything from dime-store novels to comic books to television programs as having harmful socializing effects on young children. Will the Internet soon assume that role? Certainly the concern over children's access to pornography on the Internet was the impetus behind the *Communications Decency Act* (*CDA*). In that case, the law was attempting to restrict children from reaching material that in other circumstances was illegal for them to possess. The *Telecommunications Act of 1996*, which included the *CDA*, also required manufacturers to install V-chips in all television sets made for and sold in this country after July 1999. However, hate speech is accessible and legal for both children and adults. Does the legislative emphasis on pornography and violence mean that Congress considers them to be of greater concern than hate speech on the Internet? Furthermore, are the barriers raised by the First Amendment so high that there is little hope that hate speech can be regulated? In the long run, a minor's access to hate speech may be more damaging to a civil society than his or her access to pornographic images, and at least as damaging as violent television programs. We have seen the influence that the WCOTC Web site had on Benjamin Smith in cementing the hatred he felt toward African Americans, Jews, and immigrants.

These hate Web sites are being accessed by minors. Many signers of the Knights of the White Kamellia, Realm of Texas guestbook, for example, include their age in their message. A typical signing reads: " i'm only 15 now but when i get older i plan to join the Klan To support the master race. ~ ~WHITE Power~ ~WHITE PRIDE~ ~" (Knights of the White Kamellia 1997). Resistance Records is obviously aimed at young people, indoctrinating them into the white power movement. In addition, both Stormfront and the World Church of the Creator (WCOTC) have special pages for children. The webmaster for the Stormfront Kids Page is Derek Black, who offers propaganda aimed at young readers. For example, he complained in the introduction to the site that before he was removed from public school, he had to spend most of his time tutoring slower children rather than learning himself. Now, he says, he is being homeschooled, and he has time to learn about the great accomplishments of the white race (Derek Black 2000). The WCOTC offers games and crossword puzzles for youngsters on its Web site. The crossword puzzles are designed as indoctrination tools, extolling the value of the white race and denigrating others (WCOTC 2000).

Legitimate concerns can be raised about children's access to such information. However, free speech advocates argue there are ways far short of government censorship to limit that access. The Anti-Defamation League offers a hate filter that can be downloaded from its Web site, and other commercial software filters are available for purchase. In addition, some Internet search engines offer "family friendly" browsing. However, is that enough to limit access to these sites by children? As with the V-chip in televisions, filtering software only works if it is turned on and password protected.

In other instances, such as in the case of The Nuremberg Files, private Internet service providers have chosen to remove Web sites that they believe do not meet their standards. The Stormfront Web site, for example, on its links page requests that potential linkers do not ask them to link to sites at Geocities, America Online, or some other free webhosting services because these companies have policies that censor pro-White pages. "Listing them here would only hasten that process," the site points out (Stormfront 2000). Of course, as we have seen with The Nuremberg Files site, even though one ISP elected to stop hosting it, another site, dedicated to free speech, has made it available again.

Anti-hate organizations are pressuring large Internet companies to remove sites and material that glorify hate. Rabbi Abraham Cooper of the Simon Wiesenthal Center has met with officials from such companies as Yahoo! and Amazon.com to emphasize that a private company can regulate hate material in ways that the government cannot. "Internet companies should just do what American companies have been doing for half a century: reserve the right not to peddle bigotry," he says (Guernsey 2000). However, while the companies are often willing to meet with Rabbi Cooper, they do not always agree to his recommendations. A lawyer for Yahoo! asked whether Americans "really want Internet service providers and portals deciding what they can and cannot post, if it is otherwise legal" (Guersney 2000). Experts also point out that because of a provision in the *Communications Decency Act* that the Court did not overturn, interactive computer services are not liable for material transferred over their services. The more a service monitors its users, the more it moves from being a neutral forum into becoming an editor. That editorial function would make the provider more vulnerable to lawsuits (Guernsey, 2000).

So, is the marketplace of ideas working to counter the many examples of hate speech found on the Internet? Web sites that advocate diversity and tolerance and that warn against the unfettered growth of hate are far outnumbered by those that preach hatred. As we have seen, only little can be done to eradicate the hate sites unless they advocate actual violence against specific individuals. After the 9th Circuit Court ruled in The Nuremberg Files case, a group of federal lawmakers asked the court to reconsider its ruling, arguing that it does directly incite violence. Sen. Charles Schumer of New York contended that the site undermines the *Freedom of Access to Clinic Entrances Act*, and that the court ruling could incite renewed violence against clinics and that doctors could be vulnerable to threats and violence (McGuire 2001). However, no action has been taken by the court as of this writing.

A larger question about hate as a subtext of our national conversation focuses on what hate on the Internet reveals about our prevailing national character. To some it is indicative of a culture in decline, a nation that has lost (or perhaps never even had) respect for difference and diversity. Others see Internet hate only as isolated examples of a rampant individualism. In any case, hate speech may prove to have long-term effects by reinforcing prejudice and inferiority and contributing to a social pattern of dominance and inequality (Greenawalt 1995). It may also prove to weaken the already shaky fabric of our national community and our notions of respect, trust, civic virtue, and the common or public good.

Ironically, in a discussion of Web chatrooms, a young entrepreneur spoke about the new "communities" (including hate communities) being created everyday in our cyberspace network. Community, solidarity, and commonality are terms used most frequently to describe the new on-line experiences. Feelings of isolationism and powerlessness diminish in the camaraderie of Internet relationships. Thus, organizations such as The World Church of the Creator and The National Alliance use the Internet to define and to strengthen their bond of hate and provide a sense of fellowship and identity for those threatened by our growing ethnic and cultural diversity. These sites allow the community of racists to feel safe in an insular and protected sort of way, even if it is at the expense of their victims. Is this the type of community that Alexis de Tocqueville saw in *Democracy in America* or the type of intimate loving community that Robert Bellah et al. (1986) envisioned in *Habits of the Heart*—a contemporary analysis of Tocqueville's communitarianism? Will our definition of the traditional community as the common good be so altered that it will now require a transformation of its historical meaning? Consider these questions as you reflect on the reality and presence of Internet hate communities.

In the next chapter, we will examine another way that hate makes its way into the national consciousness—through media coverage. The majority of Americans still get their news from newspapers and television news programs. However, the Internet is fast becoming the new resource for information and progress. In addition, though, it is also a place where intolerance, hatred, and venom are available for those who seek them out and even for those who do not willingly wish to broach their messages. In the final analysis, we can only hope that the excesses of Internet hate will be checked by the national community's greater desire to bank the flames of dissension and acrimony with a moral discourse truly deserving of the best in our national character and values.

— Chapter 4 —
Hate in the News

In August 1999, the headline on a *Boston Globe* column by Jeff Jacoby raised an interesting question: "Would we care about Buford Furrow if he hadn't used a gun?"

Furrow is a white supremacist who, on 10 August 1999, committed two hate crimes that garnered nationwide publicity. First, he shot seventy rounds from an Uzi submachine gun at the Jewish Community Center in Los Angeles, injuring four children and an adult. He later killed a Filipino letter carrier because he was an immigrant who worked for the federal government (Meyer, Riccardi, and Miller 1999). After fleeing to Las Vegas, he turned himself in to the FBI the next day, reportedly telling them, "You're looking for me. I killed the kids in Los Angeles" (Larrubia, Rohrlich, and Blankstein 1999, A1). Jacoby's column was prompted by the widespread publicity Furrow's crimes received in the first few weeks after they occurred. Local, national, and international media flocked to the scene. NBC's *Today* show, CBS's *Good Morning*, ABC's *20/20*, and CNN's *TalkBack Live* and *Burden of Proof* all devoted programming time to the incident, as did the network television news broadcasts and major newspapers across the country.

The emphasis on Furrow's actions illustrates the symbiotic relationship between what the media cover, and what society wants to know. Hate is a subtext of our national conversation. We crave information about hate because it is so much a part of our national culture. One primary way that hate is injected into the national psyche is through media coverage of hate crimes. By publicizing such crimes, the media alert us to the problems of hate. They editorialize against hate and interview experts about ways to overcome the scourge of hatred that infects us. However, the coverage also gives hatemongers a forum that they can use to influence the attitudes of hate sympathizers and hate spectators. This chapter will examine media coverage of hate by looking specifically at two hate crimes committed in the summer of 1999 that received national coverage—Furrow's attack on the Jewish Community Center in August, and the shooting spree carried out earlier that summer by World Church of the Creator adherent Benjamin Smith. It will focus on why the media consider hate crimes more "newsworthy" than similar crimes, and whether blanket coverage of hate crimes ends up crossing the line from analyzing how and why such events occur, to becoming infomercials for hate groups.

In the Furrow and Smith cases, the national media were reacting to incidents that were more than simple random acts of violence. Instead, these shootings were targeted at particular individuals because of their race, religion, or national origin. That is the very essence of a hate crime. Its root cause is bias against a particular individual "because of" his or her immutable characteristics. Furrow did not shoot at the children because they happened to be in any day care center; he shot them because they were in a Jewish day care center. Smith's victims were also targeted because of their race, ethnicity, or religion. One person he killed was African American, and the other was Vietnamese. His other shooting victims were young people returning from Friday night religious services at a Jewish synagogue.

As we learned in chapter 2, some state legislatures believe that hate crimes deserve enhanced punishment. The media appear to accept this notion because they tend to give hate crimes comprehensive coverage. For the most part, they consider hate crimes more "newsworthy" than random acts of violence and give them additional publicity. Not everyone agrees, though, that hate crimes deserve this extra attention. Shortly after the Furrow incident, Jacoby, the *Globe's* conservative columnist, questioned why similar crimes—parallel crimes—did not receive as much national attention. "Absent the gun control and hate-crime hooks, would the press have covered his monstrous crime so avidly?" Jacoby asked (1999, A11). He then described the circumstances of the following parallel crime.

In May 1999, Steven Abrams rammed his 1967 Cadillac through a chain link fence and drove onto the grounds of the Southcoast Early Learning Center in Costa Mesa, California. His unprovoked attack left two children dead, and two others seriously injured.

Overall, the accident killed two and injured five. After Abrams was arrested, Costa Mesa police said he told them, "I was going to execute these children because they were innocent." He blamed his actions on frustration over a failed relationship with a woman (Alexander, Leonard, and Yi 1999, A1).

In terms of sheer numbers, it could be argued that Abrams's action was more serious than Furrow's because more people were killed by Abrams's car than by Furrow's gun. However, the amount of publicity that surrounded Abrams's act pales in comparison with the media coverage given to Furrow's hate crime. Is this disparity in coverage good or bad? Should hate crimes be given so much attention? Is it because we are fascinated by hate in the same way that we all slow down when we pass an accident on the highway? Do we abhor it so much that we believe it deserves extra attention because it is senseless and horrific?

Whatever the reason, a check of the Lexis-Nexis Academic Universe database shows hundreds of print and broadcast stories mentioned Furrow in the nearly three months between the date of the shooting and 1 November 2000. Wire service reports mentioned Furrow 121 times, major newspapers 153 times, and broadcast transcripts more than 1,000 times. Because of the unusual aspects of Furrow's crime, newspapers and broadcasters from across the country sent their own reporters to cover that incident, rather than relying on the nationally distributed wire services for coverage. On the other hand, the Abrams case was publicized nationwide only by The Associated Press, so it received nowhere near the same amount of coverage. The database shows more mention of Abrams in broadcast transcripts than in newspaper articles. However, between the date of his attack on the children and 1 November 2000, he was mentioned only 136 times in broadcast transcripts (compared with more than 1,000 for Furrow), 6 times in wire service reports, and 14 times either in major newspapers or in U.S. regional papers.

That disparity in coverage led Jacoby to ask, "Does a homicidal attack on toddlers only make it to the front page when the killer uses a gun? Is attempted mass murder only newsworthy when the victims belong to an official minority group?" (1999, A11). Jacoby said in his column that he couldn't think of a "sound journalistic reason" that editors paid so much more attention to Furrow's hate crime than the parallel crime of Steven Abrams. Is he right? Should one act receive international coverage and condemnation while the other is barely mentioned?

Beginning journalism students learn that traditionally, news selection is based on six criteria: timeliness, proximity, impact, conflict, unusualness, and celebrity. Those are not the only reasons that a particular story will appear in the local newspaper or on the evening news, but they explain the vast majority of them. Most of these traditional news elements could be found in the Furrow story, but what made it more noteworthy was the additional element of hate. The media believe that one of their responsibilities is to inform and to educate the public. By focusing attention on the actions of such people as Furrow and Smith, the media can make the public aware of the simmering resentment exhibited by hate groups and their growing influence in society. The media can influence readers and viewers to examine their own attitudes about the "other." By publicizing the Furrow and Smith shootings, the media tell the public that these events are unusual in some fashion, and that we should care about them for more reasons than because they are horrific crimes.

So what do the traditional criteria for news selection mean, and why does adding the element of hate to the mix explain why Furrow's and Smith's actions received more coverage than the Abrams incident?

- Timeliness is the *when* of a story. It explains why a breaking news story, one that's happening now, leads the news at 11 P.M., even though it may not be the most "important" news item of the day. If we have already seen or heard about them, we do not care as much about the stories that were broadcast on the 6 P.M. news, or the ones that appeared in the morning newspaper. In Furrow's case, the search for the suspect received immediate blanket coverage in Los Angeles and the surrounding area. The Smith story led the news for a few days because his shooting spree occurred over a weekend, and in more than one state. More and more media began to follow the story as connections were made between the initial shootings in the Chicago area and later shootings in other parts of Illinois and Indiana.

Conversely, the Abrams story was over quickly because he was arrested right after he crashed through the fence at the day care center.
- Proximity is the *where* of a story. We are most interested in stories that happen near us. After both the Smith and the Furrow shootings, media outlets around the country added what is known as a "local angle" to make the story more interesting for their own viewers and readers by reporting on security measures that local Jewish synagogues and day care centers were implementing. The Abrams incident did not result in similar "localized" stories for two reasons. First, unlike Furrow's victims, Abrams's victims were not targeted because they were in a specific day care center. The choice of the Costa Mesa center was random. Second, there is little extra security that day care centers can put in place to prevent cars from crashing through fences that surround their playgrounds.
- Impact is *how* a story affects us; it is why local media thrive. People want to know what is happening in their community, and how it is going to affect them. However, impact is more than just whether you are going to have to pay more taxes next year. It also includes how a person reacts to an incident or event. After the Abrams, Smith, and Furrow incidents, the media explored the reactions victims had to them. However, a hate crime affects more people than a random act of violence. Hate crimes are more likely to have a psychological effect on members of targeted groups, even though they were not directly affected by the incident. After the Furrow shooting, for example, Jewish reporters wrote commentaries discussing how earlier incidences of anti-Semitic violence affected them.
- Conflict is a news media staple. Everything from war to neighborhood crime to the results of presidential elections can be, and is, covered as conflict. Both the Smith and the Furrow stories were covered as conflict in terms of the search for the suspects—the police and the FBI versus the killers. In the Smith case, police were particularly concerned about finding him because they didn't know where he would strike next. After both events, the media developed another

conflict theme by examining the negative attitudes members of hate groups hold toward the "other." The "conflict" that led Abrams to attack the children at the day care center was his anger over a failed relationship with a woman. While that is certainly serious, it does not have the importance that hatred of the "other" has on the civic conscience.

- Unusualness generally means that quirky elements are involved in the story. These stories can be lighthearted, sentimental, or just plain strange. Sometimes, however, unusualness is defined as "uniqueness." There have been too many cases in recent years in which children have been killed in schools or in day care centers. However, the Furrow and Smith stories had "unique" elements that distinguished these shootings. Those elements included the targeting of victims based on their ethnicity and their religion, and the perpetrators' involvement with the white supremacy movement.
- Celebrity is the final traditional news value. We all like good gossip. It is one of the reasons why *People* magazine and television programs such as *Entertainment Tonight* are so popular. We also all crave our own measure of celebrity. Years ago, the pop icon Andy Warhol posited that we all want our "fifteen minutes of fame." Before the shooting, Furrow and Smith were unknowns. However, media coverage of the events made them known around the world, giving them not "celebrity," but certainly notoriety. When Furrow was taken into court for his arraignment, he told his public defender, "I think they like me" (Rooney and Newman 1999). The reaction that Furrow had to his own crime is one of the reasons that critics are concerned about the amount of publicity the media give to hate crimes. They worry that the publicity may either prompt copycat crimes or lead to more recruits for the white supremacy movement.

There are plenty of other reasons that stories get covered. However, it seems clear that Jacoby's contention—that Furrow was a "poster boy" for the liberal cause of gun control legislation—was not the primary reason that the media focused so much attention on his crime. Instead, the media were reflecting society's fascination with hate and hate crimes. Through the years, the media have been credited with an agenda-setting function. They do not tell you what to think, but they do influence what you think about. Researchers Shanto Iyengar and Donald Kinder, who studied the agenda-setting influence of network television newscasts, found that "Americans' views of society and their nation are powerfully shaped by the stories that appear on the evening news" (1989, 112). In this instance, by publicizing hate crimes, the media provided Americans with plenty of material "to think about."

What types of stories were published and broadcast after Furrow's and Smith's shooting sprees? What information did the media give the American people "to think about"? Did they reveal the nature of hatred in society, or did they glorify the actions of the haters? The Lexis-Nexis Academic Database provided a wealth of stories that were published in newspapers, both in the United States and internationally, in the aftermath of the two shootings. An examination of the articles in a five-week period after each event revealed that the stories could be broken into six main categories—straight news stories, profiles of the victims and perpetrators, reactions from local and national leaders, analysis of the growing white supremacist movement, concerns about the spread of guns, and editorial commentaries about the incidents. What effect does all this coverage have on the civic good? To avoid sounding like an infomercial for hate groups, the media must balance the need to provide information to the public about the facts of an incident against the concern that they are promoting the abhorrent philosophies of the perpetrators. They must also avoid sensationalizing the incidents to the point where the public becomes as desensitized to hate crimes as it is to violent entertainment.

The first type of story about these hate crimes was the straight news story, or breaking news story, which constituted the bulk of the early coverage of the incidents. These initial stories focused on the basics of the incidents, answering such questions as what happened and where, who was injured and/or killed, and who were the suspected perpetrators of the incident. An unintended consequence of the unrelenting coverage of such breaking news events may be that it ends up helping the gunman. It could give the gunman clues to the position of people who may be trapped, and who could end up as potential hostages, or it could tip them off to the plans of the police. Guidelines issued by the Radio and Television News Directors Association (RTNDA) urge news directors to "always assume the gunman has access to your air, which means that you don't put certain things on the air if you think the gunman or the hostage holder might be watching" (*CNN TalkBack Live* 1999). For example, during the shooting at Columbine High School in April 1999, local media talked on the air with students, still trapped in the school, who had called the stations from their cell phones. If the two young men who committed that crime had still been alive and had been listening, they might have been able to pinpoint the location of those students with more disastrous results.

The second category of stories contained articles that could be accused of glorifying, or at least neutralizing, the perpetrators of the crimes. This category includes profiles of both the victims and the perpetrators. After both the Smith and Furrow shootings, the media provided stories about the impact of the shootings on the victims and their families, and covered the funerals of the victims. However, to provide "balance" to the coverage and to try to explain the motives of the perpetrators, the media also offered plenty of stories about the killers and their philosophies. These stories included profiles of Furrow and Smith that examined what may have motivated their actions, how former neighbors and girlfriends saw them, and how their parents reacted to the incidents. Friends and neighbors who are questioned for such profile stories are often reluctant to say much that reflects badly on the individual in question. In the Furrow case, for instance, a profile in *The Los Angeles Times* reported that he had mental health problems, that he was an active member of the white supremacist group Aryan Nations, and that he had a violent temper. Nonetheless, his neighbors seemed surprised that he was capable of committing such a hateful crime. One set of neighbors described him as "cheerful, with a friendly smile." The landlord of the mobile home park where he lived said, "You know, he was a wonderful tenant. He came and did his laundry. He went to work in the morning and he came home. That was all. It doesn't sound like him. He was so quiet. He was supposed to have some kind of sickness...but he didn't seem sick" (McDermott, Murphy, and Meyer 1999, A1). To many of his neighbors, Furrow appeared normal. However, as we have emphasized in this book, "normal" people are capable of hating because hate is a "normal" aspect of society. In defense of the neighbors, Hanna Rosin and David Plotz, columnists for *Slate Magazine*, questioned whether we have been conditioned by the media not to say anything negative in situations such as the Furrow shooting. "It may be that neighbors are simply following the script. Thanks to television news culture, the neighbors have undoubtedly memorized what neighbors are supposed to say (nice guy, kept to himself) and dredge that from the subconscious." As Rosin and Plotz point out, though, comments such as these sound "naïve, foolish and odd" (1999, 19A).

Legitimate questions can be raised about whether such profile stories are necessary. Do the media provide them because they are reacting to what they know is the public's vicarious interest in learning about the perpetrators of such crimes? Think again of the "celebrity" angle of news coverage. In writing such stories, though, the media may end up glorifying the perpetrators of crimes, giving them the notoriety they crave, while ignoring or marginalizing the victims.

Editors and reporters sometimes find themselves in a quandary when trying to decide how much coverage to give to a tragedy or a horrific crime. On the one hand, they do not want to be accused of harassing already-traumatized individuals. Viewers are often critical of reporters, television reporters especially, who stick microphones in the faces of victims of tragedies and ask them "how do you feel?" In addition, in the Furrow shooting, many of the victims were young children. In cases involving children, the media have an additional responsibility not to intrude unless invited by parents or other adult guardians. On the other hand, because of the nature of the incidents, the media want to inform the public as thoroughly as possible about the background and motives of the perpetrators. The public is asking, "How could this happen? How could a person attack innocent children or young men walking home from religious services? What is it about this person that allowed him to commit such a heinous crime?" In trying to answer those questions, the media end up providing that person with a platform for his or her hateful attitudes toward the "other." It is a difficult conundrum to resolve to everyone's satisfaction. News organizations must take care to balance the coverage of a hate incident with explanation and analysis. They need to help us understand the role and meaning of hate in society, and to help us dissect how hate crimes develop.

They must take care, though, to avoid describing the hatemongers in such a way that they appear to be just like the average Joe. That type of description may lead hate sympathizers and hate spectators to overlook the potential danger that hatemongers pose for society and to consider their actions as aberrations rather than symptoms of a larger problem.

The third type of story found in the Lexis-Nexis database was reaction to the shootings. These stories tended to break down into two areas. As mentioned above, many media added the element of proximity to the events by running stories about security at local Jewish Community Centers and synagogues and questioning whether similar incidents could occur in other places. The second area involved government and community leaders, from the president and attorney general on down, condemning the acts as despicable and intolerant.

The fourth type of story was analysis of the growing white supremacist and hate group movement in the country. Experts from the Simon Wiesenthal Center, the Southern Poverty Law Center, and other organizations that study and track hate groups were interviewed by newspapers and major broadcast outlets. Here, the public was able to get involved as well. WashingtonPost.com hosted an on-line chat with a hate group expert; CNN hosted *TalkBack Live* programs about hate groups, the white supremacy movement, and the World Church of the Creator. Again, this type of story has a downside. Its goal is to inform and educate the public, but it also provides a platform for the haters. In an attempt to appear "balanced" and "objective," the media often allow spokespersons for the hate groups to appear as well as anti-hate experts. For example, after the Smith shootings, Matt Hale took full advantage of interviews to publicize the World Church of the Creator, dropping the World Wide Web address for the organization into conversations whenever possible.

The fifth type of story focused on guns and gun control, raising questions about how both Furrow and Smith were able to access the weapons they used in their shooting sprees. For our purposes, these stories are less important because they focused more on the legalities of the gun purchases than on the hateful motives of Furrow and Smith. However, they likely helped convince columnist Jacoby that the media saw these incidents as another opportunity to push what he considered to be the liberal gun control agenda. Finally, the sixth type of story was commentary in the form of editorials, nationally syndicated columns, and letters to the editor of local newspapers. Most of the national commentary condemned the shootings as hateful, hurtful, and intolerant. Again, though, some focused on the issue of gun control and the need for stricter laws restricting gun ownership.

Such blanket coverage contributes to society's obsessive fascination with hate in a variety of ways. Individual readers and viewers react to the coverage in ways that fit their already existing attitudes toward the "other." For viewers and readers who consider themselves tolerant, the blanket coverage could raise awareness about the continuing hatred that some segments of society hold for the "other." Conversely, it gives the hatemongers, those people who adhere to a white supremacist ideology, a chance to advance their message that the best way to eliminate the threat from the "other" is to take drastic, violent steps. In the year following Benjamin Smith's shooting spree, the World Church of the Creator became the fastest-growing white supremacist organization. It is less clear what effect such blanket coverage has on sympathizers and spectators. The hate crimes that they learn about may either solidify their own negative attitudes or horrify them to the point where they examine and perhaps reconsider their own positions toward Jews, African Americans, Hispanics, and other minorities.

In the days after the Buford Furrow and Benjamin Smith incidents, commentators raised several concerns about the overwhelming media coverage. In a column for *USA Today*, Brian Levin asked, "[H]ow much TV coverage of hatemongers is enough? At what point does the insight we get from extensive exposure of bigotry devolve into a national infomercial to promote it?" (1999, 15A). The news media must take care not to overdo coverage of hate incidents to the point where it glorifies the philosophy or actions of the haters. When that happens, the media give the haters a propaganda platform that reinforces the fanaticism of current members and helps attract additional recruits to the hate movement. This wall-to-wall coverage may encourage violent perpetrators by giving them the by now proverbial "fifteen minutes of fame."

Floyd Cochran, a former white supremacist, appeared on CNN's *Talkback Live* soon after the Furrow shooting. Cochran now devotes his time to working against the white supremacy movement. He spoke of how his own actions as a spokesman for Aryan Nations had been covered extensively by the media: "[N]o matter where I went, I was front page news, top 6:00 story. People would print that I was educated, articulate, fun to be around, and that enhanced me among not only my racist comrades, but also in the community that I was in" (1999). Cochran argued that the media need to be more responsible in how they cover white supremacists. "[R]eport on their crimes, report on the evilness of their ideas, but you don't have to do fluff pieces, write how to contact them or put out their ideas word for word." (1999)

As Mary Glendon suggests, our society suffers both from the "exaggerated absoluteness of American rights rhetoric" and from "a near silence concerning responsibility" (1991, 45). In such circumstances, the media take their "right" to publicize information about hate groups more seriously than their "responsibility" to do so in a fashion that does not glorify the haters. As a result, the haters become cultural icons. On the same program, RTNDA President Barbara Cochran (no relation to Floyd Cochran) cited the example of Robert Matthews. He was one of the founders of The Order, a white supremacist group that robbed banks and took credit for killing radio talk show host Alan Berg in the early 1980s. Matthews died in a confrontation with the FBI. "One of the reasons that Bob Matthews is such a hero in the racist movement is, not only the crimes that he committed, but the fact that he died in a shoot-out with the FBI, and it's been repeated over and over in film footage and the story has been told. This almost takes on mythical proportions" (*CNN TalkBack Live* 1999).

In all of its coverage of the Smith and Furrow incidents, one area that the media failed to examine in depth is the growing movement toward "leaderless resistance." Instead, the media focused on the actions and influence of fringe groups such as the World Church of the Creator and The Aryan Nations. These groups, as a whole, are less likely to commit violent acts than an individual acting on his or her own. As a result, it is impossible to predict either when another hate incident will occur or whether the amount of coverage devoted to hate influences similar outbreaks of violence.

Most hate crime incidents do not receive the type of coverage the national media devoted to the Smith and Furrow shootings.

Usually, such incidents are covered only by local media, even when the story seems to be as sensational as one that is covered nationally. How many people have heard of the case of Billy Jack Gaither? In February 1999, Gaither, a thirty-nine-year-old gay man, was brutally beaten. His throat was cut, his body was bludgeoned with an ax handle, and finally he was thrown on top of a pile of tires and set on fire. Certainly his death was as horrific as that of Matthew Shepard. However, until his case was examined by *Frontline* as part of a documentary titled "Assault on Gay America," Gaither's death had not received the same type of publicity (*Frontline* 2000). Why was his story not covered? It is impossible to say exactly which stories will capture the national media's attention, and which will be covered only locally. However, it is important not to underestimate the prevalence of hate crimes based solely on the amount of coverage provided by national media.

A better gauge of how much hate is occurring is to examine hate reports distributed by The Associated Press, an international cooperative composed of newspapers and broadcast stations. The AP distributes to its members stories that have been written by its own reporters as well as articles condensed from member publications. It offers some stories nationally, whereas others are distributed only on a regional basis. In the fourteen-day period from 20 February to 5 March 2001, The AP nationally offered seven stories dealing with white supremacy, four dealing with hate crimes, and fourteen dealing with some other aspect of hate. The white supremacist stories included one that speculated about the white supremacist connection of a suspect in the murder of a Dartmouth College couple, and another concerning the possible passage of a hate crimes law in Texas. The hate crime stories included a meeting between Attorney General John Ashcroft and gay Republicans, and concerns about the increase in hate crimes in Germany. Finally, stories dealing with other aspects of hate included hate e-mails sent to Sterling Marling, the driver involved in the crash that killed NASCAR superstar Dale Earnhardt at the Daytona 500; Sen. Robert Byrd of West Virginia apologizing for using a racial epithet on a television talk show; several international stories from Germany, the Serb Republic, and Israel; and a story on attempts to quantify incidents of racial profiling.

During that same time period, local media across the country also featured a number of stories that contained elements of hate. A sampling of them demonstrates the encompassing nature of hate in society. In New York, the attorney general filed suit to test the state's law regulating access to abortion clinics. In Wisconsin, the *Milwaukee Journal Sentinel* reported on a mistrial in a hate crimes case. In Alabama, a radio talk show host who wants to return the Confederate battle flag to the state capitol building announced he may run for governor. The *Peoria Journal Star* reported that Matt Hale was denied the opportunity to take the Montana Bar examination. The *Miami Herald* reported that nooses are still used as a racial threat in Florida. White supremacists were arrested in Oregon. Finally, the *New York Daily News* reported that a cache of Nazi souvenirs was found in the home of a man who had used a picture of his mother-in-law for target practice in a Brooklyn park.

These stories reveal that hate is not confined to rural, less sophisticated areas of the country. Instead, it is a common element in society. One story, distributed by The AP, illustrates just how difficult it is to combat hate. Traverse City, Michigan, was forced to remove bumper stickers from police cars, fire trucks, and other city vehicles. The sticker featured the words "We are Traverse City," as well as human figures on a rainbow background. Critics complained that the rainbow was a symbol of gay rights. According to the story, "city offices were deluged by angry letters after launching the rainbow sticker, and the American Family Association, a conservative Christian group, said the city was endorsing homosexuality" (Flesher 2001). It is a sad commentary on the state of tolerance in our society that a symbolic message designed to combat hate ended up arousing it. As local resident M'Lynn Hartwell told AP, "[T]he furor illustrated how something was needed to pull the community together and counter 'a growing tyranny of hate and fanaticism'" (Flesher 2001).

Despite the amount of coverage devoted to issues involving hate, more can be done to bring issues involving race and ethnicity to the forefront. A study released in 2001, conducted for *American Journalism Review* and The Ford Foundation, examined the attitude that readers hold about their local newspapers. One of the questions it asked dealt with how much coverage local newspapers devoted to racial incidents and issues. The study found that among white respondents, 21 percent felt that there was "too much" coverage, 16 percent felt there was "too little," and 58 percent answered "about the right amount." In contrast, only 41 percent of nonwhite respondents answered "about the right amount." Some 35 percent felt there was "too little," and only 19 percent felt there was "too much" (Stepp 2001). When asked whether ethnic lifestyles and interests received enough coverage, 21 percent of white respondents felt there was "too little," and 61 percent felt there was "about the right amount." Conversely, 38 percent of nonwhite readers felt there was "too little," and only 43 percent felt the amount was about right (Stepp 2001).

Responses to the survey from nonwhite newspaper readers indicate that local publications need to improve coverage of issues of importance to racial and ethnic minorities. At their convention in Phoenix, Arizona, in 2000, veteran members of the National Association of Black Journalists complained that lack of diversity in the media is as much a problem now as it was in the mid-1970s when the organization was formed. In fact, for the first time since 1978, the number of African-American journalists in newspaper and broadcast newsrooms across the country has declined. Until there is true diversity in the newsrooms, there will not be diversity in the way race and ethnicity are covered. Instead, the media will continue to reinforce negative attitudes about minorities. As Denise Meredith wrote in *The Arizona Republic* after the NABJ convention, "The media inadvertently continue to foster such stereotypes as the Black youth face down and handcuffed on the nightly drug bust or the millionaire basketball player. These images hamper attempts to achieve a 'color-blind society'" (2000, B11). She argues that a more diverse newsroom would offer a "fresh perspective" on the news. "There are many issues that involve and appeal to Blacks—success despite the odds, roles of religion in our lives, small business, etc.—and these stories appeal to others who tire of reading about the latest convenience store heist" (2000, B11). It is impossible to directly link stereotypical images with the commission of hate crimes. However, they do reinforce the hatred felt at all levels of society.

Frequently, a hate crime that is covered either by national or local media—whether it concerns a church being torched, a building being painted with graffiti, or a person being threatened or intimidated—involves a common element. In most cases, the perpetrators of these crimes are members of the majority, the insiders, targeting members of the minority, the outsiders, because of their race, religion, ethnicity, or sexual preference. What happens, though, when the killers are considered "outsiders," even though they ostensibly appear to be members of the "inside" group? What happens when the killers are white, middle-class young men who have grown up with all the advantages money can buy, yet because of their fascination with the counterculture Goth movement, they are shunned by their peer group? What you get is a situation like the one that unfolded at Columbine High School in Littleton, Colorado, in April 1999.

In the Columbine case, both the local and the national media went into overdrive to cover all aspects of the crime, and it captured the nation's attention. However, even though the victims were targeted because of their talents—athletes—or their beliefs—Christians—and even though the incident took place on the anniversary of Adolph Hitler's birth, this shooting was not covered like what one might consider a "typical" hate crime. In contrast to the Smith and Furrow shootings, media outlets spent little time discussing the views of white supremacists and the hatred they held toward the "other." Instead, the media covered the Columbine story more like a typical school shooting, albeit the most deadly one to date. It was compared more often to the random shooting from the water tower at the University of Texas in the mid-1960s than to a hate crime committed by a dedicated skinhead. The coverage focused first on the hostage situation at the school, then on the grief of the affected families and the surviving students, and the fear parents experience when children are killed in a supposedly safe and secure environment. Finally, stories centered on the estrangement of young people who feel persecuted because they do not fit the traditional high school mold. Only later did the element of hate get added to the analysis. Even then, much of the coverage focused on the hatred young people feel when they are considered "different" from their peers. Among those interviewed were young men and women who dressed in "Goth" clothing. They discussed the sudden fear and isolation they encountered in their own schools because they were linked with Harris and Klebold.

Why did the Columbine shooting receive so much coverage? Mike Littwin, a staff writer for the Denver *Rocky Mountain News*, in a column that appeared about ten days after the shooting, tried to explain why it became "the school-kid shooting story that defines the trend." Among other things, he pointed out that

> [i]t has numbers. It has killers who drive BMWs. It has cultural divide—the left blames guns; the right blames video games/movies/Marilyn Mason. It's got high school culture, in which the outcasts seek revenge against the jocks. It's got hate on the Internet....Talking heads can talk comfortably about any and all of these issues. The psychologists got their shot. The newspapers get to uncover the details of who bought what gun where. And we get to see the pictures of the gun-buying prom date in her sunglasses (1999, 3B).

Another reason, though, might be that the nation was ripe for another "major" story about hate. It seems that every few years, some hateful event captures society's attention. Just a few years before Columbine, the Murrah Federal Building was blown up in Oklahoma City. Before that, it was the standoff and subsequent fire at the Branch Davidian complex in Texas. If hatred is part of our national psyche, we must crave information about it. The national media, in providing wall-to-wall coverage of these events, are giving us what we ask for.

Even several years after the Columbine shooting, all incidents of school violence are compared with it, and students who are out to make trouble threaten to commit Columbine-like attacks. Researchers say that in the years since the attack, the Columbine incident has been influential in at least four subsequent school attacks. They stop short of directly linking the crimes, but James Garbarino, a Cornell University professor, told The AP that the gunman's images have become powerful. "Dylan and Eric set out to become cultural icons for angry disaffected youth who sought revenge against the nastiness of exclusionary youth culture. Recent events suggest they succeeded in that" (Elliott 2001).

However, many of these students are not consumed with the type of hate found in dedicated white supremacist ideology. They are not even like hate sympathizers, lashing out against affirmative action programs and the people who benefit from them. Instead, these youngsters are suffering from anger and rage at being snubbed or teased or jilted. In some instances, they are also suffering from a mental illness. Sometimes these problems can be overcome by treatment or by school programs such as peer mediation. They do not have to explode into a crime in which hate can play a role. At other times, the situation deteriorates to the point where another school shooting occurs. One such shooting involved Charles "Andy" Williams, a student at Santee High School, in California, who was charged with killing several classmates, a crime he supposedly committed because he was bullied. Once again, the predictable response is horror and hand-wringing. Certainly no one should be subjected to so much bullying that he or she feels the only way out is through violence. Conversely, what type of society are we that someone would even consider shooting classmates who are guilty of bullying? What drives young men to commit such crimes? How, at such a young age, can they be so full of hate that they would shoot and kill their classmates? Does their hate give them the self-esteem that they otherwise lack? These young men fit the definition of the "dabblers" described by Levin and Paulsen in their typology of hate. They hate themselves as much as they hate their victims (1999).

One aspect of media coverage of hate crimes that needs to be mentioned briefly is the effect covering such stories has on journalists. It is sometimes difficult for journalists to maintain their distance, no matter how hard they try to be objective. The Project for Excellence in Journalism has developed a series of case studies that journalism instructors can use in class. One of the cases involves media coverage of Columbine. The focus of the case is how local television stations cover a sensitive breaking news event. One element that is examined in the case, though, is the reaction of the local journalists who covered the story. Ginger Delgado, a reporter for KUSA, told Alicia C. Shepard, who wrote the case study, that at the end of the first day, after working sixteen hours straight, "I literally walked in my apartment, slammed the door and started crying and couldn't stop. It was the images that were haunting me and the people I talked to. The somberness. You couldn't help but feel the pain and sorrow even though I didn't even know anyone involved" (2000, 13). KCNC's news director Angie Kucharski told Shepard, "Don't underestimate how horribly shaken people are to see bloody bodies and crying parents" (2000, 13). The news stations involved in the coverage brought psychologists into the newsroom to help staffers cope. KCNC anchor Bill Stuart later publicly admitted being treated for depression after covering the massacre (Shepard 2000). Whether the violence is prompted by hate or another motive, it creates pain not only in the victim, but also in the narrators and the audience caught up in the event.

When a breaking news story about hate occurs, especially one that has elements of drama as in the Furrow and Smith shootings, the news media react to what they perceive as the public's thirst for hate. The media provide breaking news and analysis for as long as the public remains interested in the story. However, the public's demand for blanket coverage does eventually abate. The national media pack up and go home, and the local community is left to deal with the aftermath. Sometimes, as in the case of Columbine, the national media return for graduation, or the reopening of the school, or the one-year anniversary of the shooting. In other cases, as in Buford Furrow's guilty plea in January 2001, the media give only a brief mention to the final resolution of the case. In this instance, the minor amount of publicity Furrow's plea and sentencing received nationally sharply contrasted with the plethora of stories surrounding the shootings. Perhaps it is because Furrow agreed to plead guilty rather than to stand trial. Such a denouement in the courtroom is much less interesting than either the frenzy that surrounded his initial hateful act or a trial in which his hateful beliefs could have been aired. In return for his guilty plea, he was spared the death penalty and instead received two consecutive life terms plus 110 years in prison without the possibility of parole.

Unfortunately, because so few media outlets covered Furrow's sentencing, the impact of his hate crimes on his victims received little notice. Both the mother of the letter carrier killed by Furrow and a former camp counselor from the community center testified at the sentencing hearing, yet their continuing pain was noted in only a few news reports. Once again, the media seemed to be responding to society's warped fascination with hate. We want to know all about the crime and the criminal, but we are much less interested in the "other" who suffers as a result. As former camp counselor Mindy Finklestein testified at the sentencing, "Buford Furrow tried to kill me. He failed, but in a way he succeeded" (Reuters 2001). Furrow succeeded because he was able to distract the nation's attention from the victim and focus it on his hate.

Stories about hate and hate crimes pose a particular challenge to the media. Their sensational nature attracts viewers and readers. Stories about hate sell, and why shouldn't they? Hate is an integral part of our national psyche. However, the media need to recognize that the way they report hate crimes affects everyone—the victims, the public, and the journalists. Without trampling on the First Amendment, it is impossible to regulate how hate crimes are covered. However, the media must take steps to expand their coverage beyond simply satisfying the public's fascination with hate. What are some of the steps the media can take? Among other things, the media should

- make the public aware of the intolerance that drives hate crimes by offering expert analysis of the political and philosophical underpinnings of these crimes;
- alert the public to the danger that hate groups pose for a civil society;
- try to avoid sensationalizing the coverage of hate incidents so it does not further harm the victims or glorify the perpetrators;
- try to avoid encouraging copycat crimes or inducing hate dabblers or sympathizers to join organized hate groups.

It is unlikely that any one medium can accomplish all of those goals simultaneously and meet its deadlines as well. That does not mean that in the aggregate, though, the media can use the excuse that they are only giving the public what it wants. In their reporting, the media need to go beyond simply reflecting the hatred in society. Is that possible? Can the media move beyond their sensational coverage of hate events? The media are part of the mainstream, and their coverage of hate reflects mainstream ideas and mainstream attitudes. In a column in *The Buffalo News*, Rod Watson urged the NAACP and other advocacy groups to challenge the media to diversify their staff and their perspective.

> Institutions tend to be inertial. They operate according to Newton's law, which means they stay at rest or keep moving at the same speed and in the same direction—in other words they keep doing the same old thing unless acted upon by some outside force. When it comes to the media, that outside force has to be the community (2000, 2B).

Sometimes the media do rise to the occasion and provide a serious examination of the underlying issues surrounding hate. More often, though, their coverage appears to be superficial and fleeting. The media won't be shaken from their inertia until the community demands more from it than sensationalism.

While important, media coverage is just one way that hate is spread throughout society and becomes part of our national conversation. Popular culture, in the forms of music, television, and film, has become a prime purveyor of hate. Our next chapter will examine how music has become the way in which young people spread and absorb the message of hate.

— Chapter 5 —
Hate and Popular Music

Who Knew?

> *I don't do black music, I don't do white music*
> *I make fight music, for high school kids*
> *I put lives at risk when I drive like this*
> *I'm sorry, there must be a mix-up ...*
> *...Fuck that, take drugs, rape sluts*
> *Make fun of gay clubs, men who wear makeup*
> *Get aware, wake up, get a sense of humor*
> *Quit trying to censor music, this is for your kid's amusement*
> (Eminem, *The Marshall Mathers* LP, 2000)

By now, you certainly feel the power of Eminem's nasty, scalding lyrics, and you probably hold a correspondingly strong feeling about whether his music has any redeeming social value. Who is this "foul-mouthed prince of hate and fury," and what does his story reveal to us about the culture of hate in contemporary America?

Eminem is Marshall Bruce Mathers III, a.k.a. Slim Shady, "monster white rap star." "God sent me to piss the world off," says Eminem, and he's achieved that fame and notoriety many times over (Larocca 2000). His CD, *The Marshall Mathers LP*, has sold at least ten million copies. As sixth grade teacher Clare Bell tells it, the eleven-, twelve-, and thirteen-year-old students in her magnet school class in Columbus, Ohio, rank Eminem as one of their favorites (Chavez 2000). He has been described as the "spokesman for the teenage male unconscious, and the inexpressible." Even the U.S. Senate Commerce Committee investigated the Eminem phenomenon, after a Federal Trade Commission report condemned the marketing of violent entertainment to children.

In January 2001, the Eminem controversy became more acute when he was nominated for several Grammy awards by the National Academy of Recording Arts & Sciences (NARAS). When the news of Eminem's nominations were announced, NARAS's Los Angeles office was inundated with protests from gay rights groups and angry parents. NARAS president Michael Greene responded to the protests, saying, "There's no question about the repugnancy of many of his songs...they're nauseating in terms of how we as a culture like to view human progress. But it [*The Marshall Mathers LP*] is a remarkable recording and the dialogue that it's already started is a good one" (Segal 2001). Greene argued that Eminem is a blessing in "heavy disguise," because he forces society into a painful examination of its own hatred and bigotry. Perhaps Greene is right—maybe a dialogue has now begun with respect to the virulent emotion of hatred. The dialogue certainly intensified after Elton John appeared with Eminem on the Grammy Awards Show. The duo performed a song together despite their ideological differences. However, was the performance just a publicity stunt, or a genuinely concerted effort to bridge one of the gaps of hatred? Actually, Eminem denies that he supports hate at all. Some observers claim he is just exploiting hatred because he knows intuitively it is embraced by his young audience. As Chris Norris writes in *Spin* magazine, "[M]any fans blow off extra-musical moralizing, assuming that hip-hop's streety, volatile lyricism will always defy polite society and that's sort of the point. With Eminem, that attitude has truly gone mainstream" (Norris 2001, 64).

Why begin this chapter with a portrait of an icon of hatred? The answer is that Eminem's incredible popularity tells us something very revealing about our national temperament and character. It also demonstrates how the cultural messages of hate are easily transmitted to the citizens of the next generation. We argued earlier that hate is an ideology, and "if by ideology we mean the mental frameworks—the languages, concepts, categories, imagery of thought, and the systems of representation—which different classes and social groups deploy in order to make sense of, define, figure out and render intelligible the way society works" (Mannheim 1952), then Eminem, by default, is one of our leading spokespersons. He is the "master comedian, true ironist, rapping about what's on everyone's mind" (Stuever 2001). In this chapter, we propose to look at how popular music helps us to decode or make sense of our society and its values. If we are forced to make sense of hatred as a societal characteristic, then what can music reveal to us about the character of that hatred?

To understand the appeal of Eminem and other performers like him, we went directly to the source—the young people themselves. Three articulate and very sophisticated fifteen-year-old females told us that Eminem and other hate promoters such as KoRn and Limp Bizkit tell it like it is! They don't follow the crowd; they don't deal in an illusory fantasy world of sweetness and love, like a Britney Spears or the Backstreet Boys. Even the hateful misogyny of Eminem's lyrics does not faze these bright young women. Their message is—embrace these musicians of hate, because they represent the truth about the way our society functions. Perhaps the young women have a point—if hatred is so endemic to the culture, then does it not make sense that the most popular music out there endorses the very hatred that we are writing about?

Hate not only shapes certain aspects of our culture, but it also serves as one subtext of our national dialogue. How is this hate, or race talk as Toni Morrison describes it, transmitted to our children? Morrison writes, "Race talk is the explicit insertion into everyday life of racial signs and symbols that have no meaning other than pressing African-Americans to the lowest level of the hierarchy." By substituting "ethnicity" or "sexual orientation" into her definition, we get ethnic talk or sexual orientation talk. The hatreds are pretty much interchangeable. Listen to the race talk of Doug Tracht, former DJ at Classic Rock 94.7 in Rockville, Maryland. In February 1999, after playing a song by black female artist Lauryn Hill, Tracht commented, "'No wonder people drag them behind trucks,' referring to the 1998 murder in Texas of James Byrd Jr., a black man who was chained to the back of a pickup truck driven by white supremacists, dragged at high speeds and decapitated. Tracht made his comment a day after the first of those men had been convicted in Byrd's slaying" (Ahrens 2000). Tracht was fired for the horrific statement, but his race talk, whether intended to be humorous or not, was heard and internalized by a huge audience of young listeners.

Race talk is reinforced by the creation of stereotypes. Walter Lippman first gave meaning to our understanding of the word *stereotype* when he asserted that people construct stereotypes or "simplifications" to help them interpret the behavior of others. Gordon Allport built on Lippman's thesis by arguing that the "human mind must think with the aid of categories" in order to "simplify" life (Beck 1999, 150–51). However, as Aaron Beck observes in *Prisoners of Hate*, "thinking in categories is the prototype of prejudice" and "simplifying through categorization readily leads to oversimplifying and consequently to distortion" (Beck 1999, 151).

Beck points out that some categorizing is rational, as when we believe that someone of "Mediterranean stock has darker hair than a person from Scandinavia" (Beck 1999, 151). It is only when these perceptions become twisted beliefs, such as Jews are "stingy" or blacks are "lazy," that the categories move beyond being reasonable or viable, according to Beck. Stereotypes are also linked to the "closed mind" phenomenon. According to this concept, a prejudiced or biased individual refuses to process contradictory information that may threaten or weaken rigid cognitive systems or beliefs. Thus, an individual who believes that Jews are "stingy" or blacks are "lazy" will never consider information that refutes those stereotypical assumptions (Beck 1999).

Our popular culture is filled with examples of ways we learn to think in distorted and unmalleable categories. Music, in particular, is a rich and fertile ground for articulating rigid categories that lead to hatred. Where exactly can we find this music of hatred? Predictably, we can locate hate music in the same place we find white supremacist political rhetoric—at the extremist fringe of society. However, it is also found at the mainstream center of our popular culture as the preoccupation and fascination with Eminem suggests. Before we examine mainstream hate music, though, an investigation into how hate is thrust upon us by the white supremacist movement is essential. Their efforts are so unabashedly incendiary and insidious that they deserve special attention in this analysis of hate music and its effects.

Resistance Records, the leading label for "hate-core music" is the latest acquisition of National Alliance leader William Pierce. Hate-core music targets blacks, Jews, Asians, and other immigrants with violent images and epithets. Its lyrics provide a stinging attack on anyone who poses a threat to whites or the white supremacist movement. The music label was originally founded by Canadian George Burdi, a member of the violently racist World Church of the Creator. However, a 1997 Canadian prosecution against Burdi for distributing hate materials dramatically weakened the impact of the music's label and forced him to sell it. First the business was sold to Willis A. Carto, the anti-Semitic leader of Liberty Lobby. Ownership changed hands once again when Pierce purchased the company in 1999. Pierce has turned Resistance Records from a once-floundering label into the "nation's premier purveyor of white power music" (Segal 2000b). Resistance Records, which boasts a catalogue of more than 250 different hate-core music titles, is now considered to be the "musical arm of the Aryan revolution." Music, says Pierce, "speaks to us at a deeper level than books or political rhetoric: music speaks directly to the soul...Resistance Records will be the music of our people's renewal and rebirth" (Segal 2000b).

Hate-core bands promoted by Resistance Records include Aggravated Assault, Brutal Attack, Plunder and Pillage, Blue-Eyed Devils, and Rahowa (the acronym for racial holy war). The following are examples of the racist lyrics found in hate-core music.

From SS Bootboys:

What can we do? Re-educate the White Race!
Cause its suspenders steel toes and white laces, see our fist fucking smash your face....
Suck it up you fucking coon, suck it up you black baboon!
Suck it up you fucking gook, suck it up you Asian puke! (Hatewatch 1999b)

From Das Reich:

White man do you understand
About all the non-Whites taking over our land
It's all a part of the Jewish plan
So wake up or this'll be the end (Hatewatch 1999a).

Resistance Records does not produce any records of its own. Rather, it provides a vast Internet-based mailing connection to fill demands for its music. The National Alliance promotes Resistance Records with a depressingly clever Web site that reads, "Surgeon General's Warning: the lyrics and images promoted by Resistance Records are not for the faint of heart or the excessively genteel" (Segal 2000b). Resistance Records claims that it fills fifty orders per day from its inventory of 80,000 CDs, thus garnering a profit of $1 million annually at the rate. If Pierce's observations are right, and if the data about Resistance Records sales are accurate, then the breadth and reach of hate-core's music may prove increasingly troubling. Jeff Berry, imperial wizard of the American Knights of the KKK, recently described how today's Klan is changing with the times. Instead of night-riding killings, which were instrumental to the Klan's historical acts of terror, the Klan is now performing a different type of nightriding which includes peddling goods over the Internet and promoting the hatred of "resistance" music.

Are the lyrics of these white supremacist groups having a measurable impact in terms of recruitment and action? It is hard to tell. Skinheads of Hammerskin Nation sponsored a major gathering of white supremacist bands on 20 April 2001, the anniversary of Adolph Hitler's birthday, in Springfield, Missouri. They believed the event would be a "powerful tool for winning new recruits to the cause" (Berkowitz 2001). Teenagers who have left the white supremacist movement talk about how that music precipitates action. "With the...lyrics echoing in their heads, a certain percentage of these still-forming youths are transformed into full-fledged haters" (Ward 1999). Randall Rojas, a twenty-three-year-old skinhead now in jail for murder, said, "You'd be doing speed and the lyrics would come into your mind, lyrics like 'Eating your insides, rah, rah, rah, smashing your brains, rah, rah, rah.' Real vulgar stuff. Hatred. I don't think any young person should listen to that stuff" (Ward, Lumsford, and Massa 1999). If the long litany of arrests for hate crimes by Hammerskin members is any indication, then this music is having some measurable impact. There are some who contend that one of the Columbine shooters, Eric Harris, also listened to such German hate bands as Rammstein and KMFDM.

The impact of Resistance Records, however, may be marginal when compared with mainstream record sales of such white artists as Eminem, Limp Bizkit, KoRn, Slipknot, and Goth rocker Marilyn Manson, all of whom proselytize some form of hate and violence. Additionally, the popularity of the Internet music directory Napster, through which as many as thirteen million listeners have downloaded music onto their computer, suggests that the reach of contemporary mainstream hate music may be phenomenally widespread. In March 2001, Napster was ordered to prevent its subscribers from swapping copyrighted songs (*Washington Post* 2001). This decision may curtail the spread of hate lyrics on-line.

However, determined swappers are likely to find other ways to share hate music.

Although mainstream artists are not as obviously racist and focused on hatred as those bands promoted by Resistance Records, their music, nevertheless, is replete with race and gender stereotypes and nihilistic hatred. Limp Bizkit sings, "I know why you wanna hate me, I know why you wanna hate me...cause hate is all the world has ever seen" (2000). KoRn offers such lyrics as, "Hate! I sing my words/ I'm fucked at dealing, with your life/dead bodies everywhere" (1996). And the lyrics from Marilyn Manson's *Irresponsible Hate Anthem*, shows how hatred can lead to random violence:

> *I'm so all American. I'll sell you suicide*
> *I am totalitarian. I've got abortions in my eyes*
> *I hate the hater, I'd rape the raper*
> *Hey victim, should I black your eyes again?*
> *Hey victim,*
> *You're the one who put the stick in my hand*
> *I am the ism, my hate's a prism*
> *Let's just kill everyone and let your god sort them out* (1996).

G. Brown of the *Denver Post* observes that, "more than two years after the shootings at Columbine High School, Marilyn Manson is still dealing with the backlash from those who believe his music shares some culpability for the tragedy" (2001).

Finally, Eminem tops the charts with misogynist hatred. In the wishful semiautobiographical song "Kim," he cuts his wife's throat and locks her in the trunk of a car. In "Kill You," he rapes and kills his mother. His mother filed a $10 million defamation suit against him for calling her a "pill-popping, welfare-collecting..." and "Kim" filed for divorce from Mathers. The "happy couple" did try for a reconciliation in order to raise their daughter—but that news was followed by another story that they were splitting up again. In May 2001, Eminem and Marilyn Manson announced they were planning to team up. We can only cringe at the new horrors their collaboration will produce.

Although Eminem insists much of his music is a joke, young boys listening to his lyrics may not understand his humor. One openly bisexual musician, the artist Moby, disputed Eminem's casual dismissal of his music's impact:

> I find it deeply disturbing that people are lending him as much support as they do. You cannot say there's no correlation between people's actions and what is seen and heard in popular culture. You can't put out homophobic and misogynist and racist stuff and say it's a joke. It's not (*Washington Blade* 2001, 18).

So is the hatred expressed by Eminem and other mainstream artists really less incendiary and dangerous than extremist lyrics from Resistance Records? The jury is still out on this question!

Contemporary rock music has always challenged conventional wisdom. It is said that "[G]eneration after generation of iconoclasts, from Joyce and Picasso to Elvis and Marilyn to punks and gangstas, have gradually pushed the limits a little further" (Ali 2000). What is interesting and frightening about this latest brand of mainstream music though, is that it is not about rebellion, as it was in the 1950s and 1960s, but rather about belligerence. David Segal writes that bands are now "transforming teen hostility and angst into entertainment." Limp Bizkit, in particular; has sarcastically named its recent music travels the "Anger Management Tour" (Segal 2000a). Slipknot's music is angry while "tapping into something very dark" (Wartofsky 2000). Thrashing, angry metal concerts—traditionally the province of boys—now feature more and more young girls surfing the mosh pits. This hatred and belligerence comes not only from the white artists previously mentioned, but also from a plethora of black rap, gangsta rap, and hip-hop entertainers, such as Public Enemy, NWA (Niggas with Attitude), who disbanded in 1992, Ice-T, Ice Cube, the Geto Boys, Snoop Doggy Dogg, 2 Live Crew, and Tupac Shakur.

Not all rap music can be criticized for hate and belligerence, as certain songs and lyrics do function as ways to engender "identity" and "self-assertion" in members of the black community. Rap originated in the mid-1970s. Using complex rhythmic lyrics, this music genre offers powerful cultural contradictions. In their essay "Rap, Black Rage, and Racial Difference," Steven Best and Douglas Kellner describe the dual impact of rap music—"at its best, rap is an indictment of racism, oppression and violence" while concurrently "celebrating black culture, pride, intelligence, strength, style and creativity." At its worst, it is "itself racist, sexist, and glorifies violence, being little but a money-making vehicle that is part of the problem rather than the solution." Gangsta rap, in particular, faces charges that its lyrics are the most violent and misogynist in the long history of popular music. Even Kevin Powell, the black editor of *Step into a World: A Global Anthology of the New Black Literature*, criticizes such music when he writes,

> [Twenty] years after the Reagan backlash on civil rights, the influx of crack and guns and the acceleration of a disturbing class divide in black America, hip-hop has come to symbolize a generation fragmented by integration, migration, abandonment, alienation and yes self-hatred (2000).

This concept of self-hatred is critical, for self-hatred, whether expressed by black or white rap artists, is often a catalyst for externalized hatred and violence. Snoop was charged in a conspiracy to murder another black man; Tupac Shakur was arrested for rape and sodomy; Eminem was arrested on assault charges for allegedly pistol-whipping a bouncer and on weapons charges for pulling a gun on a rival rap group. The East/West war between battling rappers culminated in hate and violence with the "gang-style executions" of Tupac Shakur and Notorious B.I.G. in 1996. Remember the "dabblers" from Levin and Paulsen's typology—these are the young adolescents who hate themselves as much as they despise their intended victims. Listening to music that affirms self-hatred is likely to be a contributing factor in any violent actions.

In addition to using a wide variety of styles to express hate (rap, hip-hop), the artists vary in the direction and content of their burgeoning hatreds. Popular music today proselytizes hate against dominant as well as subordinate groups. White hatred of minority culture is, of course, endemic to the white supremacist music of Resistance Records, but it is also found in the mainstream music of Eminem, Limp Bizkit, Slipknot, and KoRn. Minority hatred of white society can be found in the music lyrics of Dr. Dre, Public Enemy, and Snoop Doggy Dogg. Finally, lyrics also express white-on-white and black-on-black hatred, which, in the end, speaks to Kevin Powell's comments about the destructiveness of self-hatred.

Hate music is problematic for several reasons. White hate music, whether from Resistance Records or from mainstream artists, reinforces the burgeoning stereotypes and hatreds found particularly among young white males. Black hate music, on the other hand, can reinforce white fears. In turn, that can encourage sympathizers or spectators by fueling more hatred. Finally, hate music by both black and white artists often targets other oppressed groups, such as gays and lesbians, with a viciousness that borders on relentlessness.

White hate lyrics like KoRn's "nappy head, nappy chest, nappy chin, never seen with a happy grin," found in the song "Wicked" about Shaquille O'Neal, Mike Tyson, and Wilson Pickett, are clearly inflammatory phrases based on ugly stereotypes (1998). Henry Louis Gates Jr., an expert on African-American literature, argues, however, that ridiculous stereotypical descriptions found in popular music should just make the listener "bust out laughing" and dismiss the ridiculous hyperbole or image. Gates advanced this argument when testifying about the stereotypical lyrics of the black group 2 Live Crew, at their criminal trial on obscenity charges. However, he would probably apply that same defense—that their words are meant to be humorous—to most rap artists. Critical legal studies observers do not find Gates's humor defense very reassuring, though. They argue that even if KoRn meant the lyrics to have a humorous content (we do not know whether they did or not), the language of incendiary words "wounds" nonetheless. CLS advocates insist that humor should not be used as a defense against racism, misogyny, or hatred.

Charles Lawrence and Mari Matsuda make a related point when they argue that expressions of hatred toward historically dominant groups (whites) is distinctly different from racist hate speech directed at historically oppressed groups (blacks). Matsuda argues that hate speech against whites is neither racist nor hateful, because it is often a rebuttal to historic racism. It is also an attempt by the nondominant group member to develop a sense of self-identity. Might the hate lyrics of black performers also be an exercise in self-assertion and identity? Let's take a look.

When Ice Cube sings of white suburbanites, "it's time to take a trip to the suburb...let em see a nigga invasion...point blank for the Caucasian" (1991), is this as inflammatory as KoRn's previous lyrics? CLS supporters would not think so. When Public Enemy sings its trademark song "Fight the Power," which can be construed as a hate diatribe against white institutions, is this inflammatory or equivalent to KoRn's lyrics? Again, CLS writers would disagree. Nevertheless, it could be argued that these songs are dangerous because they threaten the comfortable safety net of white mainstream society. Additionally, they may contribute to faulty white stereotypes about minority behavior and culture. With respect to the excesses of black rap, Henry Louis Gates says, "[W]hen you are faced with a stereotype, you can disavow it or you can embrace it and exaggerate it to the nth degree. The rappers take the white Western culture's worst fear of black men and make a game out of it" (Matsuda, Lawrence, Delgado, and Crenshaw 1993). Gates does not acknowledge that white recipients of such extreme parodies do not all understand them that way—some see the parodies as truth, and this perception feeds their own fears and hatreds about the "other."

Finally, what about white and black hate music that assaults other discriminated groups? Lyrics that denigrate people because of their sexual orientation are widespread in mainstream music. In the song "Criminal," Eminem sings:

My words are like a dagger with a jagged edge
That'll stab you in the head
Whether you are a fag or lez
Or the homosex, hermafora trans-a-vest
Pants of dress—Hate fags? The answer's Yes

Marshall Mathers LP (2000)

Eminem insists that we should not take his lyrics about gays seriously. However, GLAAD, the Gay and Lesbian Alliance Against Defamation, insists that his lyrics are anything but benign. GLAAD has continued to rail against Eminem's homophobia. Its members and women's rights groups even demonstrated outside the Staples Center in Los Angeles during the Grammy Awards show with signs that read, "Hate is Not Hip!"

Listen also to the lyrics of KoRn from their *Follow the Leader* CD. "You're like a Fruity Pebble, your favorite flag is rebel. Yeeeeeeeeeehaaaaw! It's just too bad you're a fag and on a lower level" (1998). It is useful to apply Lawrence and Matsuda's interpretation when analyzing the impact of such lyrics on recipients. Just as hate speech can damage self-esteem and threaten one's sense of personal security, hate lyrics can replicate the same psychological harms. Are Lawrence and Matsuda correct—is hate against an oppressed group more problematic than hate against a dominant group?

Consider for a moment a story recounted by Lawrence in his essay, "If He Hollers Let Him Go" from the book, *Words That Wound: Critical Race Theory*. The story, an account of the experiences of a gay white male and his dealings with hate, reveals a great deal about the harms done by hate speech, and informs us about the possible effects of hate lyrics. When asked to describe the injury of racist speech, one of Lawrence's students, Michael, told how he had been called a "faggot" by a man in a subway. Lawrence writes, "Michael found himself in a state of semi-shock, nauseous, dizzy, unable to muster the witty, sarcastic, articulate rejoinder he was accustomed to making." Michael spoke about the "societal defamation" that one incendiary word "faggot" carried with it. What is even more interesting was Michael's response to Lawrence's related query about whether he had ever been verbally assaulted with a reference to his status as a white male. When asked if he had ever been called a "honky," "chauvinist pig," or "mick" (a pejorative name for a working-class Irish man), Michael responded that he had. However, those words did not carry with them the same "disorienting powerlessness" that he had experienced in the attack on his identity as a gay man (1993).

Michael's experience is telling, as we can easily apply it to a determination of which music lyrics offend and which, by inference, do not. For advocates of the CLS school, hateful lyrics against gays and lesbians are clearly more incendiary than lyrics against heterosexuals or any member of a "dominant group." In the same way that Michael did not care that he was called a honky, most whites probably do not experience any psychic wounds from listening to rap lyrics that attack white institutions—they are impervious to the harm. Matsuda explains that whites have "access to a safe harbor of exclusive dominant group interactions. Retreat and affirmation of personhood are more easily attained for members of groups not historically subjugated" (1993, 39). Hate lyrics directed against whites are not experienced personally. Rather, they are viewed as a broader threat to the economic and political status quo—hence the possible fear of a "nigga" intrusion into the suburbs, as Ice Cube warns.

Hate speech, like inflammatory hate lyrics, holds an element of the unexpected. When Michael entered the subway, he did not anticipate a verbal assault, and thus could not protect himself. Similarly, if you are listening to the radio and happen to hear the unedited version of Eminem's or KoRn's songs, you may have little time to tune out the offending hate diatribe before you have been exposed to insult and harm.

Can we also argue in this analysis that black artists such as Public Enemy or Ice-T, who deal in hateful lyrics against whites, are less reprehensible? Are they accountable in a different way for the impact of their music than Eminem or KoRn? In general, black rap music does not focus on hatred of white individuals, but rather on hatred against oppressive white institutions. Best and Kellner argue that these artists are "knowledge warriors" who use music to warn the existing power structure that the underclass may direct their anger and hatred "into political struggle and insurrection" (1999, n.p.). Thus when Public Enemy sings "Fight the Power," it is the type of hatred that is designed to mobilize blacks for positive change.

What about black-on-black hate and self-hatred? In a *Washington Post* essay titled "Raprehensible," writer Avis Thomas-Lester pondered the issue of the violent stereotypical lyrics of black hardcore rappers like DMX and their influence on black youths. She laments recommending benign "white music" to her son, for she fears it undermines pride in black culture:

> I wonder when I say yes to a CD by the white teen pop group 'N Sync but no to a recording from hard-core rapper DMX-I'm sending him a subliminal message that black music (our music) is bad, but music by white artists is okay....Am I telling him: If it's white, it's all right; if it's black, put it back? (2000, B4)

Best and Kellner, however, would argue against criticizing negative stereotypes promulgated by the black rappers themselves. For example, they insist that the word "nigger" or "nigga" is often embraced by blacks as either a "positive term of endearment and solidarity or as a political identity for a member of an oppressed class" (1999, n.p.). (Gates would probably concur.) In fact, Randall Kennedy, a Harvard law professor, has now written a book titled *Nigger: The Strange Career of a Troublesome Word*, in which he tries to "defang" the word by addressing its complicated history (Weeks 2001, C1). Will Kennedy's attempt to demystify the word work, or will the word retain its malevolent past?

A development in South Africa that addressed the impact of black-on-black hate in music is an interesting addendum to this analysis. The South African Human Rights Commission (HRC) asked the national director of public prosecutions to indict comedian Shane McCallaghan for racist songs he wrote and performed. McCallaghan's songs called Nelson Mandela and President Thabo Mbeki "kaffirs," which some consider to be the racial equivalent of "niggers" (Rossouw 2001). The HRC argued that the songs violated the right to dignity of millions of South Africans, and that they constituted hate speech as prohibited under the Promotion of Equality and Prevention of Unfair Discrimination Act. Just as other rap advocates do, supporters of McCallaghan insisted that the word was OK as long as only blacks used it. One observer also noted that "white rapper Eminem has apparently been given special dispensation from black rap artists to use the word as well" (Rossouw 2001). In fact, some in South Africa believe strongly in what writer Phumla Mthala describes as the practice of "reappropriation." This is the process by which "a group of people who have been oppressed use the same terms or phrases as their oppressors use to refer to themselves." This idea has its own critics.

What officials are more concerned about, though, are young black South Africans who are buying thousands of CDs by "angry black brothers in the United States." They cite, for example, Nastradamus, who sings,

> *I want to talk to the mayor or the governor/To the muthafuckin president/I want to talk to the FBI and CIA/And the muthafuckin congressmen./Mr. America, young black niggas want you/ I want to talk to the man, understand?/Understand this muthafucking-pack in my hand? Niggas play with Playstations/They building space stations on Mars.*

Or DMX, mentioned previously, who is also quite popular in South Africa. He sings, "Black hate white/white hate black/it's right back to the same fight." Is the issue of hate speech in South Africa comparable to the issue of hate here in the United States? That debate is just in its infancy.

What about white or black hatred toward other minority groups? In the song "Black Korea," Ice Cube includes incendiary lyrics toward Korean Americans:

> *Everytime I wanna go get a fuckin brew*
> *I gotta go down to the store with the two*
> *oriental one-penny countin motherfuckers*
> ....
> *yo yo, check it out*
> *so don't follow me, up and down your market*
> *Or your little chop suey ass'll be a target* (1991).

With these hateful lyrics, Ice Cube certainly subscribes to the "closed mind" stereotypes of Asian Americans. Finally, hate lyrics toward women, performed by both black and white artists, are perhaps the most problematic aspects of this genre of music. Black rappers such as 2 Live Crew and Snoop Doggy Dogg have consistently used derogatory lyrics toward women, calling them "ho's" and "bitches" and portraying them as good only for sexual exploitation. Snoop's "lyrics put women through a verbal shredder similar to the infamous *Hustler* cover featuring a naked woman being ground into meat" (Best and Kellner 1999, n.p.). Black women rappers such as Queen Latifah have tried to fight back with their own defiant lyrics, but the appeal of misogyny and hatred persists. In a Web article announcing the release of the white group Insane Clown Posse's newest CD, the writer begins, "Seventeen-year-old boys of the world unite. The spokesmen for violent intentions and hatred for females are back on the scene with their fifth album." In the song "Assassins," Insane Clown Posse sings, "Girl I used to love you but now you've gotta die." As the reviewer sums it up, the CD, *The Amazing Jeckel Brothers*, is nothing more than "music to strangle your ex-girlfriend to" (Maher 1999, n.p.).

Can a marketplace model of free speech (we consider lyrics as speech) really be counted on to control the deleterious effects of hate music? Many would say no. As Abraham Goldstein writes,

> [T]olerance of hate speech risks becoming a species of endorsement of such speech. It encourages the view that 'it can't be all that bad if it is

not prohibited.' Those who see efforts to regulate group libel as taking us down a slippery slope to censorship pay too little attention to a second slippery slope—one which can produce a swift slide into a "marketplace of ideas" in which bad ideas flourish and good ones die (Jacobs and Potter 1998, 111).

A growing faction of anti-hate artists such as the group Rage Against the Machine and the band Hate-Mail are among those trying to combat hate in the marketplace. In the January 2001 edition of *Vibe* magazine, black feminist poet June Jordan created a rap rebuttal to Eminem called "Owed to Eminem." In it she writes,

> *I'm the Slim Lady the real slim Lady.*
> *...But I am that I am*
> *and don't give a damn*
> *and you mess with my jam*
> *and I'll kill you*
> *I will!*
> ...
> *I'm the bitch in the bedroom the faggot*
> *You chump I'm the nigga for real so get ready to deal*
> *I'm tired of wiggas that whine as they squeal*
> *About bitches and faggots and little girls, too!*
> *I'm a Arab, I'm a Muslim, I'm a Orthodox Jew!*

There is even a Christian Rap countermovement, which appropriates the style and sound of gangsta rappers like DMX and Dr. Dre. The five-member band, Cross Movement, provides the other side of the moral marketplace with music lyrics about perdition, the soul, and the Lord. However, how many listeners will actually listen to Christian Rap, which some find "overbearing and sanctimonious"? Furthermore, how many will actually hear Jordan's comic reply to Eminem's hatred and misogyny so they can create their own impressions from her personal lyric war? Probably not a lot. Other groups like Rage Against the Machine are also losing in both the moral and economic marketplace, as their sales are nowhere close to the profits accrued by Eminem and other hate artists.

Hate, as much as we abhor it, sells in ways we cannot even imagine. In an ironic twist, in early 2001, MTV, which had been guilty of "selling" hate music videos to avid young viewers for twenty years, decided to broadcast a special program called "Fight for Your Rights: Take a Stand against Discrimination." The programming began with the film *Anatomy of a Hate Crime,* an account of the Matthew Shepard murder case. Shepard, a University of Wyoming gay male student, was abducted, tortured, and left to die in the Laramie wilderness by two male "hatemongers." The film was followed by an unprecedented eighteen hours of commercial-free scrolling of names of other victims of hate crimes. Throughout the evening, night and morning, MTV provided brief descriptions of hate incidents. The intent was to honor and remember Matthew Shepard and others like him who suffered in one form or another from hateful actions. The stories were painful reminders of the all too common incidences of virulent hatred.

The MTV program was an honorable gesture. We are left to wonder, however, whether this act of social and political consciousness can really undo or compensate for two decades in which MTV brought hate into the lives of young people through music videos. Actually, evidence of the program's failure to put a dent in hate came shortly after the program's debut. Nicholas Butterworth, president and CEO of MTVi Group, which manages MTV.com, reported that hate supporters inundated the "Fight for Your Rights" on-line message board with even more hate diatribes (Palmer 2001). One message read, "[Y]ou go ahead and fight for the minorities...because minorities are no match for the intelligence of whites" (Palmer 2001). Two weeks after the program aired, more than 6,000 messages promoting prejudice and hate had been posted on the MTV board. Many people asked, "What went wrong?" and "Why did the haters come out of the woodwork?" The answer is simple—hate is too deeply ingrained in American life. Additionally, the economic profits of hate always seem to outlast moral accountability in the marketplace of today's interests.

What can or should be done about the proliferation of hate music? Is this music a critique of hate in society? The political rap of Public Enemy seems to be, as it offers the disenfranchised a consciousness about institutional racism and inequality. This form of hate music may be valuable to some. Is hate music just an endorsement of hate, which antithetically makes it dangerous? Can we censor some hate music and not others? Censorship is not the answer, although Canada has been very successful censoring hate speech, in general. The Supreme Court of Canada ruled in *r. v. keegstra* (1995) and in *r. v. andrews* (1990) that hate propaganda would not be tolerated. In *keegstra,* a high school teacher insisted that his students refer to Jews as sadistic, materialistic, and barbaric, and rewarded them with better grades if they followed his hate-filled polemic. In *andrews,* the defendants, members of the Nationalist Party of Canada, published material insisting that "non-whites" were inferior and unclean. They also distributed mimeographed sticker cards with messages such as "Nigger go home" and "Hitler was right." In both cases, the Canadian Supreme Court upheld their convictions against free speech claims. If Canadian culture and law can accept restrictions on speech why can't the United States?

The concept or principle of hate must become less desirable and attractive to young people. We can only accomplish this task by altering or socializing our children within a different framework of values. This task, nevertheless, is quite difficult since "what's going on in the media is just a symptom of the real sickness" (Samuels, Croal, Gates, and Davis 2000, 65).

While hate music appeals to a youthful audience, the medium that attracts everyone is television. In the next chapter, we will explore how television influences our view of the "other," particularly the African-American "other."

— Chapter 6 —
Hate and Television

Since the end of World War II, television has been a focal point in American households. Nearly 100 percent of American families own at least one television set. Cable and satellite services have reduced the influence that major television networks wielded from the 1940s through the 1980s. However, even with the advent of the Internet, most Americans say they get the majority of their news from television. As a medium, television crosses all age, racial, ethnic, and gender barriers. However, the addition of more channels has not necessarily led to a hate-free, bias-free television world. Criminals continue to be a prime focus of the news, and stereotypes remain a staple in entertainment programs. The images of minorities that television has given us through the years have been as varied as the Kingfish and Steve Harvey, and the news stories about minorities have ranged from the Watts riots to the Rodney King beating to the O. J. Simpson trial. This chapter will examine what influence television programs may exert on public attitudes about racial and ethnic minorities, whether news and entertainment programs reinforce stereotypes, and finally, whether the images shown on television nurture feelings of hatred for the "other."

As we mentioned in the chapter on news coverage of hate crimes, the news media seek to inform and to educate the public. In doing so, they help to define for most of us what significant events are taking place. At the same time, as Stuart Hall and coauthors Chas Critcher, Tony Jefferson, John Clarke, and Brian Roberts point out in *The Social Production of News*, the media frame the events by offering "powerful interpretations of how to understand these events. Implicit in those interpretations are orientations towards the events and people or groups involved in them" (2000, 648). In other words, the way the news media frame the event helps the public react both to the event and to the people involved.

Hall et al. argue that this framing takes place from the point of view of the elite and powerful in society. It is accomplished by means of what ABC news anchor Carole Simpson has called "the golden rolodex." Journalists, for the most part, are expected to present an unbiased and objective view of the news and to keep their own opinions out of their reports. Instead, they rely on a cadre of "experts" to explain, analyze, and contextualize news events. These sources are often spokespersons for government agencies or major corporations, and their jobs depend on their ability to "spin" the story to put their own organization's position in the best possible light. TV journalists rely on these spokespeople because often they are able to synthesize the core of a story into a few pithy words—the prized sound bite. Hall notes that these sources end up setting the framework for the stories because there is a greater likelihood that their explanations—their spin—will be accepted. "[S]uch spokesmen are understood to have access to more accurate or more specialized information on particular topics than the majority of the population" (2000, 649), so they end up disproportionately influencing the views of the rest of us. However, as a panelist at a forum on Women, Men, and Media held at Columbia University, Simpson pointed out that these spokespeople were most often white males; thus, the viewpoints of women and minorities were "symbolically annihilated" (1991).

The cultivation theory advanced by George Gerbner posits that television holds a central place in our lives, and as such, it has become a primary source of socialization. Our own personal experiences can be displaced by what we see on television. "Audiences gradually adopt the 'symbolic reality' created by television and incorporate its images into their living environment. This symbolic reality may potentially contain both stereotypical and imprecise images" (Tamborini et al. 2000, 639).

Stories can be further distorted by the individual interpretations that members of the public bring to them. In *News Content and Audience Belief*, Greg Philo points out that how a person understands a message on television "depends in part on the beliefs which they bring to it and crucially on how those beliefs are utilized" (2000, 689). Those beliefs, often called filters, are unique to each person. In *On the Social Effects of Television*, James D. Halloran writes, "It is recognized that the viewer approaches every viewing situation with a complicated piece of filtering equipment. This filter is made up not only of his past and present, but includes his views and hopes for the future" (2000, 434). Among the filters through which people view stories are their class, race, religion, gender, ethnicity, and cultural background. As a result, the stereotypes and hatreds that individuals experience toward particular groups of people become the lenses through which they view news and entertainment programs on television, and these lenses allow them to believe the negative images.

As Richard Dyer argues in *The Role of Stereotypes*, though, it is those in power, the moral leaders of society, whether in government, industry, or media, who have the opportunity to define the stereotypes in the first place. "Who does or does not belong to a given society as a whole is then a function of the relative power of groups in that society to define themselves as central and the rest as 'other,' peripheral or outcast" (1993, 248). Walter Lippman identified stereotypes as a shorthand method of recognizing, defining, and categorizing. Misperceptions, and hatred, can arise when those stereotypes are not accurate. Sometimes, though, it is in the best interest of the elite to perpetuate these negative stereotypes. The institutional hatred engendered by the stereotypes keeps people in their place socially and economically. As James Madison argued in Federalist No. 10, the elite and the government exploit the factions in society so they can remain in control (1787). As a result, individuals who might otherwise have something in common remain divided. Instead of working to improve conditions for everyone, they fight over whether such programs as affirmative action unfairly benefit only a few. These competing factions then allow the elite to maintain their hold on the power structures of society. As Dyer writes, "[S]tereotypes express particular definitions of reality...which in turn relate to the disposition of power within society. Who proposes the stereotype, who has the power to enforce it, is the crux of the matter (1993, 248).

These stereotypes are absorbed by the culture, and then are reflected in the way television news is presented to the public. Hall, for example, argues in *Racist Ideologies and Media* that an unconscious racism is at work in the way some news stories are framed. "Every word and image of such programmes are impregnated with unconscious racism because they are all predicated on the unstated and unrecognized assumption that *blacks* are the *source of the problem*" (2000, 274). Hall is writing specifically about racism against blacks, yet his argument can easily be extended to incorporate others, such as immigrants, gays and lesbians, and ethnic minorities. This framing reinforces the type of institutional hatred we have been describing.

In "Constructing Reality from Television," Robert Wicks points out that group membership affects how people react to the information they receive from television. Earlier, we identified affirmative action as one issue that divides Americans. Wicks examined television viewers' reactions to stories about affirmative action, and he discovered that the way the story is framed affects how the viewer responds. He wrote, "Television programs have the potential to interact with predispositions, attitudes, and beliefs of certain social groups....People within certain groups can selectively process information consistent with previously held beliefs and attitudes" (1998, 26). Wicks found that minorities were more likely to "attend to, perceive, and retain" information about affirmative action when it was presented as a way to solve a social problem. On the other hand, when it was presented as "preferential treatment for certain classes of citizens" (1998, 25), some white Americans were predisposed to receive the message as an indication of reverse discrimination. The way different groups process the information can reinforce hate and fuel resentment on both sides. This difference in vision can have a profound influence on the spectators and sympathizers described in Levin and Paulsen's typology of hate, as they are already predisposed against the "other" (1999).

Even though newspapers tend to offer more in-depth coverage and analysis of events, television has become the nation's primary source for news. In the past half-century, the country has undergone significant social change and upheaval, and, as television historian J. Fred MacDonald points out, "television was better at personalizing and capturing the drama in the events of the day" (1992, 150). From its earliest days, though, television has stereotyped one of the most visible groups of the "other," African-Americans, in both news and entertainment programming. On the news, African-Americans have been underrepresented as news anchors and commentators, and overrepresented as perpetrators of crimes.

Scholars who have examined the portrayal of minorities in entertainment programs have found that since the earliest days of broadcasting, stereotypes have run the gamut from minstrel-like characters to mammies (Dates and Barlow 1990). As a result, what we believe about African-American life does not mesh with reality, but the false image is very difficult to overcome. As Oscar Gandy writes, "If biased representations within the news are relatively consistent across relatively long periods of time, far more people will have been exposed to common representations that are assumed to be fact rather than fiction" (1998, 157). These stereotypes have allowed people who are already predisposed against the "other" to shift the blame for their hate. They can point to the portrayal of minorities on television as an excuse for perpetuating hateful attitudes.

Hall et al. point out that in developing news stories, journalists rely on certain assumptions about society and how it works. One assumption is that because we are part of the same society and culture, we all hold the same perspective on an event. He calls this a "consensual viewpoint" (2000, 646). However, Hall points out that a consensual viewpoint "denies structural discrepancies" between different groups within society. "The consensual viewpoint ...carries the assumption that we also all have roughly the same interest in society and that we all roughly have an equal share of power in the society....Consensual views of society represent society as if there are no major cultural or economic breaks, no major conflicts of interest between classes and groups" (2000, 647). However, we know that discrepancies do exist. We only need to look at the reactions different segments of society had toward the acquittals of O. J. Simpson and of the police officers accused of beating Rodney King, one of the classic institutional hate crimes, to see that this is true.

News programs that emphasize crimes committed by minorities also reinforce the bias held by hate spectators and hate sympathizers. Michael Parenti writes, "Polling statistics in *USA Today* show that only 15 percent of US drug users are African-American, but data from the Black Entertainment Network indicate that 50 percent of network news stories on drugs focus on African-Americans" (1993, 11). The emphasis placed on crime news by television broadcasters, and the popularity of police and court entertainment programs, reinforce viewers' attitudes that crimes committed by minorities are among the biggest problems facing the country. Studies have also shown that people who watch a lot of television believe the world is more crime-ridden and dangerous, and that they personally are more likely to be the victim of a serious crime, than the reality borne out by FBI statistics. During Judiciary Committee hearings for U.S. Attorney General John Ashcroft, several people testifying on his behalf expressed the belief that the nation needed an attorney general who could be "tough on crime." They ignored or deliberately overlooked FBI evidence that serious crime has decreased significantly in the past decade. The "tough on crime" mantra is often an institutional buzzword for cracking down on crimes committed in inner cities. That again reinforces the stereotype that most crimes are committed by minorities.

Reporters and editors who compile the nightly news programs would deny that they set out to reinforce notions that minorities are more likely to commit crimes. They would argue that they are just following traditional news values in selecting stories that are timely, involve conflict, and impact the audience in some way. Nonetheless, television is a visual medium, and it thrives on pictures. Most media have moved away from describing the race or ethnicity of the subject of a story unless it is germane. Television reporters may not specifically say that a suspect is black or Hispanic, but by showing the person's picture, the point is made anyway:

> Television news relies on visual imagery for storytelling, even if the images may contribute to the kinds of stereotypical beliefs that advance racism and discrimination. The police sketches, like the mug shots that routinely appear on local television newscasts' crime stories, carry connotative messages of wrongdoing, of danger, of conviction-before-trial (Campbell 1995, 71).

When television news focuses on the number of black men in prison, it reinforces the belief that crimes are primarily committed by black men. When stories about welfare or the birth rate for unwed mothers are accompanied by pictures of minority women, it reinforces the attitude that the majority of unwed mothers and welfare recipients are minorities. Statistics show that neither of those statements is true. However, the coverage reinforces the attitudes already internalized by hate sympathizers and spectators. Robert

Entman points to the cumulative effect of the portrayals of African-Americans as criminal suspects in news programs: "[O]ver time, the specific realities depicted in single stories may accumulate to form a summary message that distorts social reality. Each in a series of news stories may be accurate, yet the combination may yield false cognitions within audiences" (1994, 509).

FBI statistics show that most crime is either black-on-black or white-on-white. Even so, video shown nightly on television leaves a very different impression. The negative reinforcement that black-on-white crime has on attitudes held by some whites becomes especially problematic when the victims are seen as young, defenseless, and white. Two murders in the Washington, D.C., area illustrate that point. In April 2000, Kevin Shifflett, an eight-year-old white boy, playing in his grandmother's front yard, was—for no apparent reason—stabbed and killed by a black man. After an arrest, it was learned that the suspect suffered from a mental illness. Nonetheless, local Washington media played up stories of the discovery in his room of writings in which he indicated that he hated whites and planned to kill them. A few months after this crime, a fourteen-year-old white girl sneaked out of her home to attend a party. She was found dead a few days later. The suspect arrested in that murder was also black. Pictures of him in the backseat of a police car were juxtaposed on the evening news with a school photo of the girl. The two incidents reinforce Entman's contention that over time, the messages conveyed by individual stories may distort reality.

Concerns about the way minorities are portrayed in the news are not new. The first African-American newspaper, *Freedom's Journal*, was started in 1827 in response to the way black Americans were portrayed in New York City newspapers. More than 150 years later, those concerns were echoed in the Kerner Commission Report, issued in 1968 in response to the urban riots of the 1960s. The report was commissioned by President Lyndon Johnson. One chapter focused on media coverage, and it identified the depiction of minorities as a primary area of concern. The report noted, "By failing to portray the Negro as a matter of routine and in the context of the total society, the news media have, we believe, contributed to the black-white schism in this country" (National Advisory Commission on Civil Disorders 1968, 2). As Campbell points out, what is presented in the newspaper and on television becomes reality, especially for those whites who have little or no outside contact with people of color (1998). That "reality" allows them to justify their hatred.

While some improvements in coverage have been noted in the thirty years since the Kerner Commission report was issued, much of the coverage remains negative. Studies by such scholars as Carolyn Martindale (1990a, 1990b), Edward Pease (1989), Marilyn Gist (1990), and Robert Entman (1992, 1994) demonstrate that the portrayal of African-Americans in both television news and newspapers still tends to be stereotypical. They are underrepresented when their frequency in TV newscasts is compared with their percentage in the viewing area (Campbell, Duhe, and Wiggins 1996), and they are disproportionately shown to be involved in crime, drugs, and gangs (Gist 1990).

Entman points out that television reinforces what social scientists have come to call "modern racism." Three elements come into play here. First, local television news, which relies heavily on crime stories to fill up its news hole, "tends to depict blacks as more dangerous than whites who commit similar crimes" (1994, 510). Thus, the image that viewers get shows criminals as young black men, high on drugs, who randomly attack whites. Second, political coverage by local stations shows minorities demanding "special" government favoritism. Finally, ironically, the attempt to diversify the news staff and hire minority reporters and anchors belies the need for "special" programs such as affirmative action because the on-air presence of minorities suggests that discrimination no longer impedes the progress of African-Americans (Entman 1994).

The diversity of the news staff in mainstream media was a second area of concern noted by the Kerner Report. In 1968, at the time the report was issued, fewer than 5 percent of the nation's journalists and fewer than 1 percent of the editors and supervisors were black, and most of them worked for black-owned organizations. Since then, there has been an increase in the number of reporters and editors of color, but it has not kept up with the increase in minority population. In fact, a survey by the American Society of Newspaper Editors revealed that the percentage of African-Americans working in newspaper newsrooms actually declined from 5.36 percent in 1999 to 5.31 percent in 2000 (Gonzalez 2000b).

William W. Sutton Jr., the president of the National Association of Black Journalists, said African-American journalists are leaving the industry for three reasons: "frustration at a lack of opportunity, poor pay, and a lack of respect for their ideas." As Sutton said, "Diversity is not just the color of your skin. It's a diversity of ideas and having a respect for diversity of ideas and seeing some of our ideas on air, in print or online" (Gonzalez 2000a, D1). However, without a diversity of journalists to offer these ideas, the stereotypes institutionalized by television and other media will continue to reinforce hatred.

News programs are only one way that stereotypes can reinforce the negative attitudes held about the "other" in our society. Concerns about stereotypes in entertainment programs and the effects they may have on society's perceptions of minorities have been present since the beginning days of network television. As early as 1951, the NAACP launched an ultimately successful drive to have such programs as *Amos 'n' Andy* and *The Beulah Show* removed from the air. However, as recent history has shown, it is still not easy to convince the networks to portray minorities fairly.

When television became a national medium after World War II, African-American leaders had high hopes that it would become a means for white Americans to see minorities in a new light. In his history of African Americans on television, MacDonald wrote, "[M]any felt that TV promised a new and prejudice-free era in popular entertainment" (1992, 3). However, the earliest shows featured the same stock stereotypes that had been found on radio and in film. These shows prompted the NAACP to "discourage the sponsorship and presentation of such shows even to the extent, if necessary, of resorting to the boycott of the goods, products or services of the sponsors and promoters, including radio and television stations and networks" (NAACP 1951). NAACP leader Walter White, writing in *Printers' Ink* in 1951, pointed out that such shows could be harmful. "Unhappily, the system of segregation in the United States permits far too many Americans no opportunity to know Negroes except through such media as television." According to White, what Americans were seeing on *Beulah* and *Amos 'n' Andy* reinforced "the notion that Negro lawyers are slippery cowards, Negro doctors charlatans and thieves, Negro women cackling men-chasers and tempestuous shrews, and all Negroes allergic to toil" (1951, n.p.). Both shows were eventually cancelled, yet *Amos 'n' Andy* remained in syndication until 1966. However, as social historian Mary Ann Watson pointed out, that was "long after its imprint on postwar America was securely set like an autograph in cement" (1998, 30). Neither show has disappeared entirely, either. They are both available for purchase in video stores and through video catalogs.

The concerns of the NAACP were exacerbated because these shows were popular among white viewers. "The mass audience, and consequently sponsors and stations, looked more approvingly on the mammies, coons, and Uncle Toms of the past than they did on blacks seeking approval through non-stereotyped talents" (MacDonald 1992, 23). Attempts by the networks to showcase African Americans in other formats, including variety shows, failed. The most notable attempt involved the singer Nat King Cole. Cole hosted a program on NBC that was taken off the air after a year because it was unable to attract a permanent sponsor. In the early days of television, programs tended to be sponsored by one company or product, rather than through the participatory advertising that is common today. Many advertisers were afraid to be associated with a program that showed African Americans in a positive light because they were concerned about the effects on sales in the South.

In an interview in *Ebony Magazine* after his show was cancelled, Cole lashed out against "Madison Avenue," then the center of the advertising industry, saying that "their big clients didn't want their products associated with Negroes....Madison Avenue said I couldn't be sold. That no national advertiser would take a chance on offending Southerners" (Cole 1958, n.p.). However, he pointed out that in areas where local companies were offered the chance to sponsor the program, including New Orleans and Houston, Texas, no boycotts occurred (Cole 1958). Then, in a statement that demonstrates that hate sympathizers and hate spectators are not a new phenomenon, Cole criticized industry executives as hypocritical.

> If I went down South, I would know where I stood, although I might not agree with the policies. In the North, I can walk around in various circles and people will pat me on the back and say how much they love me and

then turn around and sabotage me while my back is turned. These people use the South as a whipping boy to get themselves off the hook. It gives them an excuse for not doing what they ought to do (1958, n.p.).

The cowardice of the network and advertising executives allowed mainstream hate to flourish.

In the early days of television, many of the programs the networks produced were visual versions of previously popular radio shows. They included shows focused on ethnic groups such as Italians, Norwegians, and Jews. However, as Watson points out, there was a big difference between the way these groups were portrayed and the way African Americans were shown. The stereotypes of these ethnic groups were not designed to lead to hate the way that stereotypes of blacks did. "The contrast between these two groups of television series is stark—the laziness, greed, licentiousness, and complaisance of the black characters versus the sobriety, restraint, thrift, and strong work ethic of the white characters" (1998, 30). As Dyer noted, the most powerful in society get to define the stereotypes. Here, whites defined blacks as ignorant and foolish, and worthy of being hated. These stereotypes allowed white viewers, particularly hate sympathizers and hate spectators, to justify their negative feelings about African Americans.

According to Dates and Barlow, one of the first American scholars to identify black stereotypes used by white authors was Sterling A. Brown in his book *The Negro in American Fiction*. "Brown identified such recurring characters as the 'contented slave,' the 'wretched freedman,' the 'tragic mulatto,' the 'brute Negro' and the 'comic Negro' as the most persistent African American stereotypes to emerge from the nineteenth century and carry over into his era" (1990, 2). In *Racist Ideologies and the Media*, Hall identified a series of stereotypes used to classify minorities, including the familiar slave figure found in such films as *Gone with the Wind*, the native, who is found in cowboy movies, and the clown or entertainer, found either in situation comedies or in sports programs (2000).

Dates argued that vestiges of these stereotypes could still be found in television programs well into the 1980s. She cited the example of Nell Carter, star of the situation comedy *Gimme a Break!*, who she says fulfilled the classic mammy role. In the program, star

Nell Carter, an African-American, cares for three white children whose mother has died. In one episode, Nell was in court fighting to retain custody of the children. After falling to her knees and begging the judge to let her keep "her" children, Carter was awarded custody. Dates wrote, "For a young African-American woman to fall to her knees obsequiously begging to continue in a servant's role on network television in the 1980s was astounding—particularly after the country had experienced the civil rights movement in the 1960s and 1970s, which had engendered much soul-searching about racial issues among thoughtful people, black and white" (1990, 276). Why would Carter put herself in such a position? Dates argued that the show was a hit with crossover (white) audiences, and there were few other roles for African-American women. Nonetheless, Dates was disturbed that there was no acknowledgment of the civil or social rights issues prevalent at the time.

In his book *Primetime Blues: African Americans on Network Television*, Donald Bogle also criticizes the role Nell Carter played in *Gimme a Break!*, also considering her a stereotypical "mammy" (2001). In his essay on the book, though, John McWhorter, a fierce critic of what he considers the victimization of African-Americans, took Bogle to task:

> In Bogle's account, 'For African American viewers, *Gimme a Break!* was little more than a remake of *Beulah*.' But that is only what Bogle and assorted black commentators chose to make of it. The show was quite popular in the black American community, and it owed its popularity not least to the fact that its resemblance to *Beulah* was only superficial (2001, 34).

McWhorter than listed a variety of ways in which the two shows differed, citing Carter's sassiness, her ambition to become a singer, and her close friendship with her friend Addy. McWhorter points out, "[M]y mother, who was exquisitely alive to the realities of racism and taught college courses on the subject, regularly commented on how racially 'real' their friendship was" (2001, 34). Is Carter's the type of stereotypical performance that engenders hatred and contempt for African-Americans? Alternatively, are black critics too sensitive to any portrayal that they do not consider entirely positive? Check out the television listings, watch the show, and decide for yourself.

Stereotypes still exist on television, although they are perhaps not as blatant as they were in the 1950s. Hall points out that news programs feature stereotypical characters in new guises. "Restless native hordes are alive as guerrilla armies and freedom fighters in Africa....Dependent peoples who couldn't manage for a day without the protection and know-how of their white masters reappear as the starving victims of the Third World, passive and waiting for the technology or the aid to arrive. They are not represented as the subjects of a continuing exploitation or dependency, or the global division of wealth and labour. They are the Victims of Fate" (2000, 277).

The portrayal of African Americans in entertainment programming on television has improved since the days of *Amos 'n' Andy*. Today, it is not unusual for blacks to be shown as doctors, lawyers, and teachers. Even so, in the summer of 1999, the NAACP threatened to mobilize a boycott of the four major television networks because none of the new programs scheduled to begin that fall featured an African American in a lead role. NAACP president Kweisi Mfume described the season as "a virtual whitewash in programming" (Children Now 2000a, 1).

Because of the boycott threat, all four networks signed an agreement in the spring of 2000 promising to try to increase the number of minorities both in front of and behind the camera (de Moraes 2000). However, in the spring of 2001, three of the four members of the coalition pushing for increased diversity on television complained that the networks had not done enough. In judging the diversity records for Latinos, Native Americans, and Asians, the groups gave the networks grades ranging from a D-minus to ABC, to a C for NBC. Instead of issuing a report card, the fourth member of the coalition, the NAACP, decided to wait until summer to issue a detailed report. Nonetheless, Mfume said that at its annual meeting in July, the NAACP would again consider a boycott. Alex Nogales, president of the National Hispanic Media Coalition, also said either a boycott or legal action was possible (Waxman 2001).

As a result of the controversy over the lack of diversity on television, Children Now, a media watchdog group, commissioned two studies that examined the racial distribution of all characters in the fall 1999 prime-time lineup, and looked at race and ethnicity by program genre. Its first study, titled *Fall Colors: How Diverse Is the 1999–2000 TV Season's Prime Time Lineup?*, also examined gender, occupations by race and gender, youth characters, disability, and sexual identity (2000a). *Fall Colors II: Exploring the Quality of Diverse Portrayals on Prime Time Television* (2000b) took a closer look at specific shows, examining work and home environments, positive and negative portrayals of characters, and humor and stereotypes. Among other reasons, Children Now commissioned the studies to determine whether the racial and ethnic diversity of children's lives is reflected in what they see on television. The short answer is "no." Children Now concluded that on prime-time television

> [m]en outnumber women almost two to one. There are fewer Latinos, Asian Pacific Americans, and Native Americans than in the general population, especially among the youth characters....[W]hen programming does include people of color, it frequently does so in an exclusionary manner....[M]ost programs feature primary casts that are either all white or all Black. Racial diversity in today's prime time comes in the form of secondary and guest characters (2000a, 21).

Even the recently popular "reality" television programs perpetuate stereotypes that lead to fear, and ultimately to hatred, of black men. In an essay in *The Washington Post*, television critic Paul Farhi examined a new version of an old phenomenon—the "Bad Black Guy." Farhi pointed out that the producers of such shows as *Survivor*, *Real World*, *Temptation Island*, and *Big Brother*, all selected contestants who perpetuated the notion of black men as either overly (and overtly) sexual, violent, lazy, or antisocial. "In the ersatz terrarium of reality programming, African American men are reduced to stock figures. They play predictably to type as rogues and rascals, bad dudes and playas. While often physically attractive, and occasionally even charming, they soon enough reveal themselves as the BBG" (2001, C1). On *Survivor*, Gervase fulfilled the stereotype through his sexual exploits before the show. During the program, it was revealed that he had fathered several children out of wedlock. On *Big Brother*, William, a former member of the New Black Panther Party, antagonized his housemates and caused their food rations to be cut for a week. Finally, Stephen, on *Real World/Seattle*, slapped a female housemate on camera (2001). Even "the locksmith" on the program *Chains of Love* fits the mold of the BBG.

In the article, Farhi quoted Alvin Poussaint, a professor of psychiatry at Harvard. "These shows keep presenting images of blacks as street slick, tending toward the criminal, potentially angry. ...All it does is perpetuate the image" (2001, C1). As Farhi points out, the producers of these shows know what they are doing, and what image of black men they are allowing the audience to see. "Any good producer knows what his or her audience wants. And perhaps what the producers of reality shows know is this: This is the kind of racial 'reality' millions of Americans are willing, even eager, to accept" (2001, C1). The millions of viewers who watch these shows are so inured to these images and are so willing to accept them that the stereotypes go unnoticed until they are brought to the attention of the public. The result of the unconscious acceptance of these stereotypes is a reinforcement of the subtext of hatred that underlies our popular culture.

As pointed out above, hate sympathizers and hate spectators can easily allow the way ethnic and racial minorities are portrayed on television to influence their attitudes. However, those portrayals and the impression that they leave do not have to be negative to be damaging. Entman, for example, raised the concern that the number of African-American journalists now seen on the evening news lulls viewers into believing that minorities have made more progress than they actually have. In an earlier article in *The Washington Post*, Farhi raised the same concern about entertainment programming. He argued that despite concerns by the NAACP that too few minorities are shown on television, the real problem is not that television excludes or demeans blacks. Instead, he argues that the real problem is that television is more integrated and provides more black role models than most other American institutions:

> Indeed, TV's real problem is that it can't shake its own hopeful lies: that America is an integrated, largely harmonious, race-blind society....Why do Americans believe that black progress is greater than it is, that gaps in income, education and job status between blacks and other groups must be largely the fault of black people rather than some systemic flaw? Because television repeatedly shows us an egalitarian myth (Farhi 2000, G1).

Children Now's *Fall Colors II*, published in summer 2000, backs up Fahri's contention. It reveals that, even though the number of minorities on television is low, those who are featured are shown positively in the workplace. Further, the study found that three-quarters of characters of all races were shown as competent in the workforce. However, both male and female African Americans, whether in dramas or situation comedies, were depicted as slightly more competent than their white counterparts (Children Now 2000b). The study listed a number of characters who could serve as role models for African Americans and other minorities. They included characters such as Dr. Peter Benton on *ER*, Lt. Anita Van Buren on *Law and Order*, Dee Mitchell on *Moesha*, Chakotay on *Star Trek: Voyager*, and Lilly on *Popular*.

While the portrayals of African Americans and other minorities were found to be more positive than in the past, the study did raise concerns about other aspects of the characters they played:

> African American characters tend to be compartmentalized to sitcoms and generally are only shown in one arena—work. Asian Pacific Americans are rarely shown and their few representations lack depth and development. The few Latino characters on primetime are relegated to secondary dramatic story lines. Finally, both Asian Pacific American and Latino characters are often the victims of racial humor and stereotypes (Children Now 2000b, 26).

The study also found that when white and minority characters interacted, "they rarely acknowledged racial difference" (2000b, 26). Only three of the twenty-two programs studied addressed issues of race explicitly. When the rest mentioned race, it was usually in a humorous context, often in situations in which stereotypes were evoked, or characters of different races became the butt of jokes.

In the report, Children Now questioned the wisdom of providing the audience with a false view of a color-blind society. "For some, the picture of a colorblind society presents viewers with a goal, an endpoint for which people should be reaching. For others, the adage that we must first consider race to get beyond race applies, and there is a danger in allowing viewers to believe that racial difference—as well as inequitable conditions—is no longer a significant issue" (2000b, 9).

Is this report good news and evidence of progress, or is it bad news because the color-blind world and competent minorities found on television can be used as another reason for spectators and sympathizers to criticize affirmative action and other programs that benefit the disadvantaged? As James D. Halloran points out in *On the Social Effects of Television*, it is essential to distinguish between a gain in knowledge and a change in attitude. "It is easier to convey knowledge than to change attitudes" (2000, 437). Will changing the way African Americans and other minorities are portrayed on television lead to improved attitudes toward them in the country? Is it enough to drop a few programs such as *My Wife and Kids* into the prime-time lineup? Probably not. The industry needs to recognize that simply adding a few minority characters to ensemble shows is not enough. Minorities need to be seen as real people leading real lives, not as tokens or exaggerated stereotypes. Will this be easy? No. Is it even possible? That is questionable. Audiences must be willing to distinguish between television and the "real world." However, as even the producers of "reality" television programs have discovered, audiences are more than willing to accept hateful stereotypes.

What is needed is a change on the part of both news and entertainment programs. That task may prove to be difficult, though, because of our unconscious attitudes toward the "other." The hatred that underlies our culture makes it easy to present images that perpetuate the notion that racial and ethnic minorities are lazy, licentious, violent, and antisocial. The stereotypes are so engrained that we hardly notice when, for example, television news programs illustrate stories about welfare recipients, unwed mothers, and homeless people with black and Hispanic faces rather than white faces. Remember Callwood's contention that the misfortunes of the "other" make the rest of us feel better about ourselves. At the same time, these stereotypes prompt us to look down on—and even hate—the "other."

Over the years, the stereotypes found on television have given us a false picture of minorities. These stereotypes reinforce the hatred that allows hatemongers and hate dabblers to put aside their inhibitions and commit horrific crimes against the "other." Only when we are able to crack the cement of hardened attitudes will we be able to alleviate the hatred perpetrated by television. In our next chapter, we will examine how filmmakers have brought this conflict to the screen by describing how movies have given us a visual representation of hate crimes and their victims.

— Chapter 7 —
Hate and Film

In the television film *Anatomy of a Hate Crime: The Killing of Matthew Shepard*, which recounts the brutal murder of a gay student in Wyoming, a character announces that a hate crime could never happen there, because "hate is not a Laramie value." This refusal to recognize that hatred could thrive and transform a community like Laramie is actually symptomatic of our national refusal to acknowledge the grip that hatred has on American life. Hatred is not only a Laramie value, but, as we have argued in this book, it is also a national value.

This chapter uses the narrative texts of contemporary films to describe the reality of hate in America. Film speaks to us in ways that language cannot. Words can seldom capture the magnitude and intensity of the ways in which people experience the wounds of hate. Although writings by such CLS scholars as Mari Matsuda and Charles Lawrence make our knowledge of the scars of hate more accessible, film captures the magnitude of hatred's effects. Cinematic images can transcend the ordinary and transport the viewer to a place where each becomes the beaten, the targeted, the despised, or conversely, even the "hater." Facing the evils of hatred through our own cinematic transference is painful, but it is a process that can brilliantly capture the tragedy of real victims of hate.

Films also provide us with some explanations for the sickness that is hatred. American film has a long legacy of stereotyping the "other" which, as we have argued, is often the basis for hatred. From D. W. Griffith's notorious racist classic *Birth of a Nation* to the blaxploitation films of the 1970s such as *Sweet Sweetback's Baad Asss Song* and *Superfly*, inaccurate portrayals of blacks and other minorities have been the rule, rather than the exception. Spike Lee is the most prominent black filmmaker to use cinematic images to refute traditional black stereotypes. However, it is important to note that as early as 1919, director Oscar Micheaux was already making films that challenged those same black stereotypes. Between 1919 and 1940, Micheaux produced an extraordinary 35 feature films. One of them, *Within Our Gates* (1920), was, in part, a response to Griffith's hateful *Nation*, and told of the hideous racism of the day. Although Micheaux constructed "fully-developed black characters" in place of the "cruel stereotypes of mainstream cinema," it soon became obvious that false images die hard (DeBartolo 2000). In fact, today, racist stereotypes in film can even earn Oscar nominations, as illustrated by *The Green Mile*'s nomination for best film in 2000. *The Green Mile* tells the story of John Coffey, a black man on death row in Louisiana, circa 1935. As Tania Modleski writes, "[T]he lurid image of the monstrous black ravager of white femininity...still looms large in the white American psyche" (2000). We also see this cruel stereotype of the "black ravager" in the film *Rosewood*.

Since contemporary films serve as excellent examples of stereotyping, violence, and hatred, we will take a detailed look at the following films—*Rosewood, Do the Right Thing, Higher Learning, Bamboozled, Boys Don't Cry,* and *American History X*. A brief examination of less theatrically known films—*Followers* and *Southern Comfort*—will also follow. These films all offer succinct narrations and explanations of hate.

Rosewood is director John Singleton's powerful film of the "historically repressed" and tragic events that transpired in a small black town in Florida in the 1920s. What is astonishing about Rosewood is how little was historically documented of that act of genocidal hatred and racism. The story of Rosewood begins with an adulterous white woman's false charge that she was raped by a black man who was well known in the community. As film critic Ed Guerrero writes, "fueled by economic competition and jealousy" and ignited by hatred for the "mythical and historically indispensable black other," (1997, n.p.) a legally sanctioned lynch mob from a neighboring county entered Rosewood, murdered any black they could locate, and then proceeded to burn the entire town to the ground (Guerrero 1997). Aaron Beck contends that this type of genocide occurs when a stigmatized group (in this case, the Rosewood inhabitants) becomes prominent in the economic and cultural life of the community. Beck further posits that the hated group is then accused of trying to "usurp traditions, political authority and economic power" (Beck 1999). White vigilantes from Rosewood and neighboring towns believed that Rosewood blacks had become too prominent, and they used the alleged rape of the white housewife as the catalyst for their genocidal actions. The actual number of black Rosewood residents murdered by the vigilantes has never been accurately reported. It is only through the painful reminiscences of some 20 Rosewood survivors, who recounted their story in a *60 Minutes* expose in 1983, that we have any information at all (Guerrero 1997).

The film *Rosewood* does a brilliant job speaking to the genesis of stereotypes, prejudice, and hatred. Despite the evidence brought to law enforcement officials of the innocence of the black man falsely accused of rape, the viciously "closed minds" of the white residents could not be altered. The film shows one exception to the virulent hatred. Actor Jon Voigt plays the real-life white storekeeper John Wright, who actually protected some of the blacks from the lynch mobs in Rosewood. Singleton also gives us someone else to root for in the battle against hatred. His cinematic creation is a black World War I vet named Mann. He rides into Rosewood on horseback, valiantly fights the lynchings and murders, and saves several residents, including many children. Mann, played by actor Ving Rhames, is Singleton's revisionist Western hero. The problem is, he never really existed. Was Singleton trying to soften the horror of such systemic hatred, or was his fictional construct a way to plead the case for renewal and hope in the face of violence?

Singleton ends the film with the powerful image of a young white boy, whose father was instrumental in the lynchings, rejecting hatred and ultimately fleeing his father's home. Some regard this cinematic take as Singleton's hope that hatred will diminish in the next generation. In fact, this notion of generational hatred is critical to the analysis on hate. Author Roland Merullo worries how the legacy of hate is passed on through generations—both in the life of the perpetrator and in the life of the victim. Merullo writes,

> I am interested in the way hatred is internalized; the psychological imbalances it spawns as it mutates, echoes, and filters down through generations. In its complexity and subtlety, this process seems to me perfectly analogous to the long-term patterns of environmental damage. When a poisonous chemical is first spilled into a body of water, it has certain immediate, obvious effects—some fish die, the water becomes

undrinkable. Later, as the chemical embeds itself in the muddy bottom, the effects are more difficult to trace, but no less harmful—the internal structures of plants are altered, poisoning the fish that feed on them, harming the birds and humans that consume fish. Over time, the whole ecosystem tilts out of balance (2000).

The poisonous chemical of racial hatred is easily transmitted from one generation to the next, and that is what Singleton wants us to understand. He carefully crafts the final story line so this one white child is able to shed the toxic chemical of hate—while still reminding the audience that other children may not be as fortunate. *Rosewood* masterfully demands that we never forget the reasons for hatred and violence, and that we continue to examine our "national conscience" on such matters as tolerance and human diversity.

Do the Right Thing (1989) tells another story of hatred and racism—this time in a Brooklyn neighborhood on the hottest day of a recent summer. In the film, it is said that "the hate thrives in the heat; in a certain way, the hate becomes the heat, supplanting the cement and the sun." *Do the Right Thing* centers around the character of Mookie, a black man who works as a pizza deliveryman for Sal, the Italian proprietor of Sal's Pizzeria. We follow Mookie as he encounters various inhabitants of the Stuyvesant community—Pino and Vito, Sal's two sons who work with Mookie; Buggin' Out, who wants to organize a boycott of Sal's pizza because of the lack of racial representation on Sal's Wall of Fame; Radio Raheem, a young man whose boom box is the catalyst for the ensuing racial explosion that occurs at Sal's Pizzeria; and the deaf man who symbolizes the opposing political voices of Martin Luther King and Malcom X. We watch as Radio Raheem is brutally killed by white police officers in an act of deadly force, and we witness Mookie's final act of rage as he initiates the rebellion that leads to the burning and looting of Sal's store. This Bedford-Stuyvesant community represents a microcosm of society's larger ills, and Lee's movie forces the audience to ask what the right thing is—to engage in violent action to retaliate for racial hatreds, or to engage in nonviolence to counter that conflict and hatred. Although Mookie chooses violence, the viewer is left to wonder whether that decision is the wisest or most expedient.

In his article, "The double truth Ruth: Do the Right Thing and the culture of ambiguity," James C. McKelley describes the film as an exercise in binary thinking. McKelley's point is that African Americans are often faced with conflicting allegiances as they must mediate their cultural position within a "dominant social order of white Americanism" (1998, n.p.). For Lee, that duality is represented in one way by the opposing philosophical views of Martin Luther King and Malcolm X. King is seen as signifying forgiveness, constructive engagement, and patience within an ethic of reform. Malcolm X comes to stand for power, proactive resistance, and autonomy—an ethic of revolution. Radio Raheem, the young man whose death incites Mookie's choice of revolutionary action, is one of Lee's messengers in the presentation of this theoretical tension. Radio Raheem represents a moral dualism by wearing two brass knuckle rings inscribed with the words *love* and *hate*. When asked about the rings, Raheem answers, "Hate is always KO'd by love." However, in this world of Bedford-Stuy, hate wins the battle and Raheem is one of its casualties. Raheem's knuckle rings and the thematic tensions offered by King and Malcolm X allow the audience to explore what to do about hate. Do we choose forgiveness in the face of hatred, or do we strive for resistance in an effort to curtail the stranglehold that hatred has on our beliefs, attitudes, and actions? The answer for the viewer is as complex as Mookie's decision is at the end of the film.

Bamboozled (2000), Spike Lee's newest venture into cinematic controversy, is the penultimate accounting of racial stereotyping. In the film, Pierre Delacroix is the only black writer for a fictional television network, CNS. In an effort to draw attention to the failure of the media to address the problem of racial representation properly, Delacroix proposes a variety show that is blatantly stereotypical, hateful, and racist. The show, *Mantan: The New Millennium Minstrel Show*, is set in a watermelon patch. Its two main characters, pejoratively named Mantan and Sleep N' Eat, are described as "ignorant and lazy coons." Instead of the proposal getting Delacroix fired (which is what he wants as a form of protest), the program becomes an ironic hit with television audiences. One of the most compelling sketches in the film occurs when black actors Savion Glover and Tommy Davidson dance in blackface, a painful reminder of the insidious racism of decades past. *Washington Post* columnist Richard Cohen poignantly describes the impact of watching *Bamboozled*. "It's hard now to appreciate just how vilified, mocked, denigrated and just plain ridiculed black people were on the stage and later, in film. Racism was so pervasive, so unexceptional, that it was just seen as an unremarkable part of the American social fabric" (2000). Cohen's commentary on the film speaks to the power of a culture's impact on political and social beliefs. Lee's decision to portray the *New Millennium Minstrel Show* as an unadulterated hit is ironic evidence of what we have argued is the acceptance of hatred by mainstream America. As Cohen tells it,

> I was a racist....I grew up with Aunt Jemima and Sambo, with black servants on the screen who bowed and scraped....I can still do a fairly good imitation of Charlie Chan's chauffeur, and I have a CD on which a young Frank Sinatra sings the lyrical "Without a Song" and uses the word "darkie." He recorded it that way once and never again (2000).

Cohen's confession reveals much about the impact of the cultural influence of hatred, whether intentional or not. The searing stereotypical images remain with the audience long after the film ends. On a related note, the May 2001 opening of the long-awaited film *Pearl Harbor* created trepidation among some Japanese Americans, who feared that the film, and any possible stereotypes in it, might rekindle anti-Japanese sentiment and hatred (Accomondo 2001).

Boys Don't Cry (1999) is a brilliant film about the hatred that results from confusion and anger over matters of sexual orientation and identity. *Boys* tells the true story of Brandon Teena. Born a girl, desiring to be a male, and too poor to arrange sexual reassignment surgery, she dresses like a young man and moves to the heartland of Nebraska. Brandon, by definition, is a transgendered individual, one who has "a desire to change one's anatomic sexual characteristics to conform physically with one's perception of self as a member of the opposite sex."

In Falls City, Nebraska, Brandon befriends two alienated young men, John Lotter and Tom Nissen, and joins them in drinking, bar fights, and car theft escapades. Brandon's growing relationship with and love for Lana, John's ex-girlfriend, sets the stage for the horror and tragedy to follow. When Lotter and Nissen discover that Brandon is actually a woman, they humiliate her by forcing her to strip in front of Lana. Then, in an excruciating act of revenge and repressed desire, the two men brutally rape and beat Brandon. When she presses charges against them, authorities in Falls City fail to arrest the two men. Lotter and Nissen then commit the ultimate act of hatred and revenge by executing Brandon with six gunshots to the head as she hides in terror at a friend's farmhouse.

The sheer power of the cinematic images in *Boys Don't Cry* permits the viewer to trade places with Brandon Teena for a few brief moments. Just as we can accompany Janet Leigh into the shower in *Psycho* or watch Jimmy Stewart watch Grace Kelly in *Rear Window* (Douglas 1996, n.p.), some of us unwillingly join Brandon in experiencing the horrors of her victimization. Antithetically, others may support her punishment for what they perceive as gender dysfunctionality. As Laura Mulvey suggests in her essay "Visual Pleasure and Narrative Cinema," our responses to any film may have something to do with the differences between male and female notions of "spectatorship" (1998). Mulvey constructs an important argument about sexual difference and gaze when she points out that "the cinematic apparatus and men look at women in two ways: sadism-voyeurism, which punishes women, and fetishism-scopophilia, which fetishes the female body." For Mulvey and some male viewers of *Boys Don't Cry*, Brandon Teena may have been the "architect of her own predicament" and a worthy subject for their hateful gazes.

In *Boys*, when the two men forcibly strip Brandon down to her underwear to check out her genital identity, some viewers actually recoil at the utter humiliation and betrayal of that terrorizing moment. In fact, some believe that scene is more emotionally traumatizing than the film's account of her actual murder. At that moment, her identity as a transgendered person is front and center—the focus of the men's uncontrollable disgust and hatred. It has been said

> that Shakespeare is venerated for understanding the human heart.....When a woman impersonates a guy in Shakespeare's plays, she wins the man she loves...and everyone celebrates the union....But when a woman cross-dresses in *Boys Don't Cry*, she wins the woman she loves, then gets raped and slaughtered for upsetting the social equilibrium (Stuart 1999, n.p.).

Gender and sexual identity in America's heartland goes terribly awry and leads to hatred and violence in *Boys Don't Cry*. That hatred is expressed as Tom and John's inability to live with the ambiguity that comes when people are faced with transgendered identity. Teena's girlfriend, Lana, was able to live with the ambiguity, whereas the two men could not. *Boys Don't Cry* reminds us how difficult and painful it is to try and live according to one's own truth. Hatred cannot accept even the slightest hint of ambiguity or confusion.

After Brandon's brutal murder, officials in Nebraska refused to admit that sexual bias was a motive in her killing. Brandon's mother, Joann Brandon, eventually sued former Sheriff Charles Laux for not offering Brandon protective custody after she reported the rape and other threats to him. In 1999, a District Court judge found the county partly to blame for Brandon's death and ordered it to pay $17,360. Joann Brandon is appealing the damage amount as insufficient (O'Hanlon 2001).

The failure to admit sexual bias in Brandon's killing also infuriated gays, lesbians, and transsexuals nationwide. The National Gay and Lesbian Task Force has now joined with transsexual groups to pressure Nebraska officials to identify sexual bias crimes for what they are, and to report them under the federal *Hate Crimes Statistics Act*. In fact, a day of remembrance is now celebrated to memorialize the eighteen individuals who have been killed just since 1999 in cases of anti-transgender hatred and violence (Smith 2000). The Day of Remembrance, November 28, was the date that Rita Hester, a transgendered woman, was murdered in her Massachusetts apartment. Now activists are attempting to use the death of Hester and others to symbolize the urgency of applying hate crime laws to transgendered people.

The issue of transgendered individuals and hate came under scrutiny again in an award-winning film at the 2001 Sundance Film Festival. The new documentary film, *Southern Comfort*, received raves and "sent shock waves" through its viewers at the yearly independent film fest. *Southern Comfort* is a powerful film that closely examines, as *Boys Don't Cry* does, the poignant struggles and realities of victims of hate in the matter of sexual identity and orientation. It tells the true story of Robert Eads, a female-to-male transsexual, who ironically is dying of cervical and ovarian cancer. In the film, he poignantly reveals, "the last part of me that is female is killing me" (Mitchell 2001). The film is named for a support group that Eads and other transgendered people belong to. The group was formed in an effort to cope with the botched medical care and with the unconscious hatred and indifference the members experienced, even from their own physicians. *Southern Comfort* is set in Toccoa,

Georgia, in what is called the "trailer badlands." In the film, Eads tells an amusing story of how the local members of the KKK invited him to join their hateful organization. He responds with the good-natured comment, "I imagine it'd be quite a scene...wondering how the good old boys would react to my biological background" (Mitchell 2001). One is reminded of that painful scene from *Boys Don't Cry* in which Brandon is exposed. There is a delicious irony, however, in a story that has the hateful KKK inviting Robert to join their own ranks of intolerance.

Probably the most stunning example of cinematic hatred is the film *American History X* (1999), the story of a young working-class man, his discovery of the white supremacist skinhead movement, and his ultimate redemption from the bonds of hatred. The film is masterful at portraying the overwhelming hold and destructiveness that hate can maintain on the individual psyche. *American History X* seethes with hatred from the opening credits as Derek (actor Edward Norton) commits a brutish and horrific act of violence on a black gang member who has been vandalizing Derek's car. As the police swoop in to arrest him, the audience begins to learn, through a series of black-and-white flashbacks, of Derek's involvement in violence and hatred. We witness Derek's father, a firefighter, lamenting to him and his younger brother Danny about the injustices of affirmative action. Though the two brothers are not yet "hatemongers," the bait has been set, and their father's angry musings begin to loosen their tenuous grip on racial tolerance. Their father's murder, while putting out a fire at a crack house in a black neighborhood, is the catalyst for the violent act that eventually puts Derek in prison. (This turn of events certainly plays to negative stereotypes.) Flashbacks fill in the story of Derek's recruitment as the "lieutenant of a shadowy adult neo-Nazi" and of his induction into the skinhead movement. Derek is portrayed as both charismatic and terrifying in the ferocity of his white supremacist beliefs.

Director Tony Kaye makes the most of his narrative when he shows his central character with other skinheads, bonding and fueling their ideology of intolerance with "drugs, beer, tattoos and heavy metal." Kaye even dares to explore the sexual realm of the fascist personality by highlighting Derek's handsome, muscular body covered with hideous swastikas. In that sequence, the viewer is left with an odd and uncomfortable attraction to the sheer physicality and sensuality of Derek's body, despite the presence of his profound character flaws.

Derek's experience with a black inmate in prison triggers in him the arduous process of undoing the hatred that once defined his identity. Derek's healing process is spoiled, however, when his younger brother, Danny, is murdered in the high school bathroom by another black gang member. How will Derek mediate the world as hatred seizes another beloved family member? What was Kaye trying to tell the audience with Danny's death—that as soon as one is liberated, Derek, another succumbs, Danny, to the violence that is usually hatred's companion? At the end of the film, Kaye gives us a hazy vision of two joyous children running on the beach—obviously Derek and Danny as very young boys. To the viewer, it seems an image of betrayal, one that painfully contradicts the previous narrative. The boys are not innocent or free of the politics of prejudice and hatred—instead, they have both fallen victim to its catastrophic vices. Perhaps that is precisely the point of Kaye's creative exploration of hate and its manifestations.

What is astonishing about *American History X* is its chilling comparison to the real-life stories of T. J. Leyden, now a consultant for the Simon Wiesenthal Center, and of Gregory Withrow. Withrow's account of hatred and redemption is told in the 2000 film, *Blink*. In *Blink*, filmmaker Elizabeth Thompson documents the biography of Gregory Withrow, the son of a member of the American Nazi Party, who himself becomes a leader in the Aryan Youth Movement and an associate of Tom Metzger of White Aryan Resistance. However, when Withrow proclaims his disaffiliation with the movement some years later, he is found "nearly dead, cut up, and nailed to a board crucifixion-style" (Newitz 1998). The Matthew Shepard story redux! Like the fictional tale in *American History X*, the stories of Leyden and Withrow are crucial to our understanding of how malleable young people are in their political and social beliefs. Thompson points out that her film, *Blink*, was an inquiry into how "political identity is never a constant or a given" and how political ideologies can be transformed (Newitz 1998). While Kaye did not model his theatrical film after Leyden or Withrow, what we learn from the personalities and influences on Derek,

Leyden, and Withrow may someday help us in the difficult task of deterring hatred.

Listening to T. J. Leyden's story was quite an experience (2000). He was raised in a blue-collar neighborhood in Fontana, California, one not very different from Derek's. However, unlike Derek's father, his parents insisted on raising their children to be respectful and tolerant of all races. Nonetheless, in 1978, after his parents divorced, Leyden started "hanging" with punk rockers who vented their growing rage at rock concerts by slam-dancing and fighting with anyone who even marginally came into contact with them. Chapter 5 of this book chronicles just how intoxicating and powerful that music can be for young people. Leyden tells how neo-Nazi recruiters witnessed his rage and, at this point, seized the opportunity to mold his thinking into an ideology of intolerance and hatred. In *American History X*, Kaye shows the insidiousness of that indoctrination process with his character development of Derek. Leyden, like Derek, personified the perfect union of young, white, male violence with the seduction of extremist thinking.

Leyden moved swiftly from being a dabbler in hate, to a thrill seeker, to a full-fledged hatemonger. As he tells it, first came the clothing—the bomber jacket, the steel-toed boots, and the shaved head. Then came the "values" of the skinhead movement—the hatred, the explosiveness, and the violence. Listening to white racist CDs featuring "shit-kicker music" and attending those concerts helped Leyden and his fellow haters get "pumped up." After the concerts, they would "hunt" black, Hispanic, or gay victims for a "boot party." In skinhead vernacular, that meant mercilessly beating up someone. Leyden soon earned the distinction, like Derek, of being a "violent and militant warrior."

At age twenty-one, Leyden joined the U.S. Marines Corps, and he insists that the military made him a "better racist"—a frightening observation about such a powerful and established American institution. While stationed in Hawaii, he began an association with Tom Metzger, founder of WAR. While still in the military, Leyden became an active recruiter for the neo-Nazi movement, preaching white supremacy to fellow Marines by showing them videos and introducing them to white racist bands. He was even allowed to post a Third Reich battle flag in his locker and to place the Confederate Stars and Bars on his wall. One of his last acts as a soldier was to tattoo a Nazi storm trooper lightning bolt on his neck. Eventually, Leyden was discharged from the Corps, not because of his racist activity, but because of "alcohol-related behavior" that impaired his ability to be a good Marine. In fact, according to Leyden's own statement, "you could join an extremist group and still be in the military as long as you only participated in passive acts as defined by the base commander" (Simon Wiesenthal Center 2000, n.p.). Why did the military tolerate such hatred? Perhaps it simply demonstrates just how ingrained hatred has become and how central it is in American life.

After Leyden was discharged from the Marines, he married a woman named Nicole, who, he says, pulled him further into the world of racist skinhead beliefs. Leyden continued his connection with Metzger, learning the neo-Nazi way of inventive recruiting, which involved provoking racial slugfests. One such slugfest occurred publicly when Metzger insulted Roy Innes of the Congress of Racial Equality (CORE) on a Geraldo Rivera show. Rivera suffered a broken nose in the subsequent brawl. "White Aryan Resistance phone lines lit up with new members" after the fight, and according to Leyden, anyone who joined the movement after that became known as a "Geraldo skin" (Simon Wiesenthal Center 2000, n.p.). Leyden even took this slugfest idea to California high school campuses where he passed out hate material designed to provoke fights between white and nonwhite students.

All told, Leyden spent fifteen years actively engaged in hate. During that time, he and Nicole had two sons, who were not spared the hate proselytized by their parents. Leyden even tells how he placed a Nazi flag over one of his sons' cribs. Later, though, that very son caused Leyden to rethink his white supremacist beliefs. Just as Derek would undergo a philosophical metamorphosis in prison, Leyden radically altered his provincial and dangerous ways. One night, as Leyden tells the story, his then four-year-old son abruptly turned off a television show featuring black actors, defiantly announcing, "We don't watch shows with niggers." That proclamation began Leyden's transition to tolerance.

Can people really change? What does Kaye's film and Leyden's biography reveal? T. J. Leyden's story and Edward Norton's portrayal of Derek in *American History X* provide us with important data about the socialization process of hatred. What factors affect the cognitive process of developing attitudes? How do parent-child interactions impact a child's social adjustment? What other agents of socialization may have contributed to Leyden and Derek's behavior? As we watch these young men explore the dangerous terrain of hatred and violence, we become better equipped to prevent its manifestations.

In the summer of 2000, another interesting film dealing with hate was produced. This independent film, titled *Followers,* was written and directed by Jonathan Flicker. The film, which tells the story of a racist hazing incident, was modeled after an actual incident at a Rider University fraternity in Lawrenceville, New Jersey. *Followers* tells the tale of "nigger night," when fraternity pledges are forced to spend an evening being black. A white "pledge master" ordered white pledges to don the clothing of the Jim Crow era, wear Malcolm X hats, paint X's on their foreheads, and mock black English while cleaning the fraternity house. A message board at the film's Web site has fielded numerous responses—"[T]he sad truth is that racism is a huge problem in the Greek system," wrote one black student at the Georgia Institute of Technology (Reisberg 2000). In an interview, Flicker said, "[T]he film is not intended as a mean-spirited swipe at Greek life, but an attempt to tackle the issue of hate. It could've been a corporation, it could've been an athletics team. I used a fraternity because that's what I know" (Reisberg 2000). Flicker is speaking, then, to the universality of hate in such modern American institutions as schools and the workplace.

Followers was not the first film to address hate on campus. John Singleton's 1995 film *Higher Learning* was an earlier attempt to examine how the phenomenon of hate has found a comfortable place in academia. The film, which takes place at the mythical Columbus University, traces the lives of members of a freshman class, navigating the complexities of higher education life. Singleton interweaves three different stories into a complex narrative—those of Malik, a black athletic-scholarship student; Kirsten, a white woman, and date rape victim, now considering a lesbian relationship; and Remy, the loner, now deeply involved in the racist skinhead movement. Singleton uses their stories to illustrate how the attitudes of young adults are often laced with an ambiguity, a narrow-mindedness, and a self-righteousness that makes any dialogue about racism and sexism impossible. Actually, this is one of the shortcomings of his film—the director's own inability to rise above the creation of stereotypical character types. As Desson Howe, a *Washington Post* film critic, pointed out, "[T]he all too many white characters serve Singleton's transparent purpose as one-dimensional Bimbos, bigoted security cops, laughable lesbians, tattooed neo-Nazis, mindless meatheads or hayseed yokels" (Howe 1995, n.p.). White stereotypes are as problematic as minority ones in that they also fuel the misrepresentations that lead to hatred.

Hatred really has found an unfortunate niche on college campuses. In spite of the notion that a college community should be a place of tolerance, diversity, and intellectualism, higher institutions have frequently failed to live up to expectations. A report by the Southern Poverty Law Center found that college campuses were the third most common venue for hate crimes! In 1998 alone, there were 699 hate-motivated crimes reported on campuses, representing 9 percent of all hate crimes nationwide, and this astonishing number failed to include verbal assaults or hate speech (Corey 2000). Mark Potok, of the SPLC, commented, "We're noticing that there seems to be more and more serious [hate crimes] happening at some of the nation's most elite universities." Potok attributes this growth of hate to the fact that "many of these kids are coming from racially isolated environments and are encountering a lot of expression of identity politics" (Corey 2000). That is precisely what Singleton portrayed in *Higher Learning*.

Others argue that the 2000 Supreme Court decision in *Board of Regents of the University of Wisconsin System v. Southworth* has also contributed to the rise in campus hatred. In Southworth, a conservative student group challenged the university's policy of charging all students a mandatory activity fee, which was used to fund extracurricular programs and speeches. Conservative Christian students challenged the policy on the grounds that it forced students to support groups with beliefs contrary to their own. Christian students did not want to support gay and lesbian organizations. However, in a unanimous ruling, the Court upheld the mandatory fee. Critics of the decision now argue that "if a Ku Klux Klan group became a recognized campus group, black students would have to pay fees to support a group that would deny them their basic rights." Many believe this decision not only requires tolerance of hate on campus, but actually requires its very subsidization—all in the name of free speech! (SPLC 2000a, n.p.)

In the early 1980s, college administrators tried to curtail the spread of hate by instituting hate speech codes. It was argued that bigoted speech harmed minority students and undermined their ability to achieve academic success. However, those codes were invalidated as a result of the Supreme Court's decision in *RAV v. St. Paul* and two earlier decisions, *Doe v. University of Michigan* (1989) and *UWM Post v. Board of Regents of the University of Wisconsin System* (1991). Hate speech codes were often mocked as a way to coerce "political correctness." As Marilyn Friedman pointed out, "[C]ode critics insistently invoke the constitutional and moral halo of a right to freedom of expression, or speech" (1995, 4). Since the *RAV*, *Doe*, and *UWM* decisions, and perhaps because of them, hate now flourishes in higher education communities. Anti-Semitic hate incidents on campuses have been particularly prevalent. In the mid-1990s, a spray-painted message reading "Anti-Semitism is alive and well at FAU" was found in a men's room at Florida Atlantic University; a swastika and the words "Fuck the Jews" were discovered in the entryway to Lowell House at Harvard University; vandals drew a series of swastikas at George Washington University, and at Colorado University vandals wrote "Jews burn in Hell" on the steps of a Jewish fraternity. These incidents occurred in a short time period and represent only a fraction of the vicious anti-Semitic assaults at the nation's universities. To make matters worse, the cable network Showtime announced it would premiere the film, *The Believer*, which tells the story of a "Jewish Yeshiva student who transforms into the leader of a Neo-nazi group of skinheads" (Dempsey 2001). *The Believer*, which won a Sundance Grand Jury prize, failed to get support from such major studios as Paramount Classics, Miramax, and USA Films after the Simon Wiesenthal Center criticized its controversial content.

Racial and ethnic hatred on college campuses has also proliferated, as Flicker's film suggests. Despicable acts of hate speech and hate action took place recently at two major universities, putting the problem of hate squarely at the center of American life. At Stanford University, the Asian, Pacific-American, and the African-American communities were horrified in March 2001 by graffiti found in the history building and in Meyer Library. According to police, the following epithets were found in the buildings: "rape all asian bitches and dump them; rape all oriental bitches; nuke hiroshima; niggers don't get it; this is a whites only class; and nuke niggers." The next month, the entire Pennsylvania State University was placed on alert after a *Daily Collegian* reporter received two letters through the mail threatening a black leader on campus. More than a year before, racist e-mails had been sent to sixty-one high-achieving black students, but now a letter actually threatening LaKeisha Wolf—the most visible black student leader on campus— finally sounded the hate alarm. The letter stated that Wolf's time was "up" and read, "Don't you realize that I could have killed you 10 times by now—your monkey boy bodyguards notwithstanding" (Fletcher 2001, n.p.). The letter also urged college authorities to investigate Mount Nittany, which overlooks the Penn State campus, for the body of a black man. Several days after the letter's receipt, police discovered the bodies of two black men, although not on Mount Nittany. Officials denied there is any connection between the campus threats and the two victims, but minority students felt a visible "sense of exclusion and hostility," to say the least (Fletcher 2001, n.p.).

An incident at the University of Iowa reveals how easily we get caught up in hate stereotypes. After students there reported they had been victims of racial threats, a suspect was identified and arrested. At a news conference following the arrest, the vice-president for university relations inadvertently enraged the community by saying that she was surprised that it was a black dental student who was charged with harassing fellow black students. Ann Rhodes stated, "I figured it was going to be a white guy between 25 and 55, because they're the root of most evil. But what do I know?" A group calling itself the European/American Issues Forum filed a complaint with the U.S. Department of Education. It will be interesting to see whether or not the department responds to this claim. Nonetheless, the incident underscores that whether hate is directed at blacks or whites, it is no joking matter, at least at the University of Iowa.

Another chain of events at the University of North Dakota has dramatized the issue of ethnic hatred and bigotry. Like Native Americans across the country, Native American students there have challenged the name of the university's sports teams, the Fighting

Sioux, because they consider it demeaning and hateful. At sporting events, arch rival North Dakota State fans chant "Sioux suck" and wear T-shirts that show a stereotypical Native American between the legs of a bison. One Native American student commented, "[I]t's like we're not even human" (Brownstein 2001a, A47). Other critics have reported that derogatory use of the name extends far beyond athletic competition. They insist the pejorative name is a reflection of cumulative hatreds against all Native Americans. They cite the following incidents to support their claims: In 1972, fraternity members built an obscene sculpture of a naked Native American woman with a sign that read "Lick'em Sioux"; in 1992, onlookers at a homecoming parade performed a "tomahawk chop" gesture and yelled "go back to the reservation" as Native American children passed by on a float; and again in the fall of 2000, fraternity members dressed in cowboy and Indian garb pointed guns at unsuspecting Native American students. Proponents of the nickname argue that it must not be changed because it actually honors Native American traditions and cultures. This insensitivity to the impact that incendiary symbols and speech have on people is a critical problem in the persistence of hate.

An added dimension to the story of the hateful nickname has developed at the University of North Dakota. Ralph Engelstead, a Las Vegas casino owner and financial donor, has threatened to withdraw his offer of $100 million for the construction of a new hockey arena if the university drops the Fighting Sioux name. Questions about his motives revealed that Engelstead was found holding lavish celebratory parties on Hitler's birthday and displaying Nazi paraphernalia at his Imperial Palace hotel and casino. "The festivities featured a cake decorated with a swastika, German food, German marching music and...bartenders wearing T-shirts bearing the words, Adolph Hitler-European Tour 1939-45" (Brownstein 2001a, A47). Nevada state authorities fined Engelstead $1.5 million for harming the reputation of the state. A college spokesperson has now said that this story "could be a movie script" (Brownstein 2001a, A47).

Films that perpetuate stereotypes among young people are not the only ones that have serious implications for hatred in society. Like popular music, some films reflect the nihilism of our times. Two films that provide possible explanations for the type of nihilistic hatred expressed in songs by Marilyn Manson and Limp Bizkit are *Fight Club* and *American Psycho*. These films portray a different type of hater than the ones we read about in the first chapter. These films chronicle the stories of men who hate for no apparent reason other than to express anger for the excesses and contradictions of society. As we saw early on, a common type of hate crime offender is the thrill seeker. Thrill seekers, or dabblers, mostly young white males, tend to act in groups, out of boredom and restlessness.

This ennui is clearly shown in the film *Fight Club*, which is a stark, relentless tale about a group of young men who beat one another to a bloody pulp for no apparent reason other than to experience the strangely exotic thrill of pain. Although the men in *Fight Club* are not teenagers, their boredom, restlessness, and the excesses of their behavior are frightening displays of violence unleashed. One can only imagine a scenario in which the anger of these young men might become fused with a racial, ethnic, or gender hatred. The results would be catastrophic.

The second film, *American Psycho*, is the story of a young "status-obsessed Wall Street executive who commits frenzied murders in his spare time" (Harron 2000). Christian Bales stars as Patrick Bateman, the main character who slashes people as if he were engaging in sport. For Bateman, murder is an "essential lifestyle accessory." His hatred shows no bounds. He "targets men who [*sic*] he hates and women who [*sic*] he lusts after." Bateman also saves one of his mindless killings for an impoverished homeless black man whom he encounters during one of his late night prowlings. Some critics contend that Bateman turns to murder to establish a sense of self that is otherwise absent. This analysis may also apply to perpetrators of hate who are devoid of a significant sense of self, and who go in search of a surrogate identity.

Critical response to *American Psycho* was mixed. Some described it as an excellent film addressing the corruption and bankruptcy of modern consumerism. Others argued that such films as *Pulp Fiction* and *Natural Born Killers* did a better job connecting criminality, psychosis, and popular culture. Even the making of *American Psycho* came under scrutiny. In Toronto, where it was filmed, a victims' rights group tried to shut down the production. *American Psycho* is an important film for our study because Bateman's hatred displays a sickening lack of direction. If it were melded with an ideological anger, the results would be profoundly more devastating than the nihilistic hatred he exhibits.

Each of these films forces us to examine the omnipresence of racism, anger, and hatred, not only in others but in ourselves as well. As we study and talk about the characters on the screen, little bits of their ignorance, misunderstandings, and prejudices may become our own. Through the power of these cinematic images, we, the viewers, can begin loosening our own bonds of intolerance and hate. As Cohen offers in his response to *Bamboozled*, "The breadth and depth of American racism seems to grow in response to my knowledge of it. I can never catch up" (2000). If we are to catch up, we must pay attention to the cultural messages of hate. Film is a significant force in American culture, and as it reveals mounds of information about the attitudes, feelings, and inclinations of hate, we are far better off for that knowledge.

As we have noted in this analysis of contemporary film, many of the protagonists of hate have been young men. Are there women protagonists in the stories of hatred and violence? Our next chapter will explore the role of gender in the politics and culture of hate.

— Chapter 8 —
Hate and Gender

The previous chapters have addressed the depth and breadth of hatred, the law's responses, the symbiotic relationship between culture and hatred, and the media's attempt to cover hate. Our final discussion explores the fascinating role of gender and hate—not girls and women as victims of hate, but as the perpetrators of hate. Are girls and boys different with respect to their desires and abilities to cause harm? Are they socialized differently with respect to prejudices and hatreds? If there are differences in the socialization process, can we expect, for example, less hatred from young girls than from young boys? Can the literature on gender and moral development advise us about the respective inclinations for engaging in acts of hatred, harm, and violence? Have women played any historical role in white supremacist or other hate movements? These are just a few of the questions we hope to examine in this chapter.

The empirical data reveal, and much of our research supports, the contention that it is a young white male between the ages of eighteen and twenty-five who fits the prototype of a hate perpetrator. T. J. Leyden, Benjamin Smith, Dylan Klebold, and Eric Harris—their names roll quite quickly off the list of hate-mongers. Even the cultural narratives of hate—the murders of Matthew Shepard (*Anatomy of a Hate Crime*) and Brandon Teena (*Boys Don't Cry*)—portray how girls and boys are differently situated with respect to incipient prejudices. In both films, young women make desperate appeals to consensus and tolerance. In *Anatomy of a Hate Crime*, a girlfriend of one of the killers pleads with her boyfriend to control his homophobic rantings and threats of harm. In *Boys Don't Cry*, Brandon's own female friends try to reel in the uncontrollable violence of the two men who would eventually murder her. Will girls and women continue to shun hate action, as these stories suggest, or will they begin to "catch up" to the levels of violence perpetrated by young boys and men? Let us explore some of the research about gender and behavior to see why girls and women seem to be less engaged in acts of hate and violence.

Socialization has always been a determining factor in the feelings, attitudes, and behaviors of young people. Traditionally, boys and girls have been socialized quite differently—girls to be more passive and boys to be more aggressive. Gender identity is also influenced by what J. H. Block calls "agentic" and "communal" characteristics. "Agentic, or instrumental, characteristics—such as independence, self-reliance, and competence—are associated with the male sex. Communal, or expressive, traits—such as dependence, nurturance, cooperation, commitedness, intimacy, and emotionality—are associated with females" (Kearney-Cooke 2001, n.p.). Even the structure and nature of boys' play have generally been different from that of girls. Boys participate in games that are competitive and physical, whereas girls are often taught games that stress less competition and more consensus. Parents also respond differently to girls and boys and thus often inculcate these traditional and stereotypical attitudes and values in the respective sexes.

While some argue that socialization is the leading agent in the development of attitudes and behaviors, others look to biology for the answers. The presence of the male hormone, testosterone, and its role in aggression have long been recognized as an explanation for the variations in behavior between boys and girls. Empirical studies have shown that when high levels of testosterone are combined with low levels of serotonin, boys can manifest incredible impulsiveness and violence. Girls do have the hormone testosterone, but not nearly as much as boys. However, a Georgia State University study found that high testosterone levels in women inmates was linked to increased violence and aggressive dominance in prison. The findings, published in the journal *Psyschosomatic Medicine*, concluded that "testosterone's effects on behavior are the same in women as in men" (Nicholson 1997). Because it is only part of the picture, though, biology also has its limitations in explaining human behavior.

The literature on gender and moral development also provides some interesting observations about gender and hatred. Because hate is an emotion that can overlap with the moral decision to cause physical or even psychological harm, it is useful to explore some of the assumptions about moral development. Jean Piaget was one of the first to complete an extensive study of moral development. Among Piaget's original contributions were his recognition of four different stages of abstract thought in the cognitive development of children, and his belief that there were distinctions between moral judgments ruled by social constraints and those that arose internally (1932).

Lawrence Kohlberg (1981) built on Piaget's theories by assessing the ways that children and adolescents respond to moral dilemmas. He was particularly interested in the reasoning that children and adolescents used in making moral decisions. Kohlberg concluded that children exhibited an evolution in their moral thinking from original self-interest to a kind of principled behavior. He recognized three distinct levels (further subdivided into two other stages) in children's decision-making process:

(a) the preconventional level in which children ages seven to ten defer to adults and obey rules based on the immediate consequences of their actions;
(b) the conventional level, beginning around age ten, in which moral decisions are influenced by the opinions of others as well as the need to conform;
(c) the postconventional stage, beginning at adolescence, in which moral decisions are made according to communitarian interests and ethical standards. Kohlberg acknowledged that not all adolescents reach the postconventional stage of morality, and that fact should prove insightful to our study of hate and its consequences.

The most famous experiment in Kohlberg's study of moral development was the "Heinz dilemma." Kohlberg asked boys of various ages whether the husband of a critically ill woman was justified in stealing a drug from a pharmacist in order to save his wife's life. In the scenario, the pharmacist had charged the husband more than he could afford to pay for the life-saving drug. Thus, the stage was set for the children to decide the best way to proceed. Kohlberg found that children at the preconventional level generally responded, "If you steal the drug, you'll go to jail." He therefore concluded that children at this stage were premoral. The decisions at the conventional level included both approval and disapproval of the theft, depending on the influences of others in the group. However, it was Kohlberg's findings at the third level that proved critical. At the postconventional level, the boys' responses to the Heinz dilemma were based on the existence of a moral law that transcended society's prohibitions against theft. For them, the sanctity of human life superseded any other factors, including law or economics.

Kohlberg performed his test initially on young boys; only later did he include girls in the study. He found that most boys adhered to the postconventional response, as they said they would resort to stealing to save the dying wife. Kohlberg concluded that the boys' paramount concern was the right to life. Girls, on the other hand, responded quite differently to the Heinz dilemma. They encouraged negotiation and consensus between the husband and the pharmacist to reach a possible solution to the problem. Kohlberg concluded that the female approach to the Heinz dilemma was less developed morally than the boys' method, and consequently he "assumed that women's moral development was stunted" (Kearney-Cooke 2001). Do you agree with Kohlberg's findings that boys and girls respond differently with respect to moral dilemmas? [Try the Heinz experiment yourself and see whether gender impacts your responses!]

Kohlberg's contributions to the literature on moral development soon came under fire from other researchers. The most damaging critique came from his own colleague, Carol Gilligan, in her landmark book *In a Different Voice*. Gilligan criticized Kohlberg for devaluing the female response to moral problems. She insisted that males and females often interpret moral problems from two distinct orientations—the male approach, called the ethic of rights or justice, and the female approach, referred to as the ethic of care. Where boys endeavor to steal or harm to maximize and protect their rights, girls think in terms of contextual relationships and consensus. Young girls believe first and foremost that "no one should be hurt," and that there is a "universal responsibility to exercise care and avoid harm." Gilligan argues that this female paradigm of moral reasoning is equal to the male ethic of rights (1982).

Can Gilligan's theory of gender differences in moral development explain why more boys participate in acts of hatred and harm than girls generally do, or is she off-base here? Several new empirical studies now suggest that "both genders use both orientations" (Crandall 1999), so it would seem that boys and girls can be expected to behave more similarly than differently. Those who refute Gilligan's emphasis on how gender affects morality can now point to the resounding fact that more girls and women are showing up on the radar screen of hatred and violence.

Despite evidence from socialization theory, biology, and moral development literature, females are beginning to engage in the politics of hatred in a variety of ways. It would make sense that as women achieve parity with men in terms of resources, rights, and responsibilities, they would also begin to engage in similarly problematic behaviors. Let us take a look at female hatred and violence and examine the ways in which women unfortunately are achieving parity with men in these negative ways. Once considered an anomaly, incidents of violent behavior among women are definitely on the rise. Young girls are more involved in violent crime than they were a decade ago—their murder rate is up 64 percent, according to Jeanne Weiler of the Institute for Urban and Minority Education (1999). The Justice Department has reported that girls and women are responsible for 2.1 million violent crimes each year in the United States (Sniffen 2001). However, the numbers mask some important differences. Violent crimes committed by young girls still differ from those committed by boys in terms of their weapons of choice—boys tend to use guns in their acts, while girls rely more on knives. Boys and men tend to employ violence against strangers while committing other felonies. Girls and women tend to commit violence mostly against someone with whom they have had a prior relationship—a lover, husband, relative, or acquaintance.

However, these facts and observations are also changing. A request for data regarding female perpetrators of hate crimes from the U.S. Department of Justice and the FBI indicated that in 1998, twenty-nine such crimes were reported (Federal Bureau of Investigations 2001). It is interesting to note that when this request was made, officials at the Justice Department replied that it would take some time to find the information because data on women and hate are not routinely collected. When the data did arrive, they showed that women were charged with offenses ranging from intimidation to simple assault, destruction of property, weapons violation, and aggravated assault. Their offenses were further tabulated as antibisexual, anti-Black, anti-lesbian, anti-Hispanic, anti-Jewish, and a few antiwhite. The figure of female arrestees for hate crimes is low compared with the number of hate crimes committed by males. However, this fact may have something do with the overall business of reporting and collecting hate statistics. For example, in an article on juvenile female crime, writer Lindsay Wise reported that in Washington, D.C., "Teresa Dixon, 18, and Kuribia Maria Hampton, 16, were indicted on murder charges in the attack on Natalie Davis, 25, who died two days after her head was repeatedly smashed into the street, kicked, and stepped on" (Wise 1999). Absent from the police report was any reference to whether the race or ethnicity of the victim might have made the young women's actions a hate crime. Because society does not expect girls and women to be partners in hate, law enforcement institutions have been slow to encourage the reporting and analysis of their actual involvement in hate crimes.

The range of hate demonstrated by women is quite revealing, as it covers the continuum from passive engagements with hate speech to the more violent physical acts of intolerance and hatred. For example, in 2000, a Florida jury convicted Johanne Cuevas of felony battery. She had been charged with traveling from Orlando to Broward County for the express purpose of beating up a lesbian woman who belonged to a rival gang. Evidence was incontrovertible that Cuevas's gang despised homosexual activity and that Cuevas herself chose the victim because of her sexual orientation. Cuevas was subsequently sentenced to ten years in prison because a Florida statute now enhances a penalty when the motivating factor for a crime is hate.

In April 2001, two young women in Atlanta confessed to killing a Nigerian cabdriver who had picked them up as a late-night fare. Abebi Gray and Belinda Howard told police that on the same night they shot Tony Ehigie in the back of the head and robbed him of $40, they had also gone to the Lindbergh area of Atlanta "looking to rob some Mexicans." Gray and Howard confessed that since there were "too many" Mexicans to decide from, they chose a black cabdriver instead. It is painfully apparent that Gray and Howard's crime was prejudicially induced, although they were not, at first, charged with a hate crime. Detective Louie Torres commented after their arrest, "Can you imagine two young girls as killers? It makes no sense. That's our society today" (Good 2001). Torres's remark is evidence of society's reluctance to acknowledge the participation of women in hate. When asked about why young women would become violent against strangers, Jim DeGroot, a psychologist at the Georgia Department of Corrections, stated, "Some say as genders become more equal, they're becoming more equal on many levels" (Good 2001). This is the very argument that we are making—hate is beginning to make unfortunate inroads among females.

Even teenage girls are getting into the act of violent physical hatreds. In March 2001, one young girl received headline coverage with still another high school shooting. In fact, Elizabeth Catherine Bush, an eighth-grade student at a private Roman Catholic school in Williamsport, Pennsylvania, now has the notoriety of being the first female school shooter in more than three decades. Remember that girls traditionally use knives in the commission of violent acts. This case suggests that the times are definitely changing. Just days after the Santee, California, shooting in which Andy Williams murdered two fellow students, Bush left a Lenten Mass, walked into the cafeteria, and shot classmate Kimberly Marchese with a .22-caliber pistol that she had taken from her father. After the shooting, Bush placed the gun to her own head, but school officials stopped her from that self-destructive act. The reason given for Bush's actions—hatred against Marchese for taunting and bullying. It was reported that Marchese was a popular cheerleader who ran with a "cool crowd" from whom Bush wanted acceptance (Morse 2001).

A 1998 study by the National Institute of Child Health and Human Development found that of students in grades 6 through 10, one out of every three was adversely affected by bullying during the school day (Fitzgerald 2001). The study reported that while boys resort to hits, slaps, and pushing as part of their bullying profile, girls rely on nasty comments and spreading rumors. That observation indicates what we already suspect: Whereas girls and women are slowly entering the domain of physical hatred, as the previous incidents suggest, their true commitment to hatred rests in the realm of speech.

In Joliet, Illinois, for example, a sixty-six-year-old Franciscan nun was arrested for scrawling racist hate graffiti on the walls of the emergency room lobby at Provena St. Joseph Medical Center (Newswire 1999). Riki Wilchins, a transgendered person who was born a male and had sex reassignment surgery to become a woman, related her painful experience with hate speech. Wilchins, executive director of GenderPac, an organization based on gender rights and equality awareness, was invited to give a talk at Virginia Tech by the Lesbian, Gay, Bisexual, and Transgender Alliance. Wilchins declared, "Even the woman's [sic] community called me a self-mutilating transvestite, and said I was not welcome" (Baab 2001). Girls and women are also using speech to promote hate deception, a manipulative type of behavior that many believe fuels the already festering environment of intolerance. In 1992, three white females told police they were maliciously assaulted by a dozen black teens on their way to school in Staten Island. The women later admitted cutting themselves and fabricating the story to skip school (Jacobs and Potter 1998). In 1999, at St. Cloud University in Minnesota, a female student perpetrated a hate fraud on the college community that actually increased dissension and anger there. Jennifer Prissel, a senior at the university, reported to police that two men had assaulted her in a parking lot, punching her several times in the face, while yelling antigay slurs at her. News of the incident brought the community together, and a reward fund was started to encourage the capture of the perpetrators of this "hate" incident. Shortly after the local community had raised more than $12,000 to combat hate, Ms. Prissel told law enforcement officials that she had contrived the entire event (Gose 1999).

Two years earlier, another incident occurred when a young woman at Eastern New Mexico University fabricated a similar tale of hate. Miranda Prather told police that she was attacked after an antigay hit list had been posted at a nearby laundromat. Ms. Prather was later arrested after police learned that she had posted the antigay flyer, and had even cut herself with a kitchen knife to fake the alleged assault (Gose 1999). Why are these young women identifying themselves as victims and contriving scenarios of hate that further exacerbate intolerance? Why, in many of these stories, are young girls resorting to self-mutilation in order to mimic acts of hatred? Perhaps women are so familiar with real victimization that they need few incentives to invent false narratives of harm.

One of the most infamous examples of racial fabrication and

hate was the Susan Smith case. Smith was convicted in 1994 of drowning her two young sons. Her arrest came only after she had blamed the horrific act on a fictitious black man whom she alleged had hijacked her car. Many who heard her initial story had no difficulty accepting the accusations. Smith's despicable lies further demonized the black male and nurtured the already existing antipathy against men of color. Why, as the Smith case suggests, is it so easy to accept as truth these stories of betrayal? The answer is the alarming acceptance of racial, gender, and ethnic hatred in mainstream thinking, fostered by the media and popular culture.

When recounting examples of deception and hate, one is also reminded of the Tawana Brawley case. In 1987, in the New York town of Wappinger Falls, Brawley was discovered in a dumpster covered with dog feces and with racial slurs tattooed over her body. Brawley, who is black, accused six white police officers of abducting, assaulting, and raping her. It was later determined that Brawley had contrived the entire story—but the ramifications of the event certainly fueled the race card of hate. However, the Brawley story seems different from the Smith narrative. Critical race theorists argue that the accusations Brawley made against the white officers were in no way equivalent to the enduring damage Smith did to black men. Patricia Williams writes, "Brawley was the victim of some unspeakable crime....No matter who did it to her—and even if she did it to herself....Few will believe a black woman who has been raped by a white man....[T]he quiet, nearly invisible story of her suffering may never emerge from the clamor that overtook the quest for what happened" (MacFarquhar 1996). The Smith and Brawley deceptions promoted racial hatred on many sides, but only some agree with the analysis put forth by the critical race scholars.

Clearly, women are now involved in hate. In fact, women have always been participants in the long, unfortunate history of American hatred, as Kathleen Blee reminds us in her book, *Women in the Klan*. According to Blee, women were involved in both documented waves of Klan activity in the United States (1991). The 1860s and the 1920s were decades with two distinct movements in terms of KKK identity, and women played a significant role in both. The common thread in those two periods was the unqualified intention of Klansmen "to protect threatened white womanhood and white female purity." The first wave of Klan activity used as their initial rallying cry the notion of the imperiled southern white woman facing the violent possibility of rape by newly freed black men. This threat of sexual violation of helpless white women by black men was more than just an acknowledgment of tense white/black relations. According to some feminist analyses, it was also about the "threat to white men's sexual privileges" and about their own sense of dominion and power over women. During the first Klan wave, white women were absent from its actual membership, but they were, by their own complicity, the coalescing symbol and strategy for the organization and for the ensuing hatred by their white men.

The second wave of Klan activity played out a somewhat different scenario. By the mid-1920s, the number of both men and women in the Klan had grown to an astonishing 4 million. Although imperiled womanhood was still a rallying cry, this second Klan movement was considerably different. This Klan movement witnessed the presence of its first female leader, Elizabeth Tyler. It is sobering to learn that it was Tyler, along with Edward Clark, who was responsible for broadening the scope and magnitude of Klan hatred to include Catholics, Jews, and immigrants in addition to African Americans. Why would any woman—herself a member of a class of people so historically oppressed and often despised—lead the crusade to discover new targets for the passions of hatred? Perhaps it was the logical attempt by Tyler to divert the energies of misogynistic hatred away from women. Why would any woman want to identify with "reactionary politics"? Scholars suggest that women, like men, become interested in extremist right-wing groups because of "social marginality" (Blee 1991, 102). The answer for Blee, however, was the Klan's appeal to women "through the symbol of home, family, and women's rights." Interestingly enough, this appeal attracts white supremacist women even now.

Today, women's presence in the ever-expanding landscape of hate is flourishing in a much different domain—that of the Internet. Speech seems to remain the predominate mode of women's hatred, and it is a hatred that ranges from the vitriolic language of white supremacists to the casual expressions of racism by impressionable young girls. In fact, teenage girls have made one of the biggest contributions to the growth of female Internet users, and this fact is critical to our argument about gender and hate. As of August

2000, the number of girls and women on-line surpassed boys and men for the first time. Females, ages two and up, accounted for 50.4 percent of the total number of U.S. Internet users, according to Internet research firms Media Matrix and Jupiter Communications (Klein and Johnson 2000). Although the Internet was originally a male-dominated bastion—the early Web pioneers such as Netscape founder Marc Andreeseen, Yahoo's Jerry Yang, and AOL's Steve Case were men—women have steadily begun to find parity on-line.

How exactly have females begun to use the Internet to weave the symbols of home, family, and rights into their own tapestry of hate? According to the Anti-Defamation League (1998a), among the hundreds of Web sites devoted to promoting hate, numerous sites are now being created and run by women. In a report titled "Feminism Perverted: Extremist Women of the World Wide Web," the ADL identifies such sites as Her Race, World Church of the Creator, Women's Frontier, and Women for Aryan Unity (1998a). At the various sites women talk about their heroines—Phyllis Schlafly, Klan martyr Kathy Ainsworth, and the more recent Christian martyr Vicki Weaver, of Ruby Ridge fame. At the Her Race web site, Nancy Jensen, who says she is a National-Socialist female majoring in premed at an Ivy League university, writes: "Nature intended that women use their brains to advance their race—look at the Talmud—the Jews are the ones who advocate treating women as breeding tools and property" (ADL 1998a). For Jensen, joining her white male counterparts in the workplace is the only way to attain gender equality. What is paradoxical about Jensen's belief is that her progressive view of workplace parity is linked to a perversely vicious hatred. Her feminist contribution to gender equality is diminished by her angry racism. Jane Burton, also writing on the Her Race site, concurs with Jensen in an article on the appropriate careers for white women, which include lawyer, human resource worker, advertising writer, and real estate agent. Her views, like Jensen's, do promote the success of women in the public sphere. However, are the ideas worth it if they come with the hateful baggage of white supremacist ideology? Clearly not!

Other themes articulated by white extremist women on the Internet are hatred of miscegenation, anger at the alleged "anti-white control of the media," and a denunciation of feminism as a

Marxist-Zionist plot to destroy the white race. This attack on feminism is confusing since expanding female workplace rights is part of the white supremacist women's thinking. The World Church of the Creator's Lisa Turner, a leader in the white women's movement, speaks to several of the hateful themes mentioned above. In her Web site essay, "Lessons from the Death of Princess Diana," Turner argues that it was a sad day when "a woman of such racial beauty and purity—this English Rose—had the propensity for race-mixing relationships." Turner's racist remark that Diana "might have been pregnant with Fayed's child at her death, indicating her willingness to be ultimate traitor to the white race" (2000) leaves the reader with a chill at the vehemence of Turner's hatred.

As for her views on the media, Turner writes, "[W]hite people are subjected to anti-white images via television and motion pictures because the enemy forces have total control of the film world and business." She also contemplates a "White people's Oscars at which whites all sit together in a dazzling hall and applaud as our enemies do now for their lackeys" (2000). Turner's propaganda is grossly inaccurate as our chapter on television stereotypes and the media argues. She is also relentless in her efforts to recruit women to the white supremacist movement. Her pitch is "desperately seeking angry white females" who are willing to respond to the dictum "grow or die." As Randy Blazak, assistant professor of sociology at Portland State University, observes, "[T]hey need as many bodies as possible" (McCafferty 1999).

As more working women are facing layoffs and increased competition with minorities, white supremacists believe there is a growing pool of newly alienated women to target. Blee reports that women now compose 50 percent of all new recruits to hate groups! (McCafferty 1999) One report revealed that a group of young mothers working for the World Church of the Creator even went to a local mall and placed Creator recruitment cards in jeans pockets at a variety of clothing stores. Turner also bragged that these mothers insert hate literature in library books and in popular magazines, such as *Glamour* and *Mademoiselle*. Should we be concerned that they are finding targets for their virulent hatred? Absolutely! Turner also claims that on her e-mail list, she has more than two hundred women from various businesses and institutions —some of them college students at prestigious universities such as

Cornell, Stanford, and Harvard. As Turner writes, "They're sick and tired of the propaganda dished out in their college classrooms, like the Holocaust." You may recall from chapter 7 how Stanford University was beset with incidents of hate speech and graffiti. One is left to wonder whether it is now young women who may also be the egregious wrongdoers.

Read the following narrative of this young female high school student and listen to her hatred:

> Today, like everyday, I walked like a robot through the halls of my high-school. Today for a reason unknown to me I did look up and was not surprised to see the usual pack of 11 to 13 black students stomping through the hall in their oversized clothes and expensive shoes...they were of course followed by their adoring fans...the lost white students who admire and envy their dark skin, squalid unwashed hair and awfully incorrect English....like so many highschools, mine is being overrun with these animals....I am completely alone and passionate with my beliefs...teachers will punish me for disagreeing with them about a Shakespeare theme, but will ignore black students who throw food and expose their testicles to white females (From Jessica 2001).

This young woman seems ripe for recruitment by a group such as Turner's, and the World Wide Web is the place where she may inevitably find that connection. A current WCOTC member recently stated that "she has maintained an interest in supremacist groups since she was 13. But she had no idea how to get involved until the Web opened up a whole new world for me" (McCafferty 1999, n.p.). These sentiments illustrate how women are beginning to use the private sphere of the Internet to participate in hate as men concurrently employ the public sphere for their hate involvement.

What is particularly troublesome about women's role in hate is how the white supremacist ideology is juxtaposed with the idea of motherhood. As the primary caretakers in many families, mothers have extraordinary influence over the lives of their children. Envisioning these white supremacist women as nurturers of the intellectual and emotional life of children generates real fear and trepidation. One such mother, who recently abandoned her racist lifestyle as a member of a white supremacist group, spoke to a *20/20* reporter about the powerful influences of women and mothers as haters (ABCNEWS.com 2000).

Kirsten Kaiser spent nine years as the wife of one of the leaders of National Alliance, living with him in a separatist compound, raising three children under the tutelage of hateful beliefs, and eventually divorcing him because of the "horror" of his unrelenting hatred. One of the most difficult tasks Kaiser now faces is the challenge of undoing the "metastasizing hate" that continues to adversely affect her children. She reports that she must remain vigilant in fighting her ex-husband's continuing negative socialization of the children. Although Kaiser was able to extricate herself from the white supremacist grip, she worries about the other "numerous American women now teaching their children the message of hate" (ABCNEWS.com 2000, n.p.). For example, Christian Teague brought her six-year-old and nine-month-old daughters to the Aryan Nations 400-Man Flag Parade in Coeur d'Alene, Idaho, in the summer of 1999. Christian's six-year-old carried the Nazi flag (Benfer 1999). When anti-Nazi protesters tried to lure the girl away from her mother, Christian urged her daughter to "hold the flag up straighter and show them your heil." When the protesters became more even verbal, another "young Nazi mother cradled a baby in one hand and used the other to punch a young man repeatedly in the face until he was bloody" (Benfer 1999).

Look at the following sample clues from a crossword puzzle for children found on the World Church of the Creator Web site—it is a chilling reminder of the powerful influences of mothers over the minds of their children:

>Across:
>7. ____ are sub-human.
>12. The Jew is the human ____.
>Down:
>2. The niggers of Africa never so much as invented the ____.
>4. We must try to ____ the White race at all times. (2000, n.p.)

Mothers who direct their children to this puzzle are teaching them to hate. These mothers are a new breed of women. These new qualities of motherhood are in direct contrast to traditional behaviors. "Women, through the ages revered for their qualities of compassion, sensitivity, organization, intelligence and empathy, are now using those very same qualities as the recruiters and the new leaders of the armies of hatred" (ABCNEWS.com 2001).

Women are also serving as leaders in hate groups. "Barriers are breaking down," writes Jocelyn Benson of the Southern Poverty Law Center. "[T]hey're seeing shortcomings in male leadership, so they're turning to fill the void" (SPLC 1999). A 1999 SPLC newsletter reported the strange story of a woman named Cortney Mann, who has been the leader of the racist National Association for the Advancement of White People (NAAWP) for the past four years and "who is, bizarrely, black!" (SPLC 1999) Finally, how interesting that Carol Gilligan's identification of women's ethic of care—sensitivity, empathy, and connectedness—is now functioning as the cornerstone for white supremacist women's initiatives on hatred.

What can we conclude about the growing presence of women eager to express emotions and actions of hatred? It is interesting to note here that young girls, like their male counterparts, now even have their own all-girl metal band to articulate these hatreds. A new Canadian band calling itself Kittie, whose three female members range in age from fifteen to sixteen, have now established a presence in the male-dominated world of heavy-metal music. As Mike Ross of *The Edmonton Sun* reports on one of their performances, "Kittie does, in fact, scratch and bite its way through a set of noisy expletive-riddled songs seething with anger and alienation" (2000). Remember the young girls from the chapter on hate music who thought Eminem was great—they also rave about Kittie and its angry belligerence!

Finally, does the fact that most women practice their hatred in the relative safety of cyberspace make it less dangerous? Are women still "kinder" than men in that their hatred is mostly reserved for the realm of speech and not action? It does seem that women are prominent in the domain of hate speech. Critical race theorists such as Mari Matsuda do not believe that this type of hate is less reprehensible. Matsuda argues that "much of what we experience as reality is actually constructed by, and preserved in, language," and that "we as a culture are so certain about what hate speech is, and so certain that it is bad, that we can allow courts to treat it differently from other kinds of speech" (MacFarquhar 1996). This statement is a powerful injunction for girls and women who use the privacy of the Internet to broaden the realm of hate. Does women's willingness to engage in hate speech signal a prelude to greater and future physical acts of violence, similar to the ones committed by their male counterparts? It is hard to tell. If, however, our argument about hatred as a cultural norm is at all accurate, then women, along with men, will continue to be its unfortunate and despicable messengers.

— Chapter 9 —
The Future of Hate

We have given ourselves a break from writing about hate and have decided to visit some local landmarks. Even on our day off, though, we cannot escape the presence of hatred in our society. Our wanderings take us to Jefferson County, West Virginia, home of Harpers Ferry National Park and the Jefferson County Courthouse in Charles Town. Why are these areas associated with hate? Before the Civil War, Harpers Ferry was the site chosen by abolitionist John Brown to take his stand against the hatred of slavery. The fire station where Brown holed up before his capture remains in the park, overlooking the confluence of the Shenandoah and Potomac rivers. Less than ten miles away stands the Jefferson County Courthouse, where Brown was tried and hanged for his beliefs. A plaque commemorating his actions stands in front of the courthouse, reminding visitors of his commitment to eradicate the institution of slavery.

Our visit prompts us to question the enduring nature of hatred. We ask ourselves first, can society agree on what constitutes hate? Hate is so mainstream that when it stares us in the face, we ignore it. The advertisement placed in college newspapers by David Horowitz demonstrates how easily society can deflect discussions about hate. So what will help us recognize and acknowledge the effects of hate? We hope that by presenting the story of a victim of hate in this chapter, our readers will be better able to understand the corrosive nature of hate. Finally, we question what types of steps can be taken to overcome the hold hatred has on mainstream values and thought.

Through the course of this book, we have examined the nature of hatred, laws against hatred, and its manifestations in society and culture. Every day, though, we are inundated with additional stories of hate. From school shootings, to racist e-mails, to the fiery discussion of race reparations, we are constantly under pressure to redefine and come to terms with what constitutes hatred. Are school shootings a manifestation of hatred? If one African-American police officer uses the "n" word in an e-mail communication with another African-American officer, is it an inoffensive exchange between two peers, or is it an example of institutional hatred? Is an advertisement denouncing reparations to African Americans for the harm done by slavery an effort to raise substantive policy issues, or an in-your-face attempt to perpetuate hatred under the guise of free speech?

To help us focus on the expanding definition of hate and how it so easily finds its way into mainstream consciousness of society, let us first examine the debate over the race reparations advertisement that ran in some college newspapers in the spring of 2001. The advertisement, which was placed by David Horowitz, caused anger, resentment, rage, and hatred on campuses as diverse as Brown University, the University of Wisconsin–Madison, and the University of California at Berkeley. Horowitz is a former left-wing radical who turned right-wing conservative. Now he is the president of the Center for the Study of Popular Culture, and he previously edited *Ramparts* magazine, a well-known leftist publication that regularly attacked the United States' involvement in the Vietnam War (Powell 2001a).

Since the U.S. Supreme Court's *New York Times v. Sullivan* decision in 1964, editorial advertisements have been protected as free speech. However, student newspapers in all but a handful of the fifty-two schools to which Horowitz submitted the ad either rejected it outright or delayed publication while they sought advice from publications committees. Schools that chose not to publish the ad included Harvard, the University of Virginia, and Columbia University. The ad was titled "Ten Reasons Why Reparations for Blacks is a Bad Idea for Blacks—and Racist Too." It argued that African Americans have already been the beneficiary of a certain type of reparations—welfare and race preferences. The ad also argued that the standard of living for African Americans is better than that of their African counterparts, and that reparations would be another means of promoting the "victim" status of African Americans (Brownstein 2001b).

The ad prompted outrage on campuses where it was published. At Brown, 4,000 copies of the paper were stolen and presumably destroyed. At the University of Wisconsin–Madison, one hundred protestors stormed the office of the student newspaper, but the staff refused to give them what they wanted—an apology for running the ad (Ferdinand 2001). In addition to the protests, the ad prompted student editors and mainstream political commentators across the country to editorialize about the issue. Most of the columns were commentaries about the nature of free speech on a college campus. They defended the right of newspapers to accept (or reject) any advertisement they choose. Greg Pessin, the editor of the Duke University *Chronicle*, defended his paper's decision to publish the ad on free speech grounds. "We believe that a newspaper, a nation, and especially a university should be committed to free and open debate. We realize that this advertisement—like some of our content that appears daily—is offensive to our readers....It is important to remember the free exchange of ideas and open debate sometimes comes at the cost of comfort" (Beaver and Brush 2001).

Two perceptive commentaries focused more on Horowitz's tactics than on the nature of the ad. One was written by Jason Weinstein of the *Daily Sun* at Cornell University, which chose not to run the ad. Weinstein called Horowitz's manipulation tactics "plain-old underhanded." "He sent out $10,000 worth of advertising to college papers and in return has received millions in free advertising thanks to the knee-jerk reactions on campuses across the country. For Horowitz it's great. For the rest of the world, he's created a headache by preying on people's fears and angers. He used people's emotions as a tool for his personal gain" (2001). In a separate commentary, Bryan Nichols of the *Iowa State Daily* agreed. Calling Horowitz a "pompous self-serving publicity whore," Nichols pointed out that the ad did exactly what Horowitz desired:

> He's managed to make himself look like a paradigm of sagacity as he delivers lectures and letters to the editor on what free speech "really" means. Worst of all, he's managed to take the spotlight off of his poor arguments and refocus it on his plight to stop the 'liberal double standards' of free speech.... It allows him to look like the calm one when he was really the original instigator (2001).

Not everyone who disagreed with the ad's message believed it should be censored. For an article in *The Lantern* at Ohio State University, reporter Phil Helsel spoke with Chris Dawkins, a board member of the Urban Business Professional Association. Dawkins said the issue of slave reparations "is an important one and should be discussed openly. My feeling, contrary to some African-Americans, is that it should be published. The more dialogue we have on this subject the better it will be" (Helsel 2001). However, as is evident from the above discussion, the ad generated little dialogue on the subject of reparations itself.

Only a few commentators zeroed in on the hateful message embedded in the advertisement. Richard Cohen of *The Washington Post* was one of them. In his column titled "Specious Speech," Cohen wrote:

> Word for word, the ad makes sense. Something about it, though, is wrong. What's wrong is the message contained between the lines. What's wrong is its casual breeziness, its failure to acknowledge the pain of racism and the horror of slavery, the way it treats the commerce in human beings as something akin to a drought—a Dust Bowl for blacks (2001).

In that same commentary, Cohen also defended the free speech rights of the editors who chose to run the ad. He opposed "trashing" newspapers. Instead, he suggested, "Cancel your subscription if you like, but don't deny others the right to read what they choose." Like many liberal defenders of the First Amendment, Cohen wants to have it both ways—he wants to criticize the hateful message, but he defends the right to publish it. We must ask, though, how society can reconcile the hurt the words cause with the freedom that allows them to be disseminated. We can defend the ad on First Amendment grounds, but we cannot measure the damage it does. Will such an ad reinforce the negative stereotypes of African Americans held by hate sympathizers and hate spectators? Will it make it more difficult for African Americans to enjoy their full civil rights? There is no way to tell for sure.

Some commentators called Horowitz a publicity hound. He believes he is an ardent defender of the First Amendment. Others feel he is a hatemonger. You can decide for yourself. What is telling about the controversy over the advertisement he placed, though, is the reaction it engendered. For mainstream America, it quickly became an issue of free speech and another example of "liberal" college campuses enforcing political correctness. *The Washington Post* interviewed four college newspaper editors whose papers were offered the ad. Two accepted it; two didn't. The paper devoted a full page in a Sunday Opinion section to the interview, running long verbatim quotes from the editors. Even in that discussion, little was said about either the substance or the effect of the advertisement. Instead, the editors who chose not to run the ad defended their decision on economic grounds. Jennifer Kepka, editor of *The Eagle* at American University in Washington, D.C., said, "We would have lost advertisers and readers if we had run that ad; it was a sound business decision to reject it" (2001). To reduce the controversy over this ad to economics diminishes the harm it caused.

Why were the hateful words in the advertisement largely ignored? Was it because the words reflect the views about reparations held by many Americans, so it became safer to debate the right to publish rather than the right to reparations? Even President George W. Bush refused to address the substance of race reparations when his administration warned it would not attend the World Conference Against Racism in Durban, South Africa, in 2001, if the topics of reparations and Zionism appeared on the agenda. In the end, the administration sent only a low-level delegation instead of Secretary of State Colin Powell.

As for the ad, the emotional hurt felt by the students most directly affected was largely devalued, and what became paramount was the First Amendment rights of student editors to run the ad. In fact, those editors who chose not to run the ad, or who apologized after running it, were vilified as "cowards" by Mark Passwaters, a columnist for *The Battalion* at the University of Texas. Ironically, editors at his paper were not forced to decide whether they should run the ad because it was not sent to them (2001). Suzanne Fields, a columnist for *The Washington Times*, rejected the reaction that some African-American students felt after reading the ad. She argued that the students who experienced a physical reaction to the ad actually only had their feelings hurt, and were just trying to silence, to censor, those who disagreed with them. Note particularly the last sentence of the following quote from her column, to which we have added italics.

> Many students—and their teachers, who ought to know better—merely get their feelings hurt and demand silence from those who disagree

with them. "This racist attack on black students sets a very dangerous precedent," Kenneth Knies, a teaching assistant in the Afro-American studies department told the Brown Daily Herald. "I have talked to students who told me that they can't perform basic functions like walking or sleeping because of this ad." *(Walking and chewing gum at the same time, as in Lyndon Johnson's famous putdown of Gerald Ford, would surely be out of the question.)* (2001).

Our discussion of hate speech, however, has pointed out that it can be as harmful as hate actions. The physical reaction experienced by the victims of hate speech is often akin to suffering from post-traumatic stress disorder. Fields's decision not to acknowledge, and in fact to mock, that reaction echoes the underlying hatred found in society.

The furor over this ad demonstrates both how omnipresent hate is, and how willing society is to avoid discussing its consequences. In this case, the mainstream media allowed the message to flourish because it could not, or would not, admit that it was hateful. After the ad was published, the argument over it focused neither on the right or wrong of reparations, nor on the harm slavery has inflicted on society to this day. Instead, it became a fight over whether or not Horowitz had a "free speech" right to promulgate his hateful point of view. Those who opposed him were cast not as defenders of a civil society but as opponents of the sacrosanct First Amendment. Once again, hate was left out of the discussion.

At this juncture, we need to address head-on this critical issue of free speech versus censorship. Throughout this book, we have presented the CLS viewpoint that speech that causes harm should be restricted. Critical legal studies scholars argue that words do wound and as a result, they should be punished as the equivalent to actions. Will restricting speech truly end hatred? Should hate speech be punished in the same way as hate actions? Will punishing hate speech deter hate actions? Will punishing hate actions deter hatred? Let us examine some of these questions.

Does punishing hate actions deter hatred? We can answer this question by discussing the difference between general and special deterrence. The philosophy behind general deterrence is that imposing strict penalties on individuals who commit particular crimes will influence other people's future behavior. The failure of the death penalty to prevent killings indicates that general deterrence does not work as well as some lawmakers hope it will. The death penalty does accomplish one goal, though. It makes it impossible for the person who committed the crime—a murder perhaps—to commit another one; this is called special deterrence. In addition, imposition of the death penalty sends a message that as a society, we believe that murder is a crime against society as well as a crime against an individual.

A similar argument could be made about enhancing punishment for hate crimes. Hate crime laws in general may not deter individuals from targeting a person because of his or her race or ethnicity. What it will do, though, is serve as a notice that society abhors crimes of hate. It sends a message to the perpetrator, who may be convicted of violating a specific hate statute, that this type of behavior is unacceptable and punishable.

Will restricting or punishing speech end hatred? Probably not. The First Amendment is designed to allow different opinions on issues of importance to democracy. Certainly, hate is one of those issues. Even between the authors of this book there is disagreement about whether speech should be restricted and punished. One of us believes that tolerance of hate speech is dangerous because it damages the victim, it permits the culture of hatred to flourish, and it undermines the integrity of society. In censoring hate speech, society would be requiring its citizens to strive for a higher ethical and moral plane. The other author is a First Amendment defender. She acknowledges that it is hard to argue against the need for a better, more tolerant, more civil society. Nor does she believe that speech carries no consequences. It does hurt, and it can lead to psychological and perhaps physical harm. How many of us—whether or not we are minorities—can say we have never been teased, taunted, or bullied? How did it feel? We need only look at the school shootings at Columbine and in Santee, California, to see the effects. Nevertheless, our nation is firmly grounded in the philosophy that all opinions and views ought to be aired. Will censoring William Pierce or Matt Hale or anyone who might harbor hateful feelings make them hate less? It is more likely to drive them underground where they are apt to do more damage. Who has hurt more people—Matt Hale, who regularly spouts hate speech, or Timothy McVeigh, who kept many of his opinions to himself?

Matt Hale seeks publicity, and every time he or the KKK or another white supremacist holds a rally, dozens of protesters show up to offer opposing viewpoints. WCOTC rallies galvanize communities to oppose hate. It is the marketplace of ideas at work. As we will see later in this chapter, a hate crime in Jefferson County, West Virginia, led to some real dialogue among the races about the nature of hate and ways to combat it.

Finally, should hate speech or symbolic hate be punished in the same way as hate actions? The Supreme Court firmly rejected that approach in *RAV v. St. Paul*. As the 9th Circuit Court of Appeals decision in The Nuremburg Files case demonstrates, it is only when speech leads to immediate violence that it can be punished (American Health Line 2001). No matter how abhorrent the words are, they are protected. Unless and until there is a sea change in the Supreme Court's attitude toward speech, it is unlikely that hate speech will be punishable.

We have argued in this book that hatred is an integral part of our national psyche. However, we only hear about a small number of the hate incidents that occur every day. The ad placed by David Horowitz engendered a great deal of national media attention, as did, for example, the hate-driven school shooting at Columbine High School. Even so, most hate incidents do not make it to the national media radar screen. In fact, it takes an unusual combination of factors to involve the national media. Most hate incidents—whether they involve words or actions—are publicized only by local media. Even then, it sometimes takes a push by the victim, or a relative of the victim, for the incident to receive the attention it deserves.

That thought takes us back to Jefferson County, West Virginia. In September 2000, a hate incident occurred in which a young African-American man named Derrick Berry was threatened by a white man holding a gun. It took almost two weeks for the incident to receive any publicity. In fact, it is questionable whether it would have received any notice if Berry's sister had not contacted the local newspaper in Martinsburg, West Virginia, about the threats made against her brother. Even then, the story could have ended with the article in *The Journal*. Instead, it reverberated through the community, prompting the local chapter of the NAACP and a community civil rights organization known as FAIR (Friends

Advancing Intercultural Relations) to sponsor an open meeting on hate crimes.

It is important to point out that West Virginia is not a very diverse state. According to the 2000 Census, 95 percent of the 1.8 million people who live there identify themselves as white. Only 3.2 percent of the population are black or African-American. The percentage is a bit higher in the Eastern Panhandle of the state, where Jefferson County is located. The county, about sixty miles northwest of Washington, D.C., has grown considerably in the past ten years, 17.4 percent in comparison with the state's rate of 0.8 percent. It has become a magnet for families, mostly white, escaping from the Washington suburbs. In Jefferson County, 6.1 percent of the 42,190 residents are Black, 1.7 percent are of Hispanic or Latino origin, and another 1.4 percent reported being of two or more races (U.S. Census Bureau 2001).

Given the relatively small minority population, one might think hate should not be as much of a problem because the white population should not feel threatened. However, as the Berry incident and an incident involving the president of the school board illustrate, racism and hatred are facts of life even in communities with only a few minority residents. Hatred is mainstream, and it can happen anywhere.

As the first black president of the Jefferson County Board of Education, Larry Togans is one of the most prominent African Americans in the county. In February 2001, he received a threatening e-mail from a senior at the county high school. Ostensibly, the e-mail was sent because the board voted to change the date of the high school's graduation, and the student who sent it was upset because the new date conflicted with her planned entry into the military. However, the e-mail read in part, "[Y]a know, it's pretty bad, when people I know, myself included, who are not prejudiced, commented that there was going to be a lynching, get a rope and find a tree" (Partlow 2001). The student involved was not charged with committing a hate crime. Instead, she was charged with a misdemeanor assault. The county sheriff defended the lesser charge, saying, "[I]f it was a hate crime, the threat has to be based on the fact that it was done because of race. In this case, the threat was because he was running the school board" (Partlow 2001).

Black leaders in the county were outraged by the diminution of the threat. George Rutherford, president of the local chapter of the NAACP, said, "You talk about a lynching; to a Black person, that's a death threat" (Partlow 2001). James Tolbert, state NAACP president, also criticized the charge. "It was explicit. It was something, I think, a whole lot more serious than the police are making it" (Partlow 2001).

This incident once again illustrates the gap between the way whites and blacks perceive hate speech. White officials in the county either did not understand, or chose to ignore, the significant link between the wording of the threat and Togan's race. Critical race theorists argue that words are powerful, and as we have pointed out, they take speech very seriously. In this instance, they would advocate punishing not just the general threat, but also the words used to express the threat. The incident involving Derrick Berry included both a verbal and a physical threat. To compound the injury, after Berry had been accosted by two white men, he was subjected to a form of institutional hatred. He was stopped by police and tested for gunpowder to determine if he was the one who had perpetrated the incident.

Scholars who advance critical race theory believe that when victims of hate are urged to tell their stories in a narrative fashion, their voices and their stories become more powerful. They call this "empowerment through language: the creation of new myths to replace the old damaging ones" (MacFarquhar 1996, 44). These narratives do a better job demonstrating the urgent need for change in society than the brief description and the few quotes that one can find in a newspaper article. In that vein, we would like to offer Jacqui Puller's narrative of what happened to her brother, Derrick Berry, on the night of 4 September 2000. Puller described the hate incident for us in an interview in November 2000. As she notes, her brother was devastated by the incident, and he has been reluctant to talk about it.

Both Berry and Puller grew up in Jefferson County and attended local schools. She believes that despite the relatively small number of blacks in the county, racism and hatred are as pervasive there as everywhere else. "Being a black person, being a black woman, it's constant. You just learn over the years just to bypass it. You block it out like you block out a child crying. You just block it out, but it's always there."

Puller set up the narrative by explaining that Derrick was at his girlfriend's house on the night of the incident. The girlfriend does not have a phone, so when he wanted to make a phone call and buy some juice, he decided to walk to the convenience store at the local Texaco station. Among the people in the parking lot of the store were some white men in two tow trucks. As you read this story, imagine yourself in Derrick Berry's position. Think about how you would have reacted at the time, and how you would have felt later.

Puller described what happened:

"*Derrick was going up to the store. When the incident happened, it was roughly a little after twelve. So, he walked to the store to use the pay phone and to get some juice. Well, when he got there, he was proceeding to go into the store. That's when he noticed a bunch of guys in the parking lot. He just kept walking and that's when they yelled the remark, as far as do you need a tow. 'We tow niggers for $65.' I think it was $65, something like that. I don't know the exact price. It was a bunch of people, two tow trucks, another truck, couple of other cars, so how many was driving, plus friends?*

"*So he [Derrick] proceeded, and as they said the remark to him, he said, 'Do you all have a problem with me?'*

"*He's not a dummy, and he said there's too many of them, so he continued to walk into the store to get his juice and to use the phone. And luckily on his way out, he was standing inside the door, and he noticed a friend. A guy pulled up in a red truck, and he [Derrick] noticed a passenger, and he knew him—another white guy that he went to school with. So he asked him if he could get a ride home and they said sure. So as they proceeded to try to go out to the parking lot, and they got to one of the stop signs, that's when the incident happened.*

"*One of the tow trucks blocked them from the front, and as they proceeded to back up, another one came up and rammed them from the back, so they were totally blocked in. As they were blocked in, that's when the gentleman who was driving [the truck Derrick was in] proceeded to step out of the truck and said, 'Hey, you're blocking me in. Move so I can get my car out.' As he was going out, that's when the guy, Hanna [Brian K. Hanna, who was later charged in the incident], he comes up with a gun and puts the gun to the white guy's face/head first [the passenger in the truck]. That's when he [Hanna] started screaming the remarks.*

"*My brother said he was screaming, 'White supremacists;' 'Where's the nigger at?' 'I'm going to kill that nigger.' Also, something about he was a* skinhead. I know that was one of the remarks, too, about being a skinhead. And that's when he shot up in the air the first time. He pulled the gun from the guy's hair and shot up in the air. And then that's when he said 'where's the nigger at?' and looked in the backseat and saw my brother.

"He [Hanna] opened the back door, and that's when he put the gun to his face, my brother's face. The other guys in the truck with him [Derrick]— they were quiet, my brother was quiet. He was stunned. They didn't say anything. My brother did say that once he put the gun in his face, and he was yelling 'I'll kill you, I'll kill you,' my brother said, 'Kill me. Do what you have to do. Kill me.' But he said they weren't—you don't say anything when someone has a gun, and you don't have anything. They didn't say anything.

"He [Hanna] then shot up in the air again, continually screaming the remarks again, 'I'm white supremacist, white supremacist, we hate niggers' and this and that. That's when the gentleman he [Hanna] was with yelled at him to back off—the guy that was with the guy who had the gun.

"That's when they backed up the truck that was behind him [the truck Derrick was in]. He backed up that truck. That's how they got out. They were able to get out then. As they left the scene, they took my brother home, not thinking, or in shock, all the above, to go to the police instead. My brother's just like, 'take me home.' He has three relatives that live in that area, and he'd call someone. He was furious.

"I guess after he calmed down and thought about what happened, he proceeded to go back to the gas station. But as he was going around, that's when the police officer stopped him. When they stopped my brother, they had already talked to the white guys who was doing the shooting, and they [the white guys] reported that it was my brother that was shooting. There was a lady that was working at the Food Lion who was getting off work, who was going to her car, who heard everything. And she had called the police. The police came to the scene, but my brother had already left, but the white guys were still there. They reported it was my brother with a gun—black male, tall. On the scanner the reports are that they're looking for a black man, armed and dangerous.

"I guess that the guys must have pointed to the way my brother went, because as my brother was walking back up, that's when the cop stopped him. Instead of questioning him like they questioned the white guys, they automatically said, 'where's the gun?' and wanted to do a gunpowder test. The cops approached my brother and asked where the gun was. He said he didn't have the gun; they [the white men] were after me. That's when he started telling his story as far as the white guys threatening him. That's when *they asked him what hand do you write with. And he said I'm right-handed. They said can we do the gunpowder test. And he said do both of my hands. So that's when they put the gunpowder test on. They did it right then and there. They tested both of his hands. They discovered nothing.*

"He [Derrick] went down [to the police station] the next day with my father. Did the report. It was funny. The lady who called the incident in, she went down and gave her statement, and hers and my brother's matched almost exactly.

"After that, I asked him a couple of days later, have you talked to anyone, and no one had contacted him as far as police officers. Nothing in the paper. Nothing. I myself called The [Martinsburg, West Virginia] Journal. That's when the reporter called the police station, and they told her she couldn't report anything because they didn't want to put anything in the paper because they didn't want the guy to flee. She [the reporter] didn't write the story then. She wrote the story after they had the warrant for his arrest.

"My brother called the police station wondering what's going on, there's no arrest been made, and, how am I supposed to live knowing that this man is still free and you're not doing anything. The police officer was off duty or wasn't there or something. He knew the police officer and he called him at home. The lady, I guess it was the secretary at the station, she called my mom's house, my dad's house, and my brother was there and she got smart with him because my brother called the police officer at home. "You're going over my head,' she said.

"They finally arrested the guy, about ten days later. They haven't made any attempt to arrest the other guys who blocked them in. I guess [Hanna got arrested] because he had the gun."

In January 2001, a Jefferson County grand jury indicted both Hanna, of Ranson, West Virginia, and a second man, Jason Jacobs of Harpers Ferry, West Virginia, in connection with the incident. According to court records, Hanna was indicted on charges of violating the civil rights of another person, four counts of conspiracy to commit an offense against the state, three counts of wanton endangerment involving a firearm, shooting at another person in a place of public resort, and three counts of assault. Jacobs was indicted on charges of violating the civil rights of another person and four counts of conspiracy to commit an offense against the state (McMillon 2001).

The incident illustrates several of the points we have been making about the institutional nature of hate in our society. The police were so quick to believe the story told by the white men involved in the incident that the first thing they wanted to do when they encountered Berry was to test his hand for gunpowder. That recalls the Susan Smith incident, described in the chapter on gender. Her initial accusation—that a black man had hijacked her car and kidnapped her children—played into the stereotype of black men as criminals. In the Berry case, the white men were able to initially shift suspicion from themselves to Berry. The secretary in the sheriff's office was more concerned about Berry "going over her head" and calling the police officer at home, than about how the knowledge that no one had been arrested yet was affecting him. She displayed little sensitivity to a victim's need to discover the status of what was happening.

Narratives not only give victims of hate a voice, they also help them to demonstrate how significantly these incidents affect their lives. Puller described her brother's reaction to the incident:

"Well my brother, he's the type where he doesn't let a lot of things bother him. He'll push things away and be kind've nonchalant. And that's the way I know my brother. After the incident, a couple of days later, I stopped by the house just to check on him. He was sitting at the kitchen table. He must have been sitting there before I came in, just kind of doodling in, just sitting there, staring out into space. And I went to say something about it, about how he was doing, and he suddenly just cut me off and wouldn't talk about it. Couple of days after that was when he opened up and talked about it. He was devastated. He's a man of—nothing bothers him. He's strong, tough. But this has really eaten him up. He can't sleep at night. He still doesn't sleep."

She then explained how the incident affected her and her family. *"He's my brother, and he's alive and well. But I wake up in a dream where he's gone. Someone's knocking on my door, and he's gone....My dad's constantly having dreams. My sister, she was just, like furious. It's just hard."*

These sentiments are precisely what the Prejudice Institute/ Center for the Applied Study of Ethnoviolence has come to understand are some of the responses to being victimized because of prejudice. Some of the other stress responses to hate incidents include withdrawal, nervousness, the desire to become invisible, exhaustion, and extended use of alcohol or other drugs (Ehrlich, Larcom, and Purvis 1995).

In a plea bargain agreement in May 2001, Hanna pleaded guilty to a felony charge of wanton endangerment and two misdemeanor counts of assault. However, he did not plead guilty to the hate crime of violating the civil rights of another person (Mullin 2001). William Berry, Derrick Berry's father, said Derrick had been notified about the plea offer, and spent a great deal of time deciding whether to contest it. Derrick Berry said that when the plea bargain was first proposed, he felt as if "everyone was working against me. I felt like they were out to get me. I wanted him to be punished. I wanted him to go to trial" (2001). He felt sure that if there had been a trial, that Hanna would have been convicted because there were other witnesses to the incident. However, he finally agreed after talking the situation over with his family and representatives of the NAACP and FAIR. Berry pointed out that even though he agreed to the plea bargain, he still had the option of pursuing a civil suit against Hanna. As William Berry said, "This has affected all of our family. I don't know why it had to happen to Derrick" (Berry 2001).

Hanna was sentenced in July 2001. During the sentencing hearing, several people testified on his behalf, including an older black woman, Natalie Banks, who worked with Hanna's former wife. She testified that he regularly gave her rides home from work. "I know racism," she declared. "If Brian was a racist, I would not have gotten into his car. I don't believe that if Brian was a racist he would have let me into his car. I never saw him as mean-spirited" (Banks 2001). The chief of the local volunteer fire department testified that as a volunteer firefighter and EMS responder, Hanna never exhibited any racist tendencies and never refused to answer a call anywhere in the area.

Hanna appears to be an example of what Levin and Paulsen (1999) classified as a hate dabbler. He's a little older than the average dabbler—he was 27 at the time of the incident, and most of the time dabblers are young white men in their teens. However, he was in a classic dabbler situation. He and some of his friends saw a black man alone and on the spur of the moment decided to harass him. If Hanna and his friends had merely continued to shout insults at Derrick Berry, they would have gotten away with it. Remember, hate speech is protected. What set this incident apart was Hanna's use of a gun. When words escalate into actions or are accompanied by actions, they are no longer protected.

Judge Thomas Steptoe, who presided over the case, called the incident "bullying that rose to the level of terrorism." The civil rights violation (the hate crime) aspect of this case had been dropped as part of the plea bargain agreement. Assistant State Prosecutor Larry Crofford said he believed this incident was clearly a hate crime, but the state agreed to drop those charges because they were concerned that a jury would not reach the same conclusion. Remember that the Supreme Court's decision in *Apprendi* ruled that only juries, not judges, could determine whether a hate crime had occurred and whether a sentence should be enhanced. In a similar Jefferson County case a few months earlier, an all-white jury had refused to convict a white man of a hate crime against a black man, although they did convict the white man of assault. That decision raises questions about how effective hate crime laws and enhanced sentencing provisions will be if juries refuse to convict.

However, Judge Steptoe took the hate crime element into consideration when passing sentence. People have a right to be left alone, he pointed out. "There was no prior personal history between these two men. There was no mitigating circumstance. This was purely racial motivation." Hanna cannot blame anyone else for this incident. "He created the situation," Steptoe said. The judge then sentenced Hanna to the maximum term—six months in the regional jail on each of the two assault charges, and five years in the state penitentiary on the wanton endangerment charge, to be served consecutively (Steptoe 2001).

This case illustrates the argument of this book. Hate can happen anywhere to anyone. It is mainstream. Hanna and his friends thought nothing of harassing an innocent black man. When the police came, they lied about who shot the gun, and the police initially bought into the racial stereotype that the black man was at fault. Furthermore, this case also illustrates what a tragedy hate crimes are. Hatred unnecessarily affects innocent lives. Standing outside the courthouse after the sentencing, Derrick Berry said he feels he has gotten over the trauma of the incident, but he no longer holds the same open attitude toward all people. "I used to be color blind," he said. "I used to think that one person wasn't different from another. I've just changed. In my day-to-day reactions to people, I'm not quite as open as I used to be. I'm more suspicious of white people" (2001).

Berry has clearly suffered because of this hate crime, but so will members of Brian Hanna's family. Hanna is the father of five children, and testimony in court revealed that he was paying more than $1000 a month in child support. What's going to happen to them? In passing sentence, Judge Steptoe said, "[T]he guilty cannot hide behind the innocent to escape the responsibility of their crime." However, even Derrick Berry, when asked his reaction to the sentence, followed his initial remark that he was "relieved" with the comment, "I feel sorry for his children" (2001).

Hate is so engrained in our society and our culture, we have to wonder if anything can be done to overcome it. Some residents of Jefferson County, reacting to the hate incident involving Derrick Berry, have now made an earnest attempt to do something. After Berry was threatened, the NAACP and FAIR sponsored a seminar to educate the public about how to recognize a hate crime, and to alert them to how common hate crimes are. A core of residents and law enforcement officials who had been at the seminar then attended a series of follow-up meetings. At those meetings, they proposed ways to improve problems with law enforcement in the county, to educate citizens about tolerance, and to lobby the state legislature for expansion of hate crimes legislation to cover gays and lesbians. The group also joined the "Not in Our Town" movement, which is designed to combat hate crimes at the local level. A "Not in Our Town" rally held in the spring of 2001 attracted about seventy-five people, both black and white. Among those attending were Derrick Berry and members of his family (Casper 2001). Bob Winget, the president of FAIR, was upbeat after the rally. "Derrick Berry stood smack in the middle of that crowd, with a smile on his face. That was worth a lot. To have someone who has been a victim of hate feel like he could show up, because it wasn't real certain that he would at all. And to feel like he was welcome, and that it was a good place to be" (Winget 2001).

George Rutherford has been president of the local chapter of the NAACP since 1974. A native of Jefferson County, he served seventeen years on the West Virginia Human Rights Commission, including eight as its chairman. He is encouraged by the progress made since the Berry incident, but he is not willing to declare victory over hate yet. "In all my years in Jefferson County this effort is the first time I've seen blacks, whites, men, women, old, young, gays, lesbians, straights, even law enforcement, left religion, right religion really come together in a group, and really try to talk about the problems and to try to solve them. We've never had a diverse group like that before." What's more amazing, he said, is that the group stayed together after the first meeting. It divided into three self-selected subgroups focusing on education, law enforcement, and political action. "These type of things really give you hope," Rutherford said. "I think that if anything has been accomplished, it's that the group has come together and has begun to at least work on the issues. I would never believe it would happen" (2001).

Rutherford believes that hate crimes are much more prevalent in the county than statistics indicate. "They're not publicized because they're not reported. Also, because there's no recourse." He pins some of the blame on white juries, who he believes are unwilling to convict other whites of hate crimes, or, if they do convict, to levy any type of deterring penalty. Rutherford considers himself a victim of a white jury. "I sued the City of Charles Town because of racial slurs. I won. An all-white jury. And they gave me $1, and I never collected it. I have sat on the Human Rights Commission, and I have heard all types of cases. I have advised some people not to file complaints because of the harassment they go through. With the possibility of retaliation, it's not worth it" (2001).

Education is an important method that can be used to solve the problem of hate. However, in a joint interview with Rutherford about what is happening in Jefferson County, Winget pointed out that education must move beyond what is offered in the schools. "Education has to mean something more than public education. What do we do about all the moms and dads who are parents of the kids who are writing e-mails to the superintendent (of schools). What do we do about those folks who are fostering the next generation of hate and the next generation of racism?" Think, for example, about the women involved in the white supremacist movement who are raising their children to hate. Can tolerance education in school possibly overcome the negative messages these children receive at home?

Like Rutherford, Winget has been involved in the Civil Rights movement for decades. In the 1960s, he was among the white college students who went south during the summer to register African Americans to vote. He has learned through his years fighting hate that it takes constant reminders from the victims of hate to make any incremental progress at all. "I don't think any of us would be able to do anything were it not for black folks willingness to stand up," he said. "For me, racism doesn't equate to how do we help black folks, which is a mistake a lot of us made in the sixties. To me, racism equates to how do we white folks help each other overcome white racism. Because it is not George's problem" (Winget 2001).

Critical race theorists, though, believe that white people are incapable of overcoming racism. These scholars believe racism is "normal." It is not the action of an aberrant minority; instead, it is "an ingrained and largely unconscious feature of American culture." As we have been arguing, hate is mainstream. Theorist Derrick Bell has concluded that equality for blacks will come only when it appears to benefit white people as well. "Whites simply cannot envision the personal responsibility and the potential sacrifice inherent in the conclusion that true equality for blacks will require the surrender of racism-granted privileges" (MacFarquhar 1996, 41).

Hatred has become a "normal" aspect of our society, moving from the outskirts on the far right and the far left into the mainstream. So the mainstream establishment must demonstrate that hate crimes, hate speech, and hate incidents are not acceptable. That is the impetus behind such movements as "Not in Our Town." It demands moral guidance from community leaders. As Winget points out, law enforcement officials and political leaders need to stand up and say, "Hate crime is totally unacceptable in this community. The people who stand for law and order need to say that. Then the rest of us need to make sure that what we think are hate crimes get reported. Those folks need to have those reports on their desk" (2001). Only then can the full extent of the problem be recognized and dealt with.

If hate crimes and hate incidents are not reported, then it is easier to ignore or dismiss the problem and the effect of hate. "It's a very scary thing to stand up and be counted as a victim," Winget said. "It's very costly for victims. Those of us who haven't been victims of a hate crime get most of the benefit, because victims are willing to stand up and help us. If Derrick Berry wasn't at least willing to say that something happened, and his father wasn't willing to step up with him, nothing would happen.

The tragedy is, the people who are already suffering have to help the rest of us."

Because of victims like Derrick Berry and dedicated civil rights advocates like George Rutherford and Bob Winget, there is a chance that hatred will ease in Jefferson County. National programs such as the "Not in Our Town" movement have prompted other communities across the country to take steps to eradicate hatred. The Civil Rights Division of West Virginia's Office of the Attorney General is piloting a program aimed at young people. Called the Civil Rights Team Project, it involves training students and faculty members in middle and high schools to recognize harassment and intolerance. It provides education and awareness about issues of bias and prejudice. It also provides a way for students being harassed to alert someone before the harassment escalates to the level of violence. The program is modeled after a successful program operated by the Attorney General of Maine (Civil Rights Division 2000). The hope is that if students are educated about intolerance early, it will minimize problems both in school and later, when they reach adulthood. Will such programs as Not in Our Town and the Civil Rights Team Project ease hatred? It is too soon to tell. However, as we have shown throughout this book, more needs to be done. Hatred is so engrained in our national psyche, that it will be extraordinarily difficult to eradicate. It is so much a part of our culture that often we do not even recognize it.

Who will be the next Eminem? Where will the next Columbine-style shooting take place? Whose community center will be targeted next? Which minority group will be the next one lampooned on television situation comedies? Which hate group will be the next to discover the propaganda power of the World Wide Web? There is no quick and easy answer to the problem of hate. Enhanced penalties have not eliminated hate crimes. Demands from the NAACP have not significantly increased the number of blacks on television. Protests by gays and lesbians have not diminished Eminem's sales. To even make a dent in hate requires that political leaders refuse to play the race card; that law enforcement leaders condemn racial profiling; and that reporters and editors focus on the hate that drives society rather than giving the white supremacists who commit hate crimes their fifteen minutes of notoriety.

In reflecting on the progress made against hate, racism, and segregation in Jefferson County since the Civil Rights movement, George Rutherford related a sobering anecdote. "I can go back to around 1973. I gave a talk at a church in Shepherdstown. My kids were in high school. At that time I said that I knew that in ten years, things would be much better for everyone—the kids, the mixing of the races. A lot of the barriers would be down. There would be very little discrimination taking place. That was in 1973. And I swear, here we are now in 2001, and things are not a bit better, and I just knew back in '73 that things were going to improve within ten years. It's too engrained."

As Rutherford said, "[W]e're just as far apart now as we were thirty years ago." In another thirty years, will hate still be engrained in the fabric of the nation? It is up to us to decide.

— Epilogue —
Hate after September 11

When we first selected the title *The Landscape of Hate* for this book, we had no idea just how significant the word "landscape" would prove to be. Although we used landscape in its broadest terms, referring to the psychological, political, and cultural terrain of hatred in the United States, the devastating events of 11 September 2001, have now left us with a decimated physical landscape of hatred, painfully visible in the ruins of lower Manhattan in New York City and at the Pentagon in Virginia. There has been so much sorrow in the aftermath of this hatred that you can hear hearts breaking wherever you go in America. The culture of hatred has firmly embedded itself in the consciousness of Americans.

It would take another book to analyze the reasons some Islamic fundamentalists hate the United States so virulently that they would commit such horrific acts against innocent civilians. In this epilogue, we intend only to describe some of the incidents of domestic hatred that, sadly, have resulted in the aftermath of September 11. The stories of burned mosques, brutal assaults, and incendiary insults echo the hatred we have been documenting throughout this book. In addition, while President George W. Bush has advocated tolerance, visited mosques, and hosted Arab and Muslim leaders at the White House, the government, in the name of fighting terrorism, has taken a number of steps, that to some, seem to institutionalize hatred and intolerance. The provisions of the *USA Patriot Act*, the actions by Attorney General John Ashcroft that curtail civil liberties for suspected terrorists, and the racial profiling in the name of security at airports all contribute to the already-festering atmosphere of intolerance. These contradictory responses from the government intensify the debate about the complex nature of hatred. The September 11 attack also raised further questions about the nature of free speech and the marketplace of ideas, leading to concerns about the ability to express opinions in this time of crisis.

In the days following the September 11 attack, Arab Americans, and others who some people believed resembled Arabs and others of Middle Eastern descent, were killed or assaulted, their businesses and places of worship were vandalized, and their tranquility was shattered. The insidious inclination of marking individuals based on a faulty stereotype of physical features was frequent in the weeks and months following September 11. Ann Hull, a *Washington Post* writer, described this fear of false identification when she interviewed Greensboro, North Carolina, residents Alma Chavez and her boyfriend, both of whom are Hispanic. Hull wrote, "[T]hey don't venture out after dark, afraid that someone will mistake them for Arabs" (2001, A1).

By the middle of October, the Arab American Institute had reported a number of incidents of hate directed against actual Arab Americans, including at least two deaths. The incidents included the following: In Arizona, a Sikh man was shot to death at a gas station. On the same day in California, an Egyptian grocery store owner was shot and killed. Arrests were made in both of these cases. In Rhode Island, passing motorists threw rocks at a pregnant Muslim woman using a pay phone. In Atlanta, Georgia, four men stabbed a Sudanese man after telling him, "You killed our people in New York. We want to kill you tonight." In New York, a seventy-five-year-old man tried to run over a Pakistani woman in a store parking lot. He then followed her into the store and threatened to kill her. (Arab American Institute 2001).

Buildings, mosques, and businesses were also targeted. In Maryland, two buildings owned by a Palestinian burned to the ground. In Kentucky, Islamic meeting places were vandalized. In Ohio, a young man smashed his car through the entrance of an unoccupied mosque. In Texas, the Islamic Society of Denton was firebombed. In Virginia, hate messages were left on the answering machine of a mosque. In Rhode Island, graffiti was spray-painted on the garage door of a gasoline station owner. In San Francisco, California, a law office in the Mission District was mistaken for an Islamic Community Center. Someone threw a bag filled with blood at the building's door. The name of Osama bin Laden was scrawled on the bag (Arab American Institute 2001).

By the start of 2002, the Justice Department's Civil Rights Division had identified nine killings or "hate crimes" that it believed were directly associated with the events of September 11. There was some dispute about these numbers. The private Council on American-Islamic Relations only reported eight deaths that might have been revenge motivated, and detectives working on the actual cases disputed whether all of the deaths were actually hate inspired (Cooperman 2002). Those who disputed the numbers argued that "the notion that there has been a rash of retaliatory murders is an urban myth driven by antidiscrimination campaigners and traumatized crime victims seeking some explanation for senseless acts of violence" (Cooperman 2002, A3). This point, which challenges the validity of hate crimes, is reminiscent of the arguments made by Schlesinger and Jacobs and Potter discussed in chapter 2. This denial of hate is a dangerous trend in contemporary thinking.

Private citizens were not the only people expressing hatred. U.S. Rep. Saxbe Chambliss, R-Ga., the chairman of the House Subcommittee on Terrorism and Homeland Security, proposed, "Just turn the sheriff loose and let him arrest every Muslim that crosses the state line" (*The Washington Post* 2001, A46). Chambliss later apologized for the remark. Still another representative, John Cooksey, R-La., outraged Arab Americans and others with his suggestion that Muslim men should be subject to additional scrutiny at airports. He made his comment, "If I see someone come in that's got a diaper on his head and a fan belt wrapped around the diaper on his head, that guy needs to be pulled over," shortly after the attack (Gill 2001, 7). Even while these members of Congress were voicing their distrust and hatred, others introduced House Resolution 255, which condemned the bigotry and violence against Sikh Americans that occurred after the September 11 attack. Because of their faith, Sikh men also wear beards and turbans, and they suffered both verbal and physical assaults.

In response to the September 11 attack, Congress passed the *Uniting and Strengthening America by Providing Appropriate Tools Required to Intercept and Obstruct Terrorism Act*, or the *USA Patriot Act*. It was signed by President Bush on 26 October 2001. Some of the provisions of the act speak to the paradox of tolerance and bigotry. Section 412 of the act permits the indefinite detention of immigrants and other noncitizens. To hold a person indefinitely, the government does not need to charge him or her with terrorism. Instead, within seven days, the government only has either to show an immigration violation, such as overstaying a visa, or to charge the person with a criminal offense. If the person's home country refuses to accept him or her back, the attorney general can hold the person indefinitely if he finds "reasonable grounds to believe" that the person is involved in terrorism or an activity that poses a danger to national security (ACLU 2001).

This new policy seems in direct contradiction to the Supreme Court decision in *Zadvydas v. Davis* (2001), which concluded that the indefinite detention of immigrants would pose "serious constitutional problems." In the *Zadvydas* decision, the Court determined that the preventive detention of immigrants should not be permitted in the absence of "strong procedural protections." The ACLU has insisted that the Section 412 provisions of the *USA Patriot Act* do not provide the necessary safeguards required by the *Zadvydas* decision (2001). Soon after the *USA Patriot Act* was passed, a federal appeals court in Texas overturned the mandatory detention provision in the case of *Patel v. Zemski* (2001). Other challenges to the *USA Patriot Act* are sure to follow. One suit was filed by sixteen organizations, including the ACLU and the Center for National Security Studies. These groups were attempting to use the Freedom of Information Act to gain disclosure of information about individuals who had been arrested and detained after September 11.

In addition to enforcing the provisions of the *USA Patriot Act*, the Justice Department, in January 2002, announced that it would begin a massive search for some 6,000 men from the Middle East who remained in the United States in spite of deportation orders. People who do not leave the country after being ordered deported are considered absconders. In the past, the Immigration and Naturalization Service expended little effort seeking absconders, as the majority of its initiatives focused on other criminals among the 7.5 million undocumented aliens in the United States. This plan, which some people insisted was a practice of racial profiling in the battle against international terrorism, came under scrutiny from Arab-American and other immigrant advocacy groups (Eggen and Thompson 2002).

The passage of the *USA Patriot Act* and the "absconder initiative," as INS Commissioner James W. Ziglar called it, brought into stark relief the contrast between the administration's calls for tolerance and its concerns about hate crimes committed against Muslims, and its abrogation of the civil rights of people arrested under the provisions of the Act. The suspension of Arab Americans' civil liberties is eerily reminiscent of the internment of Japanese Americans after the bombing of Pearl Harbor. When the Supreme Court upheld the internment policy in *Korematsu v. United States* (1943), Justice Jackson wrote a scathing dissent, calling the Court majority's reasoning an example of the "ugly abyss of racism." The specter of *Korematsu* poses a frightening scenario for Arab Americans. One would hope that we would have moved beyond this generic hatred, but the racial profiling that occurred in the aftermath of September 11 demonstrates that the passions of fear and hatred may still guide institutional decision-making.

Outside of the seat of government, a less dramatic, but still troubling, response has been the chilling of free speech on college campuses and elsewhere. For example, a University of New Mexico professor received death threats and business leaders called for his resignation after he commented in class on September 11, "[A]nyone who would blow up the Pentagon would have my vote." The professor later apologized (Wilson and Cox 2001). The president of the University of Texas at Austin severely criticized a journalism professor who wrote an op-ed piece arguing that the September 11 attacks were no worse than assaults committed by the United States in Iraq and elsewhere (Wilson and Cox 2001). A political science professor at the California State University's Chico campus received "seventy hate letters" when he said the Bush administration's foreign policies may have precipitated the attacks of September 11 (Wilson and Cox 2001). Outside of academia, television stations across the country at least temporarily dropped the syndicated program *Politically Incorrect* after host Bill Maher referred to past United States military actions as "cowardly." Even newspapers and magazines fired some columnists and editorial writers for criticizing actions of the Bush administration. Katha Pollitt, a writer for *The Nation* magazine, was criticized for refusing to allow her daughter to hang out an American flag because, she said, "the flag stands for jingoism and vengeance and war" (Beam 2001, D1). The debate about these varying responses raises questions about the ability of the marketplace of ideas to thrive in an atmosphere of distrust and hatred.

Not unexpectedly, extremist groups also responded to the September 11 attack by ratcheting up their rhetoric of hate. The Neo-Nazi National Alliance distributed flyers in Chicago that showed pictures of the collapsed World Trade Center buildings, along with a demand that the United States close its borders. Disciples of hatred such as Matt Hale blamed the attack on Israeli agents and used it to stir up additional anti-Semitic feelings. Pro-life advocate Clayton Waggoner was indicted for sending anthrax hoax letters to abortion clinics.

However, much of the hate that resulted from the attack was expressed by ordinary people in e-mails sent to Arab Americans and in postings to Internet chatrooms and message boards. This reaction points out that traumatic events can trigger hatred even among people who consider themselves tolerant. Remember Levin and Paulsen's profile of hate spectators. On the day after the attack, Ali Abunimah of the Arab American Action Network wrote a commentary describing incendiary messages he received both on his own Web site and in e-mails to the network. One message that he received read: "Dear dirty towel-heads. Please take your illogical, misogynistic and murdering religion back to the Middle East. We have tolerated you disgusting people long enough in our country. I hope the US wipes out every man, women, and child Arab in the middle east [sic]....I will rest more easily when all of you are dead" (Abunimah 2001, n.p.).

Users of Internet chatrooms and message boards have expressed a wide range of opinions about the September 11 attack and its aftermath. Some of these comments have revealed a fear and hatred of Arab Americans. Others have criticized the United States for its policy toward the Middle East and its support of Israel. Internet companies such as Yahoo! have been criticized for screening these messages unfairly, using a double standard for determining which messages to remove from the boards. "In some cases, people say, anti-U.S. or anti-Israeli messages appear to be deleted faster and more frequently than anti-Arab posts" (Cha 2001, H1).

The response by some Americans to the September 11 attack demonstrates how close to the surface mainstream hatred really is. In times of crisis, our worst instincts rise to the surface and reinforce an ever-shifting hatred of the other. Popular comic strips, such as *Doonesbury* and *The Boondocks*, revealed this shifting hatred. In a series of *Doonesbury* strips appearing after the attack, title character Mike Doonesbury flies to New York to attend a memorial service for a former colleague killed in the attack. Strip author Gary Trudeau points out our fear of Arab-Americans, as he seats Mike Doonesbury next to an Arab American man on the plane. In another strip of this series, Mike Doonesbury speaks with an African-American man who admits that he feels the paradox of racially profiling the Arab-American passenger (Trudeau 2001). In *The Boondocks*, a young black male character explains why African Americans are now only the "third most-hated" ethnic group in America. The character tells his brother Riley, "America has found an ethnic group that represents, however unfair it may be, an imminent terrorist threat. Black people seem fairly harmless by comparison, at least for the time being. To put it another way, do-rags and thug mugs just aren't that big of a deal anymore" (McGruder 2001). As Fanon pointed out, we all need an "other" to legitimate our own identity.

We, too, constitute an "other." The virulent hatred felt toward the United States by some militant Islamic fundamentalists precipitated the horrific attacks of September 11. The hateful response of some American citizens toward innocent Arab Americans rounds out this vicious circular web of hatred. How do we stop it? We need to cultivate a better understanding of Islam, and we need to recognize that there is a bipolarity of feeling toward the United States. We should not be afraid to allow the "marketplace of ideas" to work. Expressions of hatred against the "other" must be balanced by questions about our own views and our country's policies. Finally, we must protect the ideals of liberty and tolerance as we use the law to investigate the crimes committed on September 11.

Walking in the halls of Hood College shortly after the attack, we noticed this statement on a bulletin board: "Let's find the cause of hatred and make it right." Perhaps in all of the thousands of words, gestures, and sentiments that have accompanied this painful and dramatic event, this statement may be the only one that makes any sense. Hatred did not begin with the September 11 assault. It began long before that, and we need to understand not only the hatred of our enemies, but the origin and reality of our own hatred. Perhaps then, as we mentioned in the previous chapter, this book can be a modest step in that direction.

References

ABCNEWS.com. 2001. Escape from Hate: Abandoning Racist Beliefs. 10 February. http://www.abcnews.go.com/onair/DailyNews/2020_rightwomen_chat.html.

Abrams v. United States, 250 U.S. 616 (1919).

Abunimah, Ali. 2001. Commentary: A Few Words. 1 October. http://www.abunimah.org.

Accomondo, Beth. 2001. Japanese-Americans Worry the Movie *Pearl Harbor* Could Inflame Racial Tensions Against Them. *Morning Edition*, National Public Radio transcript, 24 May. http://www.npr.org.

Ahrens, Frank. 2000. The Silenced Greaseman. *The Washington Post*, 9 March: C1.

Akhtar, Salman. 1995. Some Reflections on the Nature of Hatred and Its Emergence in the Treatment Process: Discussion of Kernberg's Chapter Hatred as a Core Affect of Aggression. In *The Birth of Hatred: Developmental, Clinical and Technical Aspects of Intense Aggression*. Edited by Salman Akhtar, Selma Kramer, and Henri Parens. Northvale, N.J.: Jason Aronson Inc.

Alexander, Karen, Jack Leonard, and Daniel Yi. 1999. The Death of Innocents No Accident; Tragedy: Driver Who Rammed into Costa Mesa Preschool Yard Confessed Twisted Motive, Police Say. *Los Angeles Times*, Orange County Edition, 5 May: A1. http://www.lexis-nexis.com.

Ali, Lorraine. 2000. Same Old Song. *Newsweek*, 9 October: 68.

American Civil Liberties Union. 2001. *How the USA-Patriot Act Permits Indefinite Detention of Immigrants Who Are Not Terrorists*. 23 October. http://www.aclu.org/congress.

American Health Line. 2001. Abortion: Federal Court Rules Web Site Is Free Speech. *The National Journal Group, Inc.* 29 March. http://www.lexis-nexis.com.

American History X. 1999. Screenplay by David McKenna. Dir. Tony Kaye. Perf. Edward Norton, Edward Furlong, Stacy Keach. New Line Productions.

American Psycho. 2000. Screenplay by Bret Easton Ellis and Mary Harron. Dir. Mary Harron. Perf. Christian Bale, Chloe Sevigny. Edward R. Pressman Film Corp.

Amos 'n' Andy. 1951–1953. Writers Freeman F. Gosden, Charles J. Correll. Dir. Charles Barton. Perf. Alvin Childress, Spencer Williams, Tim Moore. Hal Roach Studios.

Anatomy of a Hate Crime: The Killing of Matthew Shepard. 2000. Dir. Tim Hunter. Perf. Cy Carter, Brendan Fletcher. Team Entertainment.

Anti-Defamation League. 1998a. Feminism Perverted: Extremist Women on the World Wide Web. October. http://www.adl.org/special_reports/extemist_women_on_ web/feminism_ intro.html.

———. 1998b. *High Tech Hate: Extremist Use of the Internet.* New York: ADL.

———. 2000a. Explosion of Hate: The Growing Danger of the National Alliance. June 2000. http://www.adl.org/explosion_of_hate.

———. 2000b. Poisoning the Web: Hatred Online. June 2000. http://www.adl.org/poisoning_web.

———. 2000c. Recurring Hate: Matt Hale and the World Church of the Creator. June 2000. http://www.adl.org/special_reports/wcotc.

Apprendi v. New Jersey, 000 US 99–478 (2000).

Arab American Institute. 2001. In the Aftermath of the Tragedy: Anti-Arab and Anti-Muslim Attack Incidents. 1 October. http://www.aaiusa.org/Tragedy/incidents.

Arendt, Hannah. 1994. *Eichmann in Jerusalem: A Report on the Banality of Evil.* London: Penguin.

Asim, Jabari. 2000. Blaming the Victimology. Review of *Losing the Race: Self-Sabotage in Black America* by John H. McWhorter. *The Washington Post,* 22 August: C3.

Associated Press. 1999. Ebay Nixes Racist Domain Name Sale. *USA Today Tech Report,* 17 December. http://www.usatoday.com/life/cyber/tech/ctg901.htm, 30 November 2000.

———. 2000a. Judge Denies Motion to Dismiss Lawsuit against White Supremacist Hale. 13 July. http://www.lexis-nexis.com.

———. 2000b. Lawyer argues Hale ordered Smith to go on shooting spree. *The (Bloomington, Ill.) Pantagraph,* 7 July. http://www.lexis-nexis.com.

———. 2000c. Shooting Spree Suspect's Web Page Back Online: Site Host Includes Plea for Donations to Victims. APBnews.com, 3 May. http://www.APBnews.com:80/newscent.

———. 2000d. Violent crime plunged in 1999. *The Morning Herald,* 28 August: A1.

———. 2001. Internet Millionaire Buys Aryan Nation Compound for Human Rights Center. 7 March. http://www.lexis-nexis.com.

Baab, Amy. 2001. Speech Touches on Gender Issues at Virginia Tech Student Center. *The Collegiate Times Virginia Tech,* 6 April.

Bamboozled. 2000. Screenplay by Spike Lee. Dir. Spike Lee. Perf. Damon Wayans, Savion Glover, Jada Pinkett-Smith. 40 Acres & a Mule Filmworks.

Banks, Natalie. 2001. Testimony. *State of West Virginia v. Brian K. Hanna.* Charles Town, W.Va., 9 July.

Barclay v. Florida, 463 US 939 (1983).

Beam, Alex. 2001. Senseless Acts, Words of Nonsense. *The Boston Globe,* 27 September: D1. http://www.lexis-nexis.com.

Beaver, Bill and Silla Brush. 2001. Hubbub over Ads Continues on Campuses, in Newsrooms. *The Daily Princetonian*. University Wire, 27 March. http://www.elibrary.com/s/edumark.

Beck, Aaron T. 1999. *Prisoners of Hate: The Cognitive Basis of Anger, Hostility, and Violence*. New York: HarperCollins.

Believers, The. 2001. Screenplay by Henry Bean. Dir. Henry Bean. Perf. Ryan Gosling, Summer Phoenix. Fuller Film.

Bellah, Robert, Richard Madsen, William Sullivan, Ann Swidler, and Steven Tipton. 1986. *Habits of the Heart: Individualism and Commitment in American Life*. New York: Harper and Row.

Benfer, Amy. 1999. Nazi Family Values. 15 July. http://www.salon.com/mwt/hot/1999/aryan_compound.

Berkowitz, Bill. 2001. Heil, heil rock n' roll. 8 May. http://www.workingforchange.com.

Berry, Derrick. 2001. Personal interview with Donna Bertazzoni. Charles Town, W.Va. 9 July.

Berry, William. 2001. Telephone interview with Donna Bertazzoni. Shepherdstown, W.Va., 22 May.

Best, Steven, and Douglas Kellner. 1999. Rap, Black Rage, and Racial Difference. *Enculturation* 2 (2).

Beulah. 1950. Prod. Roland D. Reed. Perf. Louise Beavers, Henry Blair, Hattie McDaniel. Roland Reed Productions.

Birth of a Nation. 1915. Screenplay by Thomas F. Dixon Jr. Dir. D.W. Griffith, Perf. Lillian Gish, Mae Marsh. David W. Griffith Corp.

Black, Derek. 2000. Stormfront Kids Page. June 2000. http://www.stormfront.org/kids.

Black, Don. 2000. Don Black's Homepage. June 2000. http://www.stormfront.org/dblack.

Blee, Kathleen. 1991. *Women of the Klan: Racism and Gender in the 1920's*. Berkeley: University of California.

Blight, David W. 2001. A Confederacy of Denial. *The Washington Post*, 29 January: A19. http://www.washingtonpost.com.

Blink. 2001. Screenplay by Elizabeth Thompson. Dir. Elizabeth Thompson.

Block, J. H. 1973. Conceptions of sex role: some cross-cultural and longitudinal perspectives. *American Psychology* 28: 512–526. Quoted in Ann Kearney-Cooke. 2001. Gender Differences and Self-Esteem. *The Journal of Gender-Specific Medicine*. http://www.mmhc.com/jgsm/JGSM9906/Cooke.html.

Blythe, Will. 2000. The Guru of White Hate. *Rolling Stone*, 8 June: 98. Academic Search Elite, AN: 3157982.

Board of Regents of the University of Wisconsin System v. Southworth, 000 U.S.1189 (2000).

Bogle, Donald. 2001. *Primetime Blues: African Americans on Network Television*. New York: Farrar, Straus & Giroux.

Borger, Julian. 1999. Civil Rights Murder Case Reopened. *The Observer*, 22 January.

Boys Don't Cry. 1999. Screenplay by Kimberly Peirce and Andy Bienen. Dir. Kimberly Peirce. Perf. Hilary Swank, Chloe Sivegny. The Independent Film Channel Productions.

Brandenburg v. Ohio, 395 U.S. 444 (1969).

Britt, Donna. 1998. History X Offers a Closeup of Our Hatreds. *The Washington Post*, 30 October: B1.

Broder, David. 2001. Jesse Helms, White Racist. *The Washington Post*, 29 August: A21.

Brown, G. 2001. Marilyn Manson takes on critics, Columbine fallout. *The Denver Post*, 10 June. http://www.denverpost.com.

Brownstein, Andrew. 2001a. A Battle over a Name in the Land of the Sioux. *The Chronicle of Higher Education*, 23 February: A46–A49.

———. 2001b. Race, Reparations, and Free Expression: A Dispute at Brown and Other Universities Reflects Divisions among Liberal Students. *The Chronicle of Higher Education*, 30 March: A48–A50.

Buchanan, Pat. 2000. Presidential Campaign Home Page, August. http://www.gopatgo.com.

Call to Vigilance; Call to Patriots. 27 November 2000. ustkamschask@yahoo.com.

Callwood, June. 1965. *Love, Hate, Fear, Anger and the Other Lively Emotions*. New York: Doubleday & Co., Inc.

Campbell, Christopher P. 1995. *Race, Myth and the News*. Thousand Oaks, Calif.: Sage Publications.

———. 1998. News Media Coverage of Minorities. In *Contemporary Media Issues*, edited by Wm. David Sloan and Emily Erickson Hoff. Northport, Ala.: Vision Press.

Campbell, Kenneth, Sonya Forte Duhe, and Ernest L. Wiggins. 1996. African Americans in TV News in South Carolina. In *The State of Black South Carolina 1995–1996: An Action Agenda for the Future*. Columbia, S.C.: The Urban League.

Carelli, Richard. 2000. *Supreme Court Denies Racist Appeal*. Distributed by the Associated Press, 26 June. http://www.washingtonpost.com.

Casper, Sherree. 2001. Saying "No": Charles Town march encourages diversity. *The (Martinsburg, W.Va.) Journal*, 25 March, A1.

Cha, Ariana Eunjung. 2001. Online Companies Draw Fire for Removing "Offensive" Postings. *The Washington Post*, 18 November: H1.

Chains of Love. 2001. Prod. Rob Dames. Endemol Entertainment.

Chaplinsky v. New Hampshire, 315 US 568 (1942).

Chavez, Lydia. 2000. Where Is Tipper When We Really Need Her? *George*, September: 75.

Children Now. 2000a. Fall Colors: How Diverse Is the 1999–2000 TV Season's Prime Time Lineup? January. http://www.childrennow.org.

———. 2000b. Fall Colors II: Exploring the Quality of Diverse Portrayals on Prime Time Television. July. http://www.childrennow.org.

Civil Rights Cases, 109 US 3 (1883).

Civil Rights Division, State of West Virginia, Office of the Attorney General. 2000. Civil Rights Team Project. June.

CNN TalkBack Live. 1999. Bobbie Battista, host. Buford Furrow Purported to Have Ties to Aryan Nations; Does the Media Cover More Than They Should? CNN Transcript #99081200V14, 12 August. http://www.lexis-nexis.com.

Cohen, Richard. 2000. A Face on the Past. *The Washington Post*, 26 October: A37.

———. 2001. Specious Speech. *The Washington Post*, 22 March: A29.

Cole, Nat King. 1958. Why I Quit TV: After a Year on Network TV Singer Says Prejudice Is Much More Finance than Romance. *Ebony Magazine*, February: 29–34. From Black and White TV: Primary Documents. Black and White Television: African-Americans and Early TV. http://www.dorsai.org. 1998.

Conason, Joe. 2001. Ashcroft's Tough Sell: A Segregationist Group Is Banking on the Hard-on-Crime Attorney General Nominee to Drop a Murder Conspiracy Case against One of Its Own. 16 January. http://www.salon.com.

Conspiracy Against Rights. 1948. 18 *U.S. Code*. Sec. 241.

Cooperman, Alan. 2002. September 11 Backlash Murders and the State of "Hate." *The Washington Post*, 20 January: A3.

Corey, Adam. 2000. Hate on Campus. ABCNEWS.com, 12 June. http://www.ABCNEWS.com.

Crandall, Christian. 1999. Newsworthy Moral Dilemmas: Justice, Caring, and Gender. *Sex Roles: A Journal of Research*. February. http://www.findarticles.com/cf_0/m2294/3-4_40/54710012/print.jhtml.

Crofford, Larry. 2001. Personal Interview with Donna Bertazzoni. Charles Town, W.Va., 9 July.

Cuevas v. State of Florida, 770 So. 2d 703 (2000).

Dateline NBC. 2000. Web of Hate: Hate Sites on the Web Affect Everyone. National Broadcast Corporation Transcript, July. http://www.lexis-nexis.com.

Dates, Jannette L., and William Barlow, eds. 1990. *Split Image: African Americans in the Mass Media*. Washington, D.C.: Howard UP.

Dawson v. Delaware, 112 S. Ct. 1093 (1992).

DeBartolo, John. 2000. Oscar Micheaux, Micheaux Films and "Race Films." 10 December. http://www.mdle.com/ClassicFilms/SpecialFeature.

de Moraes, Lisa. 2000. TV Networks Adding Some Color for Fall. *The Washington Post*, 21 May: A1.

Dempsey, John. 2001. Showtime Buys Neo-Nazi Film. *Variety*. Distributed by Reuters Limited, 20 April.

Dennehy, Michelle. 1999. eBay Pulls Auction for Racist Domain Name. *AuctionWatch*, 15 December. http://auctionwatch.com/awdaily, 30 November 2000.

Deprivation of Rights Under Color of Law. 1948. 18 *U.S. Code*. Sec. 242.

Diamond, Sara. 1995. *Roads to Dominion: Right-Wing Movements and Political Power in the United States*. New York: Guilford Press.

Do the Right Thing. 1989. Screenplay by Spike Lee. Dir. Spike Lee. Perf. Danny Aiello, Ossie Davis, Ruby Dee, Spike Lee. 40 Acres & a Mule Filmworks.

Doe v. University of Michigan, 721 F. Supp. 852 (E.D. Mich 1989).

Douglas, J. Yellowlees. 1996. Sorry, We Ran Out of Space: Virtual Intimacy and the Male Gaze Cubed. *Leonardo* 29 No. 3: 205–215. http://web.new.ufl.edu/~jdouglas.

Dred Scott v. Sanford, 60 US 393 (1857).

Duke, David. 2000. Duke Supported Policies. *David Duke Online*, 30 August. http://www.davidduke.com/writings.

Dyer, Richard. 1993. The Role of Stereotypes. In *Media Studies, A Reader*. 2d ed. Edited by Paul Marris and Sue Thornham. New York: New York UP. First published in *The Matter of Images: Essays on Representations*. London: Routledge, 1993.

eBay. 2000. Offensive material policy. 7 June. http://www.ebay.com.

Eggen, Dan, and Cheryl W. Thompson. 2002. U.S. Seeks Thousands of Fugitive Deportees. *The Washington Post*, 8 January. http://www.washingtonpost.com.

Eggen, Dan, and David Vise. 2001. Ashcroft Firm in Defending His Record Amid Queries. *The Washington Post*, 27 January: A8.

Ehrlich, Howard J., Barbara E. K. Larcom, and Robert P. Purvis. 1995. The Traumatic Impact of Ethnoviolence. In *The Price We Pay: The Case Against Racist Speech, Hate Propaganda, and Pornography*. Edited by Laura J. Lederer and Richard Delgado. New York: Hill and Wang.

Elliott, Dan. 2001. Columbine Killers Icons to Some. Distributed by the Associated Press. APBnews.com, 16 April. http://www.APBnews.com.

Elliott, Jeff. 1999. Benjamin "August" Smith: Poised to Kill. *Monitor*, 26 July. http://www.monitor.net.

Ellison, Chris. 2000. The Nuremberg Files: Why We Must Defend This Repugnant Site. June. http://www.netfreedom.org/controversy/latest/nuremberg.asp.

Eminem. 2000. *The Marshall Mathers LP*. 6-0694906292-7.

Entman, Robert M. 1992. Blacks in the News: Modern Racism and Cultural Change. *Journalism Quarterly* 69:341–61.

———. 1994. Representation and Reality in the Portrayal of Blacks on Network Television News. *Journalism Quarterly* 71:509–20.

Eternal Jew, The. 1940. Screenplay by German Ministry of Propaganda. Dir. Fritz Hippler. Deutsche Filmherstellungs.

Fair Housing Act. 1968. 42 *U.S. Code.* Sec. 45.

Farhi, Paul. 2000. TV's Skin-Deep Take on Race: False Harmony, Not Lack of Black Shows, Called Problem. *The Washington Post*, 13 February: G1.

———. 2001. Reality TV Broadcasts "Bad Black Guy" Stereotype. *The Washington Post*, 20 February: C1.

Fanon, Franz. 1967. *Black Skin, White Masks.* Translated by Charles Lam Markmann. New York: Grove Press.

Federal Bureau of Investigation. 2001. *Uniform Crime Report, Hate Crime Statistics, 1999.* Washington, D.C. http://www.fbi.gov.

Ferber, Abby L. 1999. *White Man Falling: Race, Gender and White Supremacy.* Lanham, Md.: Rowman and Littlefield.

Ferdinand, Pamela. 2001. Free-Speech Debate Splits Liberal Brown: Anti-Reparations Ad at Center of Controversy. *The Washington Post*, 21 March: A33.

Fields, Suzanne. 2001. Brown's Much Ado about the Ad; Students' Fury, after PC Sensitivities Scorned. *The Washington Times*, 26 March: A17. http://www.elibrary.com/s/edumark.

Fight Club. 1999. Screenplay by Jim Uhls. Dir. David Fincher. Perf. Brad Pitt, Edward Norton Fox, Helena Bonham Carter. Art Linson Productions.

Finn, Peter. 2000. Neo-Nazis Sheltering Web Sites in the U.S.: German Courts Begin International Pursuit. *The Washington Post*, 21 December: A1.

Fitzgerald, Jim. 2000. New York Signs Hate-Crime Law. Associated Press, 10 July.

Fitzgerald, Susan. 2001. 1 Student in 3 Affected by Bullying at School. Distributed by Knight Ridder News Service, 25 April.

Flesher, John. 2001. Mich. Town Scraps Bumper Stickers. The Associated Press, 23 February. http://www.washingtonpost.com.

Fletcher, Michael. 2000. Unsolved Killings, Unresolved Pain. *The Washington Post*, 26 September: A3.

———. 2001. Racial Threats Have Penn State Campus on Edge. *The Washington Post*, 3 May. http://www.washingtonpost.com.

Followers. 2000. Screenplay by Jonathan Flicker, Dir. Jonathan Flicker. Castle Hill Productions.

Ford, Jack. 2000. Right Women. 12 July. http://abcnews.go.com/onair/2020/2020_rightwomen_feature.html.

Fraleigh, Douglas, and Joseph S. Tuman. 1997. *Freedom of Speech in the Marketplace of Ideas.* New York: St. Martin's Press.

Freedom of Access to Clinics. 1994. 18 *U.S. Code* Sec. 248.

Friedman, Lawrence. 1984. *American Law: An Introduction*. New York: WW Norton & Company.

Friedman, Marilyn, and Jan Narveson. 1995. *Political Correctness: For and Against*. Lanham, Md.: Rowman & Littlefield Publishers, Inc.

From Jessica. 2001. http://women.wpww.com/Writings/Jessica.html. January 8.

Frontline. 2000. Frontline—Assault on Gay America: The Life and Death of Billy Jack Gaither. http://www.pbs.org/wgbh/pages/frontline/shows/assault/etc/synopsis.htm.

Gandy, Oscar H. Jr. 1998. *Communication and Race: A Structural Perspective*. New York: Oxford University Press.

Ghosts of Mississippi. 1996. Screenplay by Lewis Colick. Dir. Rob Reiner. Perf. Alec Baldwin, James Woods, Whoppi Goldberg. Castle Rock Entertainment.

Gill, James. 2001. Fine Minds Struggle; Then There's Cooksey. *The Times-Picayune*, 21 September: 7. http://www.lexis-nexis.com.

Gilligan, Carol. 1982. *In a Different Voice: Psychological Theory and Women's Development*. Cambridge, Mass.: Harvard University Press.

Gimme a Break! 1981–1987. Written by Susan Beavers. Dir. Hal Cooper. Perf. Nell Carter, Dolf Sweet. Alan Landsburg Productions.

Gist, Marilyn. 1990. Minorities in Media Imagery. *Newspaper Research Journal* (autumn): 52–63.

Glendon, Mary Ann. 1991. *Rights Talk*. In *Freedom of Speech in the Marketplace of Ideas*. 1997. Douglas Fraleigh and Joseph S. Tuman. New York: St. Martin's Press.

Glod, Maria. 2001. Base Probing Display of Black Mannequin. *The Washington Post*, 6 June: B7.

Golden, Larry. 2001. China Crisis and Racism. 11 April. RACE-POL@listserv.ilstu.edu.

Gone with the Wind. 1939. Screenplay by Sidney Howard. Dir. Victor Fleming. Perf. Clark Gable, Vivian Leigh, Olivia DeHavilland, Leslie Howard. Selznick International Pictures.

Gonzalez, Daniel. 2000a. Black Journalists in Phoenix to Discuss Media Roles, Goals. *The Arizona Republic*, 17 August: B2. http://www.lexis-nexis.com.

———. 2000b. Minority Journalists in Great Demand. *The Arizona Republic*, 18 August: D1. http://www.lexis-nexis.com.

Good, Joshua. 2001. Slaying Suspects Linked to Other Robberies. *The Atlanta Journal-Constitution*, 19 April: 1A.

Gose, Ben. 1999. Hate-Crime Hoaxes Unsettle Campuses. *The Chronicle of Higher Education*, 8 January: A55–56.

Green Mile, The. Screenplay by Frank Darabout. Dir. Frank Darabout. Perf. Tom Hanks, David Morse, Michael Clarke Duncan, Gary Sinise. Warner Bros.

Greenawalt, Kent. 1995. *Fighting Words: Individuals, Communities, and Liberties of Speech*. Princeton: Princeton University Press.

Guernsey, Lisa. 2000. Mainstream Sites Serve as Portals to Hate. *The New York Times*, 30 November 2000. http://www.nytimes.com.

Guerrero, Ed. 1997. Rosewood review. *Cineaste*, (winter) 23: 45.

Hale, Matt. 2000a. The Insane Teaching of Equality. 13 June. http://www.wcotc.com/literature.

———. 2000b. The Value of Hatred. 13 June. http://www.wcotc.com/literature.

———. 2000c. WCOTC World Headquarters 24-hour Hotline. September 2000. http://www.creator.org/hotline.html, 1 December 2000.

Hall, Stuart. 2000. Racist Ideologies and the Media. In *Media Studies, A Reader*. 2d ed. Edited by Paul Marris and Sue Thornham. New York: New York UP. First published in *Silver Linings*. London: Lawrence & Wishart, 1981.

Hall, Stuart, Chas Critcher, Tony Jefferson, John Clark, and Brian Roberts. 2000. The Social Production of News. In *Media Studies, A Reader*. 2d ed. Edited by Paul Marris and Sue Thornham. New York: New York UP. First published in *Policing the Crisis: Mugging, the State and Law and Order*. Basingstoke: Macmillan Education Ltd., 1978.

Halloran, James D. 2000. On the Social Effects of Television. In *Media Studies, A Reader*. 2d ed. Edited by Paul Marris and Sue Thornham. New York: New York UP. First published in *The Effects of Television*. London: Panther Books, 1970.

Harron, Mary. 2000. The Risky Territory of "American Psycho." *The New York Times*, 9 April:13.

Hate Crimes Laws: A Comprehensive Guide. 1994. *A Publication of the Anti-Defamation League*. New York: Anti-Defamation League.

Hate Crimes Laws: A Comprehensive Guide. 1999. Anti-Defamation League. June 2000. http://www.adl.org.

Hate Crimes Sentencing Enhancement Act. 1994. Title XXVII of the *Violent Crime Control and Law Enforcement Act of 1994*, PL 103–322.

Hate Crimes Statistics: Uniform Crime Reports. 1998. http://www.fbi.org. 2001.

Hatewatch: Racist Music. 1999a. Das Reich. http://hatewatch.org/wpmusic.html. 16 February.

———. 1999b. SS Bootboys. http://hatewatch.org/wpmusic.html. 16 February.

Helsel, Phil. 2001. Slavery Ad Causes Anger on Campuses. *The (Ohio State University) Lantern*. University Wire, 2 April. http://www.elibrary.com/s/edumark.

Hernandez, Greg. 1998. Man Convicted of E-Mail Hate Crime Released; Courts: Ex-UCI Student Has Served More Time Than Maximum Sentence Allows. He Still Faces Car Theft Charges. *Los Angeles Times*, 14 February. Electric Library, http://www.elibrary.com/s/edumark/. March 1998.

Higher Learning. 1995. Screenplay by John Singleton. Dir. John Singleton. Perf. Laurence Fishburne, Omar Epps, Ice Cube. Columbia Pictures.

hooks, bell. 1995. *killing rage: Ending Racism*. New York: Henry Holt and Company.

Horowitz, Craig. 1996. Anti-Semitic Violence Is Increasing. In *Hate Crimes*, edited by Paul Winters. San Diego, Calif.: Greenhaven Press.

Horsley, Neal. 2000. The Nuremberg Files. June. http://www.netfreedom.org/nuremberg.

Howe, Desson. 1995. Higher Learning. *The Washington Post*, 13 January.

Hull, Anne. 2001. A Changed America/Immigration. In N.C., Anxiety and Animosity Put an Edge on an Old Dream. *The Washington Post*, 25 November: A1.

Human Rights Watch. 2000. Special Issues and Campaigns: Freedom of Expression on the Internet. 26 June. http://www.hrw.org/hrw/worldreport00/special/internet.html.

Ice Cube. 1991. Black Korea. *Death Certificate*. Priority Records. 049925715514.

Ingall, Marjorie. 1998. i will hunt all of you down & kill you. *Mademoiselle*, September: 136–147.

Insane Clown Posse. 2001. *The Amazing Jeckel Brothers*. 7-3145246582-5.

Issues 2000. 2000. Pat Buchanan on Civil Rights. *Issues 2000: Every Presidential Candidates' View on Every Issue*, August. http://www.issues2000.org/Pat_Buchanan_Civil_Rights.htm.

Iyengar, Shanto, and Donald Kinder. 1989. *News That Matters: Television and American Opinion*. Chicago: University of Chicago Press.

Jacobs, James B., and Kimberly Potter. 1998. *Hate Crimes: Criminal Law and Identity Politics*. Oxford, England: Oxford University Press.

Jacoby, Jeff. 1999. Would We Care about Buford Furrow If He Hadn't Used a Gun? *The Boston Globe*, 23 August: A11. http://www.lexis-nexis.com.

Jesdanun, Anick. 2001. Yahoo! to Ban Nazi Artifacts from Auctions. Distributed by the Associated Press, 2 January. http://www.washingtonpost.com.

Jordan, June. 2001. Owed to Eminem. *Vibe*, February, 66.

Kearney-Cooke, Ann. 2001. Gender Differences and Self-Esteem. *The Journal of Gender-Specific Medicine*. http://www.mmhc.com/jgsm/JGSM9906/Cooke.html.

Kepka, Jennifer. 2001. Why We Did (or Didn't) Publish the Ad. A Look at Journalism School of Hard Knocks. *The Washington Post*, 1 April: B3.

Kettle, Martin. 2001. Echoes of Slavery as Bush Nominees Back Confederacy. *The Guardian*, 12 January. http://www.guardianunlimited.co.uk/archive.

Klein, Alec, and Carrie Johnson. 2000. Web Now a Female Address. *The Washington Post*, 10 August: A1.

Knights of the White Kamellia, Realm of Texas. 1997. Guestbook. Knights of the White Kameillia Web site, November. http://members.aol.com/realmoftex.

Kohlberg, Lawrence. 1981. *The Philosophy of Moral Development: Moral Stages and the Idea of Justice.* San Francisco: Harper & Row.

Korematsu v. United States, 319 US 432 (1943).

KoRn. 1996. *Life Is Peachy.* 074646755426.

———. 1998. *Follow the Leader.* 0-7464690012-3.

Laris, Michael. 2000. Va. Hits Ads Linking Immigration, Sprawl. *The Washington Post*, 21 September. http://www.washingtonpost.com.

Larocca, Amy. 2000. How Little Marshall Mathers Became A Badass. *George*, September: 76.

Larrubia, Evelyn, Ted Rohrlich, and Andrew Blankstein. 1999. Community Center Shootings; Suspect Scouted 3 Prominent L. A. Jewish Sites as Targets; Buford Furrow Tells Authorities Security Too Tight at Museum of Tolerance, Skirball, University of Judaism. Source Says He Found Granada Hills Center by Chance and Stated That the Kids Got in the Way! *Los Angeles Times*, Home Edition, 13 August: A1. http://www.lexis-nexis.com.

Lawrence, Frederick. 1999. *Punishing Hate: Bias Crimes under American Law.* Cambridge, Mass.: Harvard University Press.

Lederer, Amy, and Richard Delgado. 1995. *The Price We Pay: The Case against Racist Speech, Hate Propoganda, and Pornography.* New York: Hill and Wang.

Lee, Martin. 2001. No Trespassing in the land of the free; Demographics: A backlash against nonwhite immigrants is likely to get worse as the economy weakens. *The Baltimore Sun*, 14 January. http://www.baltimoresun.com.

Levin, Brian. 1999. Some hatemongers don glossy veneers. *USA Today*, 5 August:15A. http://www.lexis-nexis.com.

Levin, Jack, and Monte Paulsen. 1999. Hate. In *Encyclopedia of Human Emotions.* Vol. 1, edited by David Levinson, James J. Ponzetti Jr., and Peter F. Jorgensen. New York: Macmillan Reference.

Leyden, T.J. 2002. *Confessions of a Skinhead.* Lecture, Museum of Tolerance, Los Angeles, Calif. 11 July.

Limp Bizkit. 2000. *Chocolate Starfish and the Hot Dog Flavored Water.* 606949075927.

Linda Chavez. 2001. Biography by Eagles Talent Connection, Inc., May. http://eaglestalent.com.

Littwin, Mike. 1999. A Story That, Sadly, Invites Excess. *Denver Rocky Mountain News.* 2 May: 3B. http://www.lexis-nexis.com.

MacDonald, J. Fred. 1992. *Blacks and White TV: African Americans in Television Since 1948.* 2d ed. Chicago: Nelson-Hall Publishers.

MacFarquhar, Lisa. 1996. The Color of Law. *Lingua Franca*, July/August: 40–47.

Madison, James. 1787. Federalist No. 10. The Same Subject Continued (The Union as a Safeguard against Domestic Faction and Insurrection). *The New York Packet*, 23 November. http://www.law.ou.edu/hist/federalist.

Maher, Brendan. 1999. Insane Clown Posse, The Amazing Jeckel Brothers. January 9. http://www.popmatters.com/music/reviews.

Mallaby, Sebastian. 2000. Le Net, C'est Moi. *The Washington Post*, 27 November: A21.

Mannheim, Karl. 1952. *Ideology and Utopia: An Introduction to the Sociology of Knowledge*. New York: Harcourt, Brace and Company.

Manson, Marilyn. 1996. Irresponsible Hate Anthem. *Antichrist Superstar*. Interscope Records. 606949008628.

Martel, Brett. 2000. Feds Say Raid Followed Allegations That Duke Gambled Away Donations. The Associated Press, 17 November. http://www.washington post. com.

Martindale, Carolyn. 1990a. Changes in Newspaper Images of Black Americans. *Newspaper Research Journal* (winter): 40–49.

———. 1990b. Coverage of Black Americans in Four Major Newspapers, 1950–1989. *Newspaper Research Journal* (summer): 96–112.

Masters, Brooke A., and Patricia Davis. 2000. Va. Slaying of Boy, 8, Is Probed for Bias. *The Washington Post*, 8 September: B9.

Matsuda, Mari J. 1993. Public Response to Racist Speech: Considering the Victim's Story. In *Words That Wound: Critical Race Theory, Assaultive Speech and the First Amendment*, by Mari J. Matsuda, Charles R. Lawrence III, Richard Delgado, and Kimberle W. Crenshaw. Boulder, Colo.: Westview Press Inc.

Matsuda, Mari J., Charles R. Lawrence III, Richard Delgado, and Kimberle W. Crenshaw. 1993. *Words That Wound: Critical Race Theory, Assaultive Speech and the First Amendment*. Boulder, Colo.: Westview Press Inc.

McCafferty, Dennis. 1999. Desperately Seeking Angry White Females. October. http://www.salon.com/news/feature/hate/print.html.

McDermott, Terry, Kim Murphy, and Josh Meyer. 1999. Community Center Shootings; Suspect Is Called Racist Loner; Profile: Friends Say Buford Furrow Had Mental Health Problems. *Los Angeles Times*, Home Edition, 12 August: A1. http://www.lexis-nexis.com.

McGruder, Aaron. 2001. *The Boondocks*. Distributed by United Press Syndicate. 14 November. http://www.ucomics.com/boondocks.

McGuire, David. 2001. Lawmakers Ask Court to Shut Down Anti-Abortion Site. Newsbytes.com, 13 April. http://www.newsbytes.com.

McKelley, James.1998. The double truth Ruth: Do the Right Thing and the culture of Ambiguity. *African American Review*, 32 No. 2: 215.

McMillon, Dave. 2001. Grand jury indicts W.Va. men on civil rights charges. *The (Hagerstown, Md.) Morning Herald*, 18 January: B1.

McWhorter, John. 2000. *Losing the Race: Self-Sabotage in Black America*. New York: The Free Press.

———. 2001. Gimme a Break! Blacks, Television, and the Decline of Racism in America. *The New Republic*, 5 March: 30–37.

Mendels, Pamela. 1998. Governments Expand Restrictions on Internet, Report Says. *Cyberlaw Journal*, 18 December. http://www.nytimes.com/library/-tech/98/12/cyberlaw/18law.html. February 1999.

Meredith, Denise. 2000. Media Diversity Means Get Right Story, Get Story Right. *The Arizona Republic*, 19 May: B11. http://www.lexis-nexis.com.

Merullo, Roland. 2000. Hatred and Its Sly Legacy. *The Chronicle of Higher Education*, 1 December: B10.

Meyer, Josh, Nicholas Riccardi, and T. Christian Miller. 1999. First a Loner, Then a Separatist; Profile: Suspect Buford Furrow Jr. Found Camaraderie with a White Supremacist Group. *Los Angeles Times*, Home Edition, 22 August: A1. http://www.lexis-nexis.com.

Mississippi Burning. 1988. Screenplay by Chris Gerolmo. Dir. Alan Parker. Perf. Gene Hackman, Willem Dafoe, Frances McDormand. MGM.

Mitchell, Elvis. 2001 Genders That Shift, but Friends Firm as Bedrock. *The New York Times*, 21 February: B3.

Modleski, Tania. 2000. In Hollywood, Racist Stereotypes Can Still Earn Oscar Nominations. *The Chronicle of Higher Education*, 17 March: B9.

Montana Blocks Hale from Bar Examination. 2001. *The Peoria Journal Star*, 1 March.

Morello, Carol. 2001. In Virginia Town, Free Speech Hits a Wall: Charlottesville Debates Merit of Proposed Public Chalkboard. *The Washington Post*, 11 February: A1.

Morgenstern, John. 2000. Distinguishing Hate Crimes: Social Justice or First Amendment Foul? A Report on Hate Crime in America and an Analysis of American Hate Crime Legislation. June 10. http://firms.findlaw.com/JPMorgen/Memo3.htm.

Morin, Richard. 2001. Misperceptions Cloud Whites' View of Blacks. *The Washington Post*, 11 July: A1.

Morin, Richard, and Sharon Warden. 1995. Americans Vent Anger at Affirmative Action. *The Washington Post*, 24 March: A1. http://www.washingtonpost.com.

Morrison, Toni. 1992. *playing in the dark: whiteness and the literary imagination*. Cambridge, Mass.: Harvard University Press.

Morse, Jodi. 2001. Girlhood Interrupted. *Time*, 19 March: 28.

Mullin, Sarah. 2001. Hate crime suspect pleads guilty. *The Martinsburg (W.Va.) Journal*, 25 May: B1.

Mulvey, Laura. 1998. Visual Pleasure and Narrative Cinema. In *Feminism and Film Theory*. Edited by C. Penley. New York: Routledge.

My Wife and Kids. 2001. Dir. Andy Cadiff. Perf. Damon Wayans, Tisha Campbells. Wayans Brothers Entertainment.

NAACP. 1951. Resolution Concerning *The Beulah Show* and *Amos 'n' Andy*. From Black and White TV: Primary Documents. Black and White Television: African-Americans and Early TV. http://www.dorsai.org. 1998.

National Advisory Commission on Civil Disorders. [1968] 1988. *The Kerner Report.* New York: Pantheon Books. (Originally published by Bantam Books.)

National Alliance. 2000a. The National Alliance homepage. 13 June. http://www.natall.com.

———. 2000b. National Alliance Goals. 13 June. http://www.natall.com/what-is-na.

———. 2000c. Who is the National Alliance. 13 June. http://www.natall.com/who-is.

Natural Born Killers. 1994. Screenplay by Quentin Tarantino. Dir. Oliver Stone. Perf. Woody Harrellson, Robert Downey Jr., Juliette Lewis. Warner Bros.

Neiwert, David. 2001. Hate Group Loses Property to Two Who Won Lawsuit. *The Washington Post*, 14 February: A3.

New York Times Co. v. Sullivan, 76 US 254 (1964).

Newitz, Annalee. 1998. Aryan to Anti-Racist: Political Sympathies and Elizabeth Thompson's *Blink*. Bad Subjects: Political Education for Everyday Life. Issue #36. http://www.eserver.org/bs/36/newitz.html.

Newswire. 1999. Chicago-Area Nun Arrested over Racist Graffiti at Hospital. 12 August. http://www.afgen.com/racist_nun.html.

Nichols, Bryan. 2001. "Reparations" Author Trying to Make Himself a Martyr. *Iowa State Daily*. University Wire, 29 March. http://www.elibrary.com/s/edumark.

Nicholson, Michelle. 1997. Testosterone Linked to Violence in Female Inmates. Georgia State Univ. 23 September. http://www.eurealert.org/releases/psych-inmate.html.

Norris, Chris. 2001. Eminem. *Spin* 17 No. 1: 60–66.

Noto v. United States, 367 US 290 297 (1961).

O'Hanlon, Kevin. 2001. Brandon Teena's Mother Sues Sheriff. The Associated Press, 13 January.

Omi, Michael, and Howard Winant. 1986. *Racial Formation in the United States*. New York: Routledge & Kegan Paul.

Palmer, Kimberly Shearer. 2001. MTV: Battling Hate Online. *The Washington Post*, 1 February: C4.

Parenti, Michael. 1993. *Inventing Reality: The Politics of the News Media*. 2d ed. New York: St. Martin's Press.

Partlow, Bob. 2001. Slur "not child's play." *The Herald Mail*, 24 February: A1.

Passwaters, Mark. 2001. Not Printing Controversial Ad Violates First Amendment. *The (University of Texas) Battalion*. University Wire, 28 March. http://www.elibrary.com/s/edumark.

Patel v. Zemski, 275 F.3d. 299 (2001).

Pearl Harbor. 2001. Screenplay by Randall Wallace. Dir. Michael Bay. Perf. Ben Affleck, Josh Harnett, Cuba Gooding Jr. Touchstone Pictures.

Pease, Edward F. 1989. Kerner Plus 20: Minority News Coverage in the Columbia Dispatch. *Newspaper Research Journal* (spring): 17–37.

Philo, Greg. 2000. News Content and Audience Belief. In *Media Studies, A Reader*. 2d ed. Edited by Paul Marris and Sue Thornham. New York: New York UP. First published in *Seeing and Believing: The Influence of Television*. London: Routledge, 1990.

Piaget, Jean. 1932. *The Moral Judgment of the Child*. New York: The Free Press, 1965.

Pierce, William. 1997a. The Campaign against "Hate Crime": Who Are the *Real* Haters. 13 June 2000. http://www.natall.com/free-speech.

———. 1997b. Who Are the Haters? *Free Speech*, 3 (September):9. http://www.natall.com/free-speech/fs979c.html. June 2000.

———. 2000. Images. American Dissident Voices broadcast transcript, 10 June. http://www.natvan.com/pub/061000.txt.

Plessy v. Ferguson, 163 US 537 (1896).

Potok, Mark. 2000. Internet Hate and the Law. *Intelligence Report*, Southern Poverty Law Center (winter): 48–9.

Powell, Kevin. 2000. My Culture at the Crossroads. *Newsweek*, 9 October: 66.

Powell, Michael. 2001a. A Radical Transformation: Former '60s Agitator David Horowitz Has Changed His Politics, but Not His Tone. *The Washington Post*, 28 March: C1.

———. 2001b. The Rebels of the Right: Some Politicians Still Seek to "Explain" the Confederacy. *The Washington Post*, 16 January: C1.

Puller, Jacqui. 2000. Interview with Donna Bertazzoni and Janis Judson. Bolivar, W.Va., 13 November.

Pulp Fiction. 1994. Screenplay by Roger Avary. Dir. Quentin Tarantino. Perf. John Travolta, Samuel Jackson, Uma Thurman. Miramax Films.

Purnick, Joyce. 2000. Park Rampage Stirs Anguish on 2 Fronts. *The New York Times*, 19 June: B1.

Quindlen, Anna. 2000. Sexual Assault, Film at Eleven. *Newsweek*, 3 July: 68.

r. v. andrews, 3 S.C.R. (1990).

r. v. keegstra, 2. S.C.R. (1995).

Raspberry, William. 2000. Hate Crimes, Thought Police. *The Washington Post*, 11 September: A23.

RAV v. City of St. Paul, 505 US 377 (1992).

Real World/Seattle, The. 1998. Dir. Alan Cohn. Bunim-Murray Productions.

Reisberg, Leo. 2000. Coming to a Campus Near You: Racist Hazing with Deadly Consequences. *The Chronicle of Higher Education*, 14 April: A66–67.

Reno v. ACLU, 117 S.Ct. 2329 (1997).

Reuters. 2001. Furrow Gets Two Life Terms for Gun Rampage. 26 March. http://www.lexis-nexis.com.

———. 2000. German Urges Global Rules on Hate on Web. *New York Times* on the Web. 28 June. www10.nytimes.com/library/tech.

Rooney, Brian, and Kevin Newman. 1999. Unrepentant Killer? *ABC World News Tonight with Peter Jennings*, Transcript #99081201-j04, 12 August. http://www.lexis-nexis.com.

Rosewood. 1997. Screenplay by John Singleton. Dir. John Singleton. Perf. Jon Voight, Ving Rhames, Don Cheadle. Warner Bros.

Rosin, Hanna, and David Plotz. 1999. What neighbors really don't know. *The Baltimore Sun*, 26 August: 19A. http://www.lexis-nexis.com.

Ross, Loretta. 1995. White Supremacy in the 1990s. http://www.publiceye.org/eyes/whitesup, 5 September 2000.

Ross, Mike. 2000. Kittie Lets the Fur Fly. *The Edmonton Sun*, 8 September: WE21. http://www.lexis-nexis.com.

Rossouw, Rehana. 2001. Have We Lost Our Sense of Humour? *Crossfire*, 2 February.

Rutherford, George. 2001. Interview with Donna Bertazzoni. Shepherdstown, W.Va., 6 April.

Rutstein, Nathan. 1993. *Healing Racism in America: A Prescription for the Disease*. Springfield, Mass.: Whitcomb Publishing, Inc.

Sack, Kevin. 2001. A Bitter Alabama Cry: Slow Justice Is No Justice. *The New York Times*, 12 April: A12. http://www.lexis-nexis.com.

Samuels, Allison, N'Gai Croal, David Gates, and Alisha Davis. 2000. Battle for the Soul of Hip-Hop. *Newsweek*, 9 October: 58–65.

Santana, Arthur, and Allan Lengel. 2001a. D.C. Police Probe Blue E-Mail: Racist, Vulgar Messages Sent on Patrol Car Computers. *The Washington Post*, 28 March: A1.

———. 2001b. D.C. Officers Upbraided over E-Mails. *The Washington Post*, 29 March: B1.

Sawyer, Diane, Cynthia McFadden, and Sam Donaldson. 1999. A Deadly Hate. *ABC 20/20* transcript. 7 July. http://www.lexis-nexis.com.

Schlesinger, Arthur M. Jr. 1991. *The Disuniting of America*. Knoxville, Tenn.: Whittle Direct Books.

Schorow, Stephanie. 1998. The End of Childhood. *The Boston Herald*, Art & Life, 18 November: 59.

Segal, David. 2000a. Limp Bizkit, Managing Their Anger Well. *The Washington Post*, 11 December. http://www.washingtonpost.com.

---. 2000b. The Pied Piper of Racism. *The Washington Post*, 12 January: C1.

---. 2001. Grammys' Discordant Note. *The Washington Post*, 5 January: A12.

Shepard, Alicia C. 2000. Columbine School Shooting: Live Television. Project for Excellence in Journalism. http://www.journalism.org. December.

Simon Wiesenthal Center. 1999. Wiesenthal Center Head: Pat Buchanan Is Preeminent Guru of America's Haters. 22 September.

---. 2000. The Making of a Skinhead. 20 July. http://www.wiesenthal.com/tj.

Simpson, Carole. 1991. Panelist at Women, Men and Media Symposium. Columbia University, October.

Smith, Gwen. 2000. Day of Rememberance Celebrated in 14 Cities. 29 November. http://www.gender.org/vaults/rod_2000_2.html.

Sniffen, Michael. 2001. Female Crime Rate Declines. The Associated Press. 5 December.

Souchard, Pierre-Antoine. 2000a. France Calls for Net "Zoning." Distributed by The Associated Press. *The Washington Post*, 21 November: E15.

---. 2000b. Yahoo! Ordered to Block French Users. The Associated Press, 20 November. http://www.washingtonpost.com.

Southern Comfort. 2001. Dir. Kate Davis. Perf. Robert Eads, Lola Cola. Q-Ball Productions.

Southern Poverty Law Center. 1999. All in the Family. *Intelligence Report* (summer). http://www.splcenter.org/intelligenceproject/ip-4k2.htlm.

---. 2000a. Subsidizing Hate. *Intelligence Report* (spring): 2. http://www.splc.org.

---. 2000b. The Year in Hate. *Intelligence Report* (winter): 6–7.

---. 2001. The Year in Hate. *Intelligence Report* (winter). http://www.splc.org.

Stephenson, Crocker. 2000. Missionaries of Hate. *Milwaukee Journal Sentinel*, 19 March. http://www.lexis-nexis.com.

Stepp, Carl Sessions. 2001. Signs of Progress. Report by *American Journalism Review* and The Ford Foundation, March.

Stepp, Laura Sessions. 2001. A Lesson in Cruelty: Anti-Gay Slurs Common at School. Some Say Insults Increase as Gays' Visibility Rises. *The Washington Post*, 19 June, A1.

Steptoe, Thomas P. 2001. Sentencing decision. *State of West Virginia v. Brian K. Hanna*. Charles Town, W.Va., 9 July.

Stormfront. 2000. June. http://www.stormfront.org.

Stuart, Jan. 1999. River of Tears: Moving Performances Fuel a Powerful *Boys Don't Cry. The Advocate*, 26 October. http://www.geocities.com/brand0n93/movie.

Stuever, Hank. 2001. The Kids Are Alright. *The Washington Post*, 18 February: F4.

Sullivan, Andrew. 1999. What's So Bad About Hate. *New York Times Magazine*, 26 September. http://www.nytimes.qpass.com/qpass-archives.
Survivor. 2000. Prod. Mark Burnett. Host Jeff Probst. Survivor Productions.
Sweet Sweetback's Baad Asss Song. 1971. Dir. Melvin VanPeebles. Perf. Melvin VanPeebles. Yeah Productions.
Tamborini, Ron, Dana E. Mastro, Rebecca M. Chory-Assad, and Ren He Huang. 2000. The Color of Crime and the Court: A Content Analysis of Minority Representation on Television. *Journalism Quarterly* (autumn) 77: 639–53.
Tasker, Fred. 2001. Nooses as Racial Threats Still a "Disturbing" Reality: Bigotry, 1991 Law Prompt a Rapid Rise in Lawsuits. *Miami Herald*, 2 March. http://www.miami.com/herald/content/news/national/digdocs/075875.htm.
Tatum, Beverly. 1997. *Why Are All the Black Kids Sitting Together in the Cafeteria? And Other Conversations About Race*. New York: Basic Books.
Temptation Island. 2001. Prod. Tom Colamaria. Host Mark Walberg. Rocket Science Laboratories.
Terminiello v. Chicago, 337 US 1 (1949).
Thomas-Lester, Avis. 2000. Raprehensible. *The Washington Post*, 5 November: B4.
Thomasson, Emma. 2000. Berlin Conference Urges Action on Web Hate Sites. Distributed by Reuters, 26 June. http://www.foxnews.com/vtech.
Triumph of the Will. 1934. Screenplay by Leni Riefenstahl and Walter Ruttmann. Dir. Leni Riefenstahl. Leni Riefenstahl studio film.
Trudeau, Garry. 2001. Doonesbury. Doonsbury Electronic Town Hall—Daily Dose. 13 October. http://www.doonesbury.ucomics.com.
Turner, Sister Lisa. 2000. Lessons from the Death of Princess Diana. January 8. women:wpww.com/Writings/prindi.html.
United States v. Morrison, 000 U.S. 99-5 (2000).
U.S. Census Bureau. 2001. Jefferson County, W.Va. Quick Facts from the U.S. Census Bureau, May. http://quickfacts.census.gov/qfd/states.
U.S. Newswire. 2001. ADL Detects Rise in Online Racist Speech in Aftermath of Cincinnati Riots. U.S. Newswire, 26 April. http://www.usnewswire.com:80.
UWM Post v. Board of Regents of the University of Wisconsin System, 774 F. Supp. 1163 (1991).
U.S. Public Law 101-275. 101st Cong. 2d sess., 23 April 1990. *Hate Crimes Statistics Act*.
U.S. Public Law 103-322. 103rd Cong., 2d sess., 13 September 1994. *Violent Crime Control and Law Enforcement Act*.
U.S. Public Law 104-104. 104th Cong. 2d sess., 8 February 1996. *Telecommunications Act of 1996*.
U.S. Public Law 104-155. 104th Cong., 2d sess., 3 July 1996. *Church Arsons Prevention Act*.

U.S. Public Law 107-56. 107th Cong. 1s sess., 26 October 2001. *USA Patriot Act.*

Violence Against Women Act. (1994) Title IV of the *Violent Crime Control and Law Enforcement Act of 1994.* PL 103-322.

Vise, David, and Dan Eggen. 2001. Democrats, Ashcroft Duel on Racial Issues. *The Washington Post*, 18 January: A1.

Ward, Erik K., John Lunsford, and Justin Massa. 1999. Sounds of Violence. SPLC Intelligence Report. http://www.splcenter.org/intelligenceproject/ip-416.html.

Wartofsky, Alona. 2000. Slipknot: Metal's Bad Noose Bearers. *The Washington Post*, 6 February: G5.

Washington Blade. 2001. Controversial Eminem performs at Grammy Awards. 23 February: 18.

Washington Post. 2001. Hall of Shame. 22 November: A46.

Watson, Mary Ann. 1998. *Defining Visions: Television and the American Experience since 1945.* Fort Worth, Tex.: Harcourt Brace & Company.

Watson, Rod. 2000. Community Holds the Key to Diversifying Newsrooms. *The Buffalo News*, Final Edition, 24 August: 2B. http://www.lexis-nexis.com.

Waxman, Sharon. 2001. TV Networks Get Poor Marks on Diversity. *The Washington Post*, 25 May: C5.

Weeks, Linton. 2001. Anatomy Of a Word: Harvard Professor Hopes to Take Away a Racial Epithet's Sting. *The Washington Post*, 11 December: C1.

Weiler, Jeanne. 1999. Girls and Violence. ERIC Clearinghouse on Urban Education Number 143, May.

Weinstein, Jason. 2001. Weighing In on the Horowitz Debate. *Cornell Daily Sun.* University Wire, 2 April. http://www.elibrary.com/s/edumark.

White, Walter. 1951. Negro Leader Looks at TV Race Problem. *Printers' Ink*, 24 August: 31. From Black and White TV: Primary Documents. Black and White Television: African-Americans and Early TV. http://www.dorsai.org. 1998.

Wicks, Robert H. 1998. Constructing Reality from Television. Paper presented to the Communication Theory and Methodology Division of the Association for Education in Journalism and Mass Communication, 5 August.

Wilson, Robin, and Anna Maria Cox. 2001. Terrorist Attacks Put Academic Freedom to the Test. *The Chronicle of Higher Education*, 5 October: A13.

Winget, Robert. 2001. Interview with Donna Bertazzoni. Shepherdstown, W.Va., 6 April.

Wisconsin v. Mitchell, 113 S. Ct. 2194 (1993).

Wise, Lindsay. 1999. Violent Crimes by Female Juveniles Rise Faster Than Male Rate. Scripps Howard News Service, 11 July.

Within Our Gates. 1920. Screenplay by Oscar Micheaux. Dir. Oscar Micheaux. Perf. Evelyn Preer, Flo Clements. Micheaux Book and Film Co.

World Church of the Creator. 2000. Creativity Crossword Puzzle. http://www.wcotc.com/kids/cpuzzle. 13 June.

Yates v. United States, 354 US 298 (1957).

Young-Bruehl, Elisabeth. 1996. *The Anatomy of Prejudices*. Cambridge, Mass.: Harvard University Press.

Yuhn, A. 1995. Judge Dismisses Charges in Internet Fantasy Case. Associated Press, 23 June.

Zadydas v. Davis, 185 F. 3d 279 (2001).

Index

2 Live Crew, 106, 108, 113
9th US Circuit Court of Appeals, 64, 178
18 USC 241, 42-43
18 USC 242, 42-43

absconder initiative, 196–197
Abrams, Steven, 78–82
Abrams v. United States, 55
affirmative action,1, 9, 16, 21–22
Ainsworth, Kathy, 165
Akhtar, Salman, 4
Allport, Gordon, 101
Amazon.com, 74
American Civil Liberties Union (ACLU), 196
American Family Association, 90
American History X, 136, 143–146
American Psycho, 152
American Society of Newspaper Editors, 124
American University, 175
Amos 'n' Andy, 125–126
Anatomy of a Hate Crime, 115, 135, 155
Anti-Defamation League (ADL), 35, 57–60, 71, 73, 165
ADL model hate crime statute, 35-36
Apprendi v. New Jersey, 40-41
Arab American Institute, 194
Arendt, Hannah, 18
Aryan Brotherhood, 38–39
Aryan Congress, 48
Aryan Nations, 48, 84, 88, 168
Ashcroft, John, 3, 16, 20, 26–27, 89, 122, 193
Avants, Ernest, 50

Backstreet Boys, 101
Baker, Jake, 56

Bakker, Rev. Jim, 59
Bamboozled, 136, 139–140, 153
Barclay v. Florida, 38–39
Barr, Sen. Bob, 16
Baumhammers, Richard, 10
Beck, Aaron, 3, 15, 23, 102, 136
Believer, The, 149
Bell, Derrick, 189
Bellah, Robert, 175
Berry, Derrick, 178, 180
Berry, Jeff, 104
Berry, William, 185
Best, Steven, 106–107, 111
Beulah Show, 125
bias-motivated crime, 31, 35–36
Big Brother, 130
bilingual education, 20
Birth of a Nation, 135
Black, Derek, 73
Black, Don, 53, 59, 67
Black Entertainment Network, 121
Black Liberation Army, 38-39
Black Panthers, 1
Blanton, Thomas E. Jr., 50–51
Blee, Kathleen, 163–164, 166
Blink, 144
Block, J.H., 156
Board of Regents of the University of Wisconsin v. Southworth, 148
Bob Jones University, 26
Bogle, Donald, 128
Boondocks, 199
Boys Don't Cry, 136, 140–142
Branch Davidian, 93
Brandenburg v. Ohio, 33, 65
Brandon, Joann, 142
Brawley, Tawana, 163
Britt, Donna, 1
Brown, John, 171
Brown University, 172

Brzonkala, Christy, 44
Buchanan, Pat, 19–20, 24
Burdi, George, 102
Bush, George, 3
Bush, George W, 9, 21, 25, 34, 175, 193, 195
Butler, Richard, 48
Byrd, James, 1, 11
Byrd, Sen. Robert, 89

California State University, Chico, 197
California State University, Los Angeles, 57
Callwood, June, 9, 11
Carter, Nell, 127–128
censorship, 73, 176
Center for Democracy and Technology, 71
Center for New Community, 58
Center for the Study of Popular Culture, 172
Chains of Love, 130
Chambliss, Robert, 50
Chambliss, Saxbe, 195
Chaney, James, 50
Chaplinsky v. New Hampshire, 33
Chavez, Linda, 20, 25
Cherry, Bobby Frank, 50
Child Online Protection Act, 68
Children Now, 129–130, 132
Christian Rap, 114
Christian Right, 18–19, 21
Church Arsons Prevention Act, 43
Civil Rights Act of 1964, 34
Civil Rights Cases, 33
Civil Rights Movement, 188, 191
Civil Rights Team Project, 190
Clark, Edward, 164
closed-mind, 102, 137
Cochran, Floyd, 87
Cohen, Richard, 139, 153, 174
Cohn, Judge Avern, 56
Cole, Nat King, 126
Collins, Addie Mae, 50
Columbia University, 118, 172

Columbine High School, 92–95, 178, 190
Commerce Clause, 45
Communications Decency Act, 54, 70, 72, 74
Confederate, 26
Congress, 32, 34, 73
Congress of Racial Equality, 146
Cornell University, 173
Council of Conservative Citizens, 16, 26
critical legal studies (CLS), 55–56, 62, 65–66, 108, 135, 176
critical race theory, 169, 180, 189
Crofford, Larry, 186
cyberspace regulation, 69–72

Dartmouth College, 89
Dates, Jeanette, 127
Dawson v. Delaware, 38–39
Deal, Justin, 10
death penalty, 95, 177
Decauter, Joseph E., 50
Dee, Henry, 49
Dees, Morris, 48
DeLaBeckwith, Byron, 49
DeLaughter, Bobby, 49
Del Dotto v Olsen, 47
Diallo, Amadou, 39
Diamond, Sara, 8
DMX, 111–112, 114
Dr. Dre, 107, 114
Doe v. University of Michigan, 149
Do the Right Thing, 12, 136, 138–139
Doonesbury, 199
Dred Scott v. Sanford, 32
Dukakis, Michael, 18
Duke, David, 19, 23–24, 59
Duke University, 173

e-mail, 53, 56–57
Eads, Robert, 142–143
Eastern New Mexico University, 162
e-Bay, 70
Edwards, William Jr., 49

Eminem, 99–101, 105–107, 109, 111–112, 114, 190
Equal Protection Clause, 41
Eternal Jew, 4, 12
Ethnic Intimidation Act of 1990, 35
Evers, Medgar, 49
Evers, Myrlie, 49

FAIR (Friends Advancing Intercultural Relations), 178–179, 185
Fair Housing Act, 43
Fall Colors, 130–131
Fanon, Franz, 11–12
Farhi, Paul, 130–131
FBI, 27, 44, 122-123, 159
feminazis, 8
Ferber, Abby, 21
Fight Club, 152
fighting words, 33
First Amendment, 5, 9, 32, 38, 63, 67, 174, 177
Flicker, Jonathan, 147
Followers, 136, 147
Fourteenth Amendment, 32, 38, 41
Freedom of Access to Clinic Entrances Act, 75
Freedom's Journal, 123
Free Speech Online Blue Ribbon Campaign, 66
Friedman, Lawrence, 32
Friedman, Marilyn, 149
Furrow, Buford, 77–82

Gaither, Billy Jack, 89
Gandy, Oscar, 121
Gates, Henry Louis, 108–109
gender bias hatred, 45-46, 152
gender and moral development, 156–159
GenderPac, 162
Georgia State University, 156
George Washington University, 149
Gerbner, George, 118
Geto Boys, 106
Ghosts of Mississippi, 49
Gilligan, Carol, 158–159

Gimme a Break!, 127
Glendon, Mary, 88
Goldstein, Andrew, 113–114
Gone With the Wind, 127
Goodman, Andrew, 50
Gore, Al, 21, 59
Grammy Awards, 99–100, 109
Green Mile, The, 136
Greene, Michael, 100
Griffith, D.W, 135

Hale, Matt, 23–24, 28–30, 58, 62–63, 86, 177, 198
Hall, Stuart, 117–19, 121, 127, 129
Halloran, James D., 118–119, 133
Hanna, Brian K, 181–183, 185–187
Harris, Eric, 92–93, 104, 155
Harvard University, 21, 149, 172
Harvey, Steve, 117
hate-core bands, 102–103
hate crimes, 27–28, 49, 78, 81, 83, 91–92, 148, 159, 189, 194–195
Hate Crimes Prevention Act of 1998, 46–47
Hate Crimes Sentencing Enhancement Act, 44
Hate Crimes Statistics Act, 43, 142
hate dabbler, 14–15, 23, 94, 133, 185
hatemonger, 14–15, 24, 77, 86, 133, 145
hate spectator, 17–19, 22–24, 34, 77, 86, 131, 174
hate speech, 5, 54, 57, 65, 68, 110, 164, 169, 185
hate speech codes, 149
hate sympathizer, 17-19, 23–24, 34, 54, 77, 86, 93, 131, 174
Hatewatch, 103
hatred of the "other", 7, 28, 125
Hawkins, Yusef, 39
Heinz dilemma, 157–158
Helms, Jesse, 17
Her Race, 165
Hier, Rabbi Marvin, 19
High Tech Hate: Extremist Use of the Internet, 57

Higher Learning, 136, 147–148
Hill, Lauryn, 101
Hitler, Adolf, 4, 12, 104
Hobbes, Thomas, 52
Holmes, Justice Oliver Wendell, 55
Hood College, 199
Horowitz, David, 171
Horsley, Neal, 64
Horton, Willie, 3, 18
House Subcommittee on Terrorism and Homeland Security, 195
Human Rights Watch, 167–168

Ice Cube, 106, 108, 113
Ice-T, 106, 111
identity politics, 51–52
Immigration and Naturalization Service, 196
Innes, Roy, 146
Insane Clown Posse, 113
Iyengar, Shanto, 83

Jackson, Wharlest, 50
Jacobs, James, 51–52
Jacobs, Jason, 183
Jacoby, Jeff, 77–79, 82
Jefferson County Board of Education, 179
Jeffords, James, 17
Jensen, Nancy, 165
Jim Crow, 26
John, Elton, 100
Johnson, Lyndon, 123
Jones, Russ & Laura, 37
Jordan, June, 114
Justice Department, 25, 43, 46, 194

Kaiser, Kirsten, 168
Kaye, Tony, 143
Keenan, Jason, 48
Keenan, Victoria, 48
Kellner, Douglas, 106–107, 111
Kennedy, Randall, 112
Kerner Commission, 123–124
Kinder, Donald, 83
Kingfish, 117

King, Martin Luther, 138–139
King, Horace, 48
King, Rodney, 117, 121
Kittie, 169
Klebold, Dylan, 92–93, 155
Knights of the White Kamellia, 73
Kohlberg, Lawrence, 157–158
Koon, Stacy C., 43
Korematsu v. United States, 197
KoRn, 104–5, 107–9, 111
Kozinski, Judge Alex, 65
Ku Klux Klan, 16, 23, 42, 54, 143, 163–164

Lampkin, Mary, 48
Laux, Charles, 142
Lawrence, Charles, 65–66, 108, 110, 135
Lawrence, Frederick, 41, 52
Lee, Spike, 12
Lepine, Mark, 46
Lesbian, Gay, Bisexual, and Transgender Alliance, 162
Levin, Brian, 87
Levin, Jack, 9, 14, 17–18, 62, 94, 107, 120, 185, 198
Lexis-Nexis Academic Database, 79, 83, 86
Leyden, T. J., 144–146, 155
Liberty Lobby, 103
Lifton, Robert K., 44
Limp Bizkit, 104–107, 152
Lippman, Walter, 101, 119
Log Cabin Republicans, 27
Lott, Trent, 16
Lotter, John, 140–141

MacDonald, J. Fred, 120, 125
MacFarquhar, Lisa, 163, 169, 180
Machado, Richard, 53, 56–57
Madison, James, 2, 11, 119
Maher, Bill, 197
Malcolm X, 138–139
Mandela, Nelson, 112
Manson, Marilyn, 104–105, 152
Marine Corps, 145

marketplace of ideas, 54–55, 74, 199
Massachusetts Institute of
    Technology, 57
Matsuda, Mari, 56, 65–66, 108, 110,
    135, 169
Matthews, Robert, 88
Mbeki, Thabo, 112
McKelley, James C., 138–139
McNair, Denise, 50
McWhorter, John H., 5, 42, 128
McVeigh, Timothy, 177
Merullo, Roland, 137
Metzger, John, 48
Metzger, Tom, 48, 144
Mfume, Kweisi, 129
Micheaux, Oscar, 136
Mississippi Burning, 37, 50
Moby, 106
Montana State Bar Association, 63
Moore, Charles, 49
Moore, Harry & Hariette, 49
Moore, O'Neal, 49
Morrison, Toni, 11–12, 101
MTV, 114–115
multiculturalism, 4, 9, 21
Mulvey, Laura, 141
Murphy, Gregory D., 31
Museum of Tolerance, 2
My Wife and Kids, 133

NAACP, 11, 49, 71, 125–126, 129,
    185, 190
Napster, 104
Nation of Islam, 1, 8
National Academy of Recording Arts
    and Sciences, 99–100
National Alliance, 23, 54, 60–62, 102
National Association for the
    Advancement of White People,
    16, 23
National Association of Black
    Journalists, 125
National Gay and Lesbian Task
    Force, 142
National Hispanic Media Coalition,
    129

National Institute of Child Health
    and Human Development, 161
National Public Radio, 20
Natural Born Killers, 152
Nazi, 12, 35, 69–72
Neo-Nazi, 9, 18, 48, 60
New Black Panther Party, 130
New Right, 19
New York Times v. Sullivan, 172
Nissen, Tom, 140–141
normalization of hatred, 18, 189
Norton, Gale, 26
North Dakota State
Not in Our Town, 189–190
Noto v. United States, 33–34
Nuremberg Files, 64, 66, 74–75, 178

O'Connor, Justice Sandra Day, 41
Ohio State University, 173
Omi, Michael, 34

Parenti, Michael, 121
Pataki, George, 39
Patel v. Zemski, 196
Paulsen, Monte, 9, 14, 17–18, 62, 94,
    107, 120, 185, 198
Pearl Harbor, 140
penalty enhancement, 37–42, 177
Pennsylvania State University, 150
Piaget, Jean, 157
Pierce, William, 13, 23–24, 60–62,
    102, 177
Plessy v. Ferguson, 33
Point of View Diner, 2
political correctness, 174
Politically Incorrect, 197
Pollitt, Katha, 197
Potok, Mark, 148
Potter, Kimberly, 51–52
Poussaint, Alvin, 131
Powell, Kevin, 107
Powell, Lawrence M., 43
Prejudice Institute/Center for the
    Applied Study of Ethnoviolence,
    184

Project for Excellence in Journalism, 94
Promotion of Equality and Prevention of Unfair Discrimination Act, 112
Psycho, 141
Public Enemy, 106-107, 109, 111, 115
Puller, Jacqui, 180
Pulp Fiction, 152

Queen Latifah, 113

r. v. andrews, 115–116
r. v. keegstra, 115–116
race reparations, 172–176
race talk, 101
rage, 4
Rage Against the Machine, 114
rap music, 106
Radio and Television News Directors Association, 84
Ramsey, Charles, 25
RAV v. St. Paul, 34, 36–37, 39, 52, 178
Real World, 130
Reagan, Ronald, 3, 34
Rehnquist, Chief Justice William, 45
Reno v. ACLU, 54
Republican Party, 17
Resistance Records, 102–105
Rivera, Geraldo, 146
Robertson, Carole, 50
Rogers, Creed, 49
Rosewood, 136-137
Ross, Loretta, 17, 24
Ruby Ridge, 165
Rutherford, George, 180, 187–189
Rutstein, Nathan, 33

Scalia, Justice Antonin, 37
scapegoating, 3
Schafly, Phyllis, 165
Schlesinger, Arthur, 51–52
Schwerner, Michael, 50
self-hatred, 5, 107, 111
September 11, 2001, 193–199

Shakur, Tupac, 106–107
Shepard, Matthew, 1, 89, 115, 135, 144, 155
Shifflett, Kevin, 31, 123
Simon Wiesenthal Center, 19, 53, 74, 86
Simpson, O. J., 117, 121
Singleton, John, 136
Skinheads, 59, 143, 145
Skinheads of Hammerskin Nation, 104
Slipknot, 104, 107
Smith, Benjamin, 28–30, 58, 78, 155
Smith, Susan, 163
Snoop Doggy Dogg, 106–107, 113
socialization of hatred, 146–147
South African Human Rights Commission, 112
Southern Comfort, 136, 142–143
Southern Poverty Law Center, 15–16, 48, 53, 86, 148, 169
Spears, Britney, 101
St. Cloud University, 162
Stanford University, 149–150
Steptoe, Judge Thomas, 186
stereotypes, 61, 101–102, 119, 121, 125, 127, 129, 133, 136, 139
Stevens, Justice John Paul, 54
Stormfront, 59
Sullivan, Andrew, 1, 13, 30
Superfly, 135
Supreme Court, 32–33, 37, 40, 45, 49, 63, 65, 149
Survivor, 130
Sweet Sweetback's Baad Asss Song, 135

Tatum, Beverly, 2
Teague, Christina, 168
Teena, Brandon, 140–142, 155
Telecommunications Act of 1996, 54, 72
Temptation Island, 130
Terminiello v. Chicago, 33
Thomas Jefferson Center for the Protection of Free Expression, 24
Thompson, Elizabeth, 144

Index 227

Tocqueville, Alexis de, 75
Togans, Larry, 179
Tracht, Doug, 101
Triumph of the Will, 4
Turner Diaries, 13, 60
Turner, Lisa, 166
Tyler, Elizabeth, 164

Uniform Crime Report, 44
University of California at Berkeley, 172
University of California at Irvine, 53
University of Colorado, 13
University of Iowa, 150
University of New Mexico, 197
University of North Dakota, 150-151
University of Virginia, 172
University of Wisconsin at Madison, 172
University of Texas, 175
Urban Business Professional Association, 174
usegroups, 56–57
U.S. Department of Education, 150
United States v. Morrison, 44–45, 47
USA Patriot Act, 193, 195-196
UWM Post, v. Board of Regents of the University of Wisconsin, 149

Viktora, Robert, 36–37
Violence Against Women Act, 44–46
Voting Rights Act of 1965, 34

Warhol, Andy, 82
Weathermen, 1
Weaver, Vicki, 165
Wesley, Cynthia, 50
West Virginia Human Rights Association, 187
White Aryan Resistance, 48, 144–145
White, Ben Chester, 50
White, Walter, 125
Wilchins, Riki, 162
Williams, Charles "Andy", 94
Williams, Patricia, 65, 163
Winant, Howard, 34

Winget, Bob, 187–190
Withrow, Gregory, 144
Within Our Gates, 136
Wisconsin v. Mitchell, 34, 37–39, 50
Women for Aryan Unity, 165
Women's Frontier, 165
World Church of the Creator, 23, 54, 58, 60, 62–63, 73, 75, 86–88, 102, 165–168
World Conference Against Racism, Racial Discrimination, Xenophobia and Related Intolerance, 175
World Wide Web, 57, 58, 64, 72

Yahoo, 69, 74, 198
Yates v. United States, 33–34
Young-Bruehl, Elisabeth, 12–14, 29, 45

Zadvydas v. Davis, 196

Teaching Texts in Law and Politics

David Schultz, *General Editor*

The new series Teaching Texts in Law and Politics is devoted to textbooks that explore the multidimensional and multidisciplinary areas of law and politics. Special emphasis will be given to textbooks written for the undergraduate classroom. Subject matters to be addressed in this series include, but will not be limited to: constitutional law; civil rights and liberties issues; law, race, gender, and gender orientation studies; law and ethics; women and the law; judicial behavior and decision-making; legal theory; comparative legal systems; criminal justice; courts and the political process; and other topics on the law and the political process that would be of interest to undergraduate curriculum and education. Submission of single-author and collaborative studies, as well as collections of essays are invited.

Authors wishing to have works considered for this series should contact:
    Peter Lang Publishing
    Acquisitions Department
    275 Seventh Avenue, 28th floor
    New York, New York 10001

To order other books in this series, please contact our Customer Service Department at:
    800-770-LANG (within the U.S.)
    (212) 647-7706 (outside the U.S.)
    (212) 647-7707 FAX

or browse online by series at:
    WWW.PETERLANGUSA.COM